Jesse Stuart

Jesse Stuart

HIS LIFE AND WORKS

by Everetta Love Blair

UNIVERSITY OF SOUTH CAROLINA PRESS

COLUMBIA 1967

The publishers gratefully acknowledge the following permissions to quote:
The poems "The August sassafras leaves are turning red" and "The winds are kind to white bones on a hill" (Nos. 3 and 7 in the sequence *Young Kentucky*) first appeared in *Poetry* magazine, which has granted permission for their use. All poetry from *Man With A Bull-Tongue Plow* by Jesse Stuart; Copyright, ©, 1934, 1959, by Jesse Stuart; Dutton Paperback Series; reprinted by permission of E. P. Dutton & Co., Inc. Passages from *The Thread That Runs So True* by Jesse Stuart; copyright 1949 by Jesse Stuart, Preface © 1958 by Jesse Stuart; reprinted by permission of Jesse Stuart and Charles Scribner's Sons. Passages from "Angel in the Pasture" by Jesse Stuart; reprinted by permission of *Esquire Magazine;* © 1959 by Esquire, Inc. The poem "It Is Most Painful Now As I" by Jesse Stuart; reprinted by permission of the *Saturday Evening Post;* © 1959 The Curtis Publishing Company. Passages from "Are We A Nation of Digits?" by Jesse Stuart; reprinted by permission of the *Saturday Evening Post;* © 1962 The Curtis Publishing Company. The poem "Freedom Lanes" by Jesse Stuart; reprinted by permission of *American Forests* magazine. Passages from "Challenge in Cairo" by Jesse Stuart; reprinted by permission of Jesse Stuart and *NEA Journal.* Quotation from all other works by Jesse Stuart reprinted by permission of Jesse Stuart and McGraw-Hill Book Company. Passages from "Man With a Hoe" by Malcolm Cowley, *The New Republic,* Oct. 31, 1934; reprinted by permission of Malcolm Cowley. Passages from letters by Donald Davidson quoted by permission. Material from an article by Everetta L. Blair previously published in *The Georgia Review,* Fall 1961, used with permission.

*To the readers of Jesse Stuart
throughout the World*

Foreword

,••••••••••••••••••••••••••••••••••••••,

In the early winter of 1944 my wife, Naomi Deane, and our two-year-old daughter, Jane, and I took a train from Washington, D. C., to New York City to see my movie agent and our friend, Annie Laurie Williams. I was in the Writers Unit of the United States Naval Reserve, stationed in Main Navy, Washington, D. C. Annie Laurie Williams had just sold movie rights of my novel *Taps for Private Tussie* to Metro-Goldwyn-Mayer. Upon arrival at Annie Laurie Williams' apartment, we were introduced to her close friend, Mrs. Arnold D. Blair. Little did I dream then, upon our meeting, that Everetta Love Blair would some day spend years writing my biography.

At this time Annie Laurie Williams was very depressed about her husband Maurice Crain, a radio operator and gunner on a B-17 Air Force bomber, who had been shot down in Germany and was a prisoner of war. He was a prisoner of war in "Stalag 17" for two and one half years, where he encouraged his prison mates to write; at this time Mrs. Blair's husband, Arnold, was with the First Army in Europe, a major in the 39th Infantry Regiment, Ninth Infantry Division, under General Louis Craig. Colonel William C. Westmoreland was the Chief of Staff. Everetta Love Blair at this time was a feature writer for First Army Information in New York City.

Annie Laurie and I had planned to talk about the future plans for the movie, *Taps for Private Tussie*. But all our talk was about World War II, when the end would come, and whether Maurice would get out of "Stalag 17" alive after his long imprisonment. Mrs. Blair was having anxious moments, too, about her husband. While we talked of War first, books and movies second, our two-year-old Jane took a liking to Mrs. Blair, who played with her over Annie Laurie Williams's divan bed. Jane's laughter, for she knew nothing about war and that her father and his only brother were in it, too, was one of the bright spots at our meeting. Jane wouldn't let Mrs. Blair rest. And when we left the apartment, I knew very little about Mrs. Blair except that it was evident she loved children. It was not until many years later that I came to know her as a writer and a woman of integrity and determination.

After World War II ended, Major Blair was sent to troubled Korea. Then he was given an assignment in Japan, where Mrs. Blair joined him in 1949. When the war broke out in Korea in 1950, when the Communist aggressors from North Korea invaded South Korea, Major Blair found himself in another war. And his wife, a Texan by birth, a dutiful wife of an officer, who helped her country in every way she could except for carrying a rifle in combat (and I believe she could have done this), became a feature writer at General Headquarters Public Information Office, Far East Command, in Tokyo. She served under General Douglas MacArthur until his removal from command by President Harry. Truman. Then she served under his successor, General Matthew B. Ridgway, until her husband was reassigned to the States in November 1951.

On two separate occasions, for a period of more than a week each time, Everetta Love Blair served on special assignments at the war front, interviewing troops at regimental and battalion headquarters, some of the men in slit trenches, and making tape

recordings of Special Services shows that were performed for the
men just behind the lines, in the summer and fall of 1951.

"It was supposed to be a 'quiet time,' " she told me, "but artil-
lery guns usually supplied an *obligato* for the shows, and when
I stayed with the nurses at the Mobile Army Surgical Hospitals,
I saw that there had been plenty of action. I just can't ever say
enough for the wonderful morale of those troops I saw at the
front and the units that supported them, the doctors and nurses, and the Special Services and USO casts that put on their
shows for the men in the face of great danger."

Being woman, she hadn't been a soldier, but she had been ex-
posed to the dangers on the war front, too, and had written
about and tape-recorded the life she saw there. She was given
a citation of honor, a Certificate of Achievement, by the General
Headquarters when she left the Far East in November 1951.

With Maurice Crain back safely from "Stalag 17," and a
long time in his recovery after he returned, Naomi and I often
visited Annie Laurie Williams and Maurice Crain, both of whom
are literary agents, in New York City. Through them we heard
about Everetta and Arnold Blair, who was now Lieutenant Colonel Blair. From Japan, Lt. Col. Blair had been transferred to Fort
Jackson, Columbia, South Carolina. Later he was eligible for retirement. The Blairs could have lived on his retirement pension
and enjoyed a restful life. But being people of action, unlike some
retired people, they chose to return to school. They entered the
University of South Carolina, each of them seeking Master's degrees. Mrs. Blair had majored in English and journalism at the
University of Texas. She wanted the M.A. in English. Col. Blair
was a graduate of The Citadel and had majored in civil engineer-
ing along with the military. Math and science teachers were
badly needed, so he decided to teach math. He worked toward
the Master's in education.

"When I was in Japan, and before the Korean War broke out,
I attended meetings of literary and other cultural groups from
the various embassies there," Mrs. Blair ("Eve") said to me. "I
was asked why America hadn't produced other writers like

Whitman and Emerson with a positive, inspirational approach. This made me wonder. I thought about it a great deal over there, where you came in contact with the literature of many lands, and you could get a better perspective on our own literature, and see what America needed to supply on the world literature scene. I began to search for that writer. I searched for a well-known American author who had an optimistic viewpoint in his work, an individualist, who showed faith in humanity instead of the skepticism and futility shown by so many writers today.

"In an introductory section in a Southern Literature text book at the University of South Carolina, I found a statement by a critic, Randall Stewart, who said that there were two writers in contemporary American literature who wrote in the tradition of Whitman—Thomas Wolfe and Jesse Stuart. I had always loved the writing of Thomas Wolfe, but Wolfe was dead, his writing completed, at the age of thirty-eight. In the text book, I found two short stories by Jesse Stuart, 'Uncle Jeff' and 'Another April.' This was the beginning. I was really excited. I was sure that I had found the writer I wanted, but I did much more research on you.

"I recalled having met you at Annie Laurie Williams' apartment, the author of *Taps for Private Tussie*. Later I had read that work, and a short story of yours in the Saturday Evening Post, and I thought of you then as an outstanding American humorist. I didn't know your poetry. When I found your sonnet collections, *Man With a Bull-Tongue Plow* and *Album of Destiny*, at McKissick Library and at Richland County Library in Columbia, I was tremendously moved.

"I remembered a bit of conversation that I had managed to get in with you that evening at Annie Laurie's, though you say you recall only the talk of the war and my playing with Jane. I asked you whether you knew of a small book called *Five Acres and Independence*. My husband had written me from Europe to send him a copy of it because, like most men in combat, he had been dreaming of settling on a piece of land and being independent after the war. No one had been able to tell me about this book, but you knew of it. You told me just where to go to buy a copy. I remembered that conversation and how your eyes lit up up when you talked about the land, 'the wonderful feeling of being a part of the land.' You described your hill farm in Kentucky and spoke longingly of returning to it. Your sonnet collections were filled with this love of the land, love of nature, and the sort of pride in your region and in all of America that the writer for whom I was seeking would have in his work. I was convinced. A study of your life and work was approved for my M.A. thesis at the University of South Carolina, with Dr. Milledge Seigler as director. It was his class in Southern Literature in which I found your short stories."

After Lt. Col. Blair received his Master's in education at the university, he continued to teach math in a Columbia, South Carolina, area high school, the Brookland-Cayce Senior High School. After Everetta Love Blair received her M.A. degree at the University of South Carolina, she decided to continue her study of my life and of all I had written and to earn a doctorate in English at the University of South Carolina. She chose for the subject of her dissertation *"Jesse Stuart: A Survey of His Life and Works."* This was approved by the late Dr. Havilah Babcock, then head of the University of South Carolina English Department.

There have been many theses written on my work and four dissertations, but no one has ever read the body of what I have written with such a passion as Everetta Love Blair. No one has ever fine-tooth-combed what I have written as much as she has. If there was one phase of one book, a story or a poem, she was not sure about, she wrote me direct. How many letters passed between us, perhaps she knows. I am sure several hundred would be a safe estimation. Within those letters must be another thesis or dissertation, or book. I've written to her more fully than to anyone, explaining my thoughts and desires in my work, in answer to her probing questions.

She was the third woman to receive a Ph.D. in English (there have been three since) from the University of South Carolina since its founding in 1801. To achieve this degree was a high challenge and a continuous struggle, but these battles were mild compared with those of her pioneer Kentucky, Virginia, and Tennessee ancestry that moved on to Texas soon after the Civil War to develop new land in a state that had fought for its independence as a nation, and to become a part of the United States. These battles were mild, too, to the experiences she had known in the Korean War. She was now on a different front, an English Front. These were difficulties of a different kind. But she persisted, she endured. And no one rejoiced more than she when she reached her goal and was awarded the Ph.D. In all of her work, her trials and tribulations, I wonder if ever there was another Career Soldier's wife who did this?

She received her Ph.D. after eight solid years of work. She read 32 books, 340 short stories, 2000 poems, and over 200 articles, in covering my works, while finishing her required graduate courses, some additional to those required today. Then she spent two more years, using her research material, and adding to it, to do this biography, *Jesse Stuart and His Works*. Rightfully it has been published by the University of South Carolina Press. I have not read this biography. But I certainly did read her thesis and her dissertation, which I regarded, and without bias, as high-quality work. I don't see how she has had the patience to read all I have written, for my bibliographer, Dr. Hensley Woodbridge, Southern University, Illinois has listed approximately three thousand published items. She has written me so many letters that I feel she has an acute understanding of all that I have tried to do in my writing, teaching, and my living among the people I've written about in my Appalachian area of America. She has lived with all I've written. She and her husband have visited in our home, and she has interviewed a number of the persons who were characters in my books, as she toured our region. She has been present at a number of major events in my life in recent years, including the awarding of my fellowship in the Academy of American Poets in 1961 in New York City.

So in this foreward (my first one in a book about me) I

have tried to give you a glimpse into the character of Dr. Everetta Love Blair, who did this book, and the order of events which have led up to her writing it. You can be the judge of her book on a writer who, I am sure, must be difficult to write about.

JESSE STUART

W-Hollow
Greenup, Kentucky
May 3, 1967

Acknowledgments

································

I SHOULD like to express my deep gratitude to Dr. John R. Welsh, of the University of South Carolina English Department, the principal director of my Ph.D. dissertation, *Jesse Stuart—A Survey of His Life and Works;* and to my other directors at the University—Dr. W. Yeaton Wagener of the English Department, and Dr. Robert D. Ochs, Head of the University's History Department, and to Dr. Daniel W. Hollis, of the History Department—who have given so generously of their time in my behalf.

I am grateful, especially, to the late Dr. Havilah Babcock, Head of the English Department of the University of South Carolina, whose unfailing interest and encouragement through the years enabled me to continue with my project.

To Dr. Milledge Seigler, in whose class in Southern Literature I received the inspiration to write about Jesse Stuart, I express my special appreciation; and to Dr. Alfred Rawlinson and the staff of McKissick Library for the many courtesies extended, my deep appreciation; also, to Dr. Hensley Woodbridge, former Librarian of Murray State College, Murray, Kentucky, my appreciation for his invaluable Bibliography of Jesse Stuart's works, and for his patience in supplying needed information.

I am indebted greatly to Donald Davidson, Jesse Stuart's beloved professor at Vanderbilt University, who has given graciously of his time to supply me with details of Stuart's days at Vanderbilt, and with his opinions of Stuart and of his writing, in answer to my requests. The late Robert Hillyer, Mark Van Doren, Robert Penn Warren, John Hall Wheelock, Mrs. Hugh Bullock, president of the Academy of American Poets, and Paul Green, have given aid and encouragement in my work, for which I am most grateful. The noted historian, the late David Ogg, of New College, Oxford, a Scot, and my former professor, provided a devoted interest and invaluable advice in the progress of my book. It is my great regret that he is not here for its publication. But I am happy, indeed, that Mrs. Ogg will be with me in America for the event.

My deepest thanks must be expressed to Jesse Stuart himself, whose generous cooperation in providing me with the answers to myriads of questions, and in sending additional memorabilia, from time to time, for my project, has enabled me to present what I hope to be a close and revealing study of a writer of ever-increasing importance.

I could not conclude my acknowledgments without declaring my heartfelt gratitude to my husband, Arnold Blair, for his great forbearance and aid through my years of research and of writing; to the many friends in Columbia and elsewhere who have stood by and encouraged, not only out of friendship for me but also admiration for Jesse Stuart; lastly—but certainly not leastly—to the fleet of typist-friends who have contributed long hours toward the production of this manuscript.

In the words of Stuart, I shall now "Be in a joyful mood and walk . . . [beneath the pines] Into Spring's cool solitudes . . ."

EVERETTA L. BLAIR

Columbia, South Carolina
June 1965

Contents

Introduction

How do you criticize or teach a flowing river? It was perfectly clear that Jesse Stuart was a river of poetry—and heaven knew what more! It would have been silly for me to try to persuade Jesse to write like T. S. Eliot or like my friends of the Fugitive group.

> —Donald Davidson, writing of his former student at
> Vanderbilt University.

Poet, novelist, short story writer, educator, and social philosopher, Jesse Stuart is considered by many critics to be one of the most dynamic and original figures in contemporary American literature. These critics hold that Stuart's strongly personalized writing has in it such deep insight into the basic character of mankind, such truth applicable to the general experience of all men living, that he must be placed in the realm of those writers considered universal and, as borne out by the steady publishing of his books in numerous foreign languages, must be looked upon as a strong contender for a lasting place in world literature.

Other critics relegate Stuart to the ranks of the regionalists because all of his work, with the exception of one or two short stories, have sprung from one source—the hills and people of his native northeastern Kentucky. These critics confine him to the category of the frontier humorist and dismiss his mountain characters as caricatures portrayed in much the same light as the "crackers" in Augustus B. Longstreet's *Georgia Scenes.* Some would put him even further back than Longstreet into the oral tradition of the earliest "tall story" humorist of the frontier.

Thus critical opinions are widely divergent upon the subject of Jesse Stuart. He is truly a controversial figure in today's literary scene.

Writing in an age as unpropitious for him as was the period of classicism for Robert Burns, Stuart has contributed since 1934, and continues to contribute, against the stream of modern formalism, a powerful flow of romantic, bardic, and individualistic poetry and prose which has won literary honors for him in each of the fields which he has entered—poetry, the short story, autobiography and the novel.

Against aesthetic distance, obscurantism, and depersonalization Stuart opposes intense subjectivity, clarity, and lyricism, showing mysticism and a close communion with Nature. In addition, he displays a deep concern for the individual in such warmly human and humanitarian works as his classic about school teaching, *The Thread That Runs So True.* In the hilarious *Taps for Private Tussie,* his best-selling novel which has appeared in a number of foreign editions, he combines broad humor and lyricism with social criticism.

Is Jesse Stuart, then, a "marvelous phenomenon" of his times, as poet-critic Donald Davidson and other distinguished analysts have termed him, a writer who has achieved universality in his own way, outside the influence of a modern school or cult, or is he to be considered only as a regionalist because of his indigenous source material, a throw-back to the oral tradition of the frontier? This is the problem with which one is confronted when writing of Jesse Stuart.

My long study of Stuart began soon after my return from an

extended period of living overseas where, in various discussion groups, I had gained an invaluable perspective on the position of contemporary American literature in relation to the literature of Europe and of the Far East.

I began a search for the present-day figure who would exemplify a strong American tradition, such as that of Whitman. In a class in Southern Literature at the Universiy of South Carolina, I found in the textbook *Literature of the South* Randall Stewart's critical opinion that Jesse Stuart and Thomas Wolfe should be considered as writing under the influence of Whitman, and I turned eagerly to the examples of Stuart's work in that volume. These were two of his most celebratd short stories, the poetic and tender *"Another April"* and the ruggedly realistic *"Uncle Jeff."*

Deeply impressed, I found and read his early volumes of poetry, *Man With a Bull-Tongue Plow* and *Album of Destiny*, his powerful autobiography *Beyond Dark Hills*, and his first short story collections, *Head o' W-Hollow* and *Men of the Mountains*, filled with gusty humor and the individualism of pioneer America. Stuart's prose was as poetic as a folk ballad and often reminiscent of the free verse of Whitman. Pastoral, romantic, individualistic, strong and uninhibited, at times startlingly realistic and contradictory to his mysticism, but thoroughly American and a humanist— this was Jesse Stuart! Yes, Randall Stewart could say he was writing in the tradition of Whitman.[1] My search was at an end. I determined to begin a thorough study of Jesse Stuart and to write about him—"a subject rich and massive," as Davidson, who was Stuart's most helpful professor at Vanderbilt, commented approvingly when I wrote to him for information.[2]

The most rewarding study has come, naturally, from Stuart's autobiographical works. There is little to be found about him as yet in libraries, and so, for further information, I went to his publishers in New York. Annie Laurie Williams, the agent for the

---

[1] Lines from the poem "One Body" in *Hold April* (1962) seem especially to be in the spirit of Whitman: "Body and spirit are together life, Body and spirit are together dream."

[2] Donald Davidson, letter to the author April 26, 1953.

filming and the televising of Jesse Stuart's works, arranged for me to have access to the files of E. P. Dutton and Company, publishers of Stuart's earlier books, to those of Charles Scribner's Sons, publishers of the long prose work, *The Thread That Runs So True* (1949); and to those of McGraw-Hill, publishers since 1950, of Stuart's longer prose works, short story collections, and juvenile books.

In the files of these publishers I found a wealth of material, voluminous stacks of correspondence and of newspaper clippings, containing stories and reviews, both favorable and unfavorable; and, there established in small, quiet rooms in these offices, I began taking notes. (In succeeding years, since the beginning of my study in 1953,[3] I have kept these notes up to date, with additional visits to the publishers.)

Most important of all to my study of Jesse Stuart's life and work has been the wholehearted cooperation which I have received from Stuart himself. Through the years, he has taken time from his busy schedule of writing, lecturing, farming, and participating in community activities to grant me personal interviews, and to write innumerable letters, some of them necessarily lengthy, in answer to my many questions. He has lent me personal copies of his books, which were doubly valuable and interesting because of his notations in them, and he has from time to time mailed me newspaper clippings and copies of periodicals containing articles written by him or about him, and other material which would have a bearing upon my study.

In my consideration of Stuart's life and of his personality as relating to his work, I have been most fortunate in having had a series of interviews with the author, some of them upon occasions that were of definite significance in his career. These interviews were a brief meeting with Stuart in 1944, in the company of Miss Williams in New York, following her sale of *Taps for Private Tussie* to the Metro-Goldwyn-Mayer Company for filming; in

---

[3] The writer's study of Jesse Stuart was interrupted in 1954 when she joined her husband, an army officer, during his assignment in the Far East, and it was not resumed until spring of 1957.

1953 at Spartanburg, South Carolina, following his address to the South Carolina Teachers' Association; in 1956, along with Mrs. Stuart and their daughter Jane, in New York, upon Stuart's first trip away from home, following his near-fatal heart attack in 1954; and in 1959, at Nashville, Tennessee, where Jesse Stuart and Robert Penn Warren were the featured speakers at the Vanderbilt Literary Symposium, the event that marked Stuart's first return to Vanderbilt since his year of graduate work there in 1931–32; in March 1960, at Columbia, South Carolina, when Stuart visited the University of South Carolina for "Jesse Stuart Day," and in June 1960, at Stuart's home, "W-Hollow," Greenup, Kentucky,[1] where my husband and I were guests of the Stuarts and were shown the settings for many of Stuart's stories and introduced to a number of his "real-life" characters who have appeared in his writing; two meetings in New York, 1961, one of which was for his Award ceremony given by the Academy of American Poets; and one in 1963 when he visited the University of South Carolina a second time.

All of Stuart's published works have been considered in this survey—11 long prose works, both autobiographical and fictional; four volumes of poetry and six of short stories; *A Jesse Stuart Reader* and *Save Every Lamb,* which are collections of tales, reminiscences, poetry, and short stories; a recent textbook for the short story *Short Stories For Discussion,* for which he is co-editor and short story contributor; five juvenile novels; as well as his lectures, essays, and additional writings. I have also studied certain poems and short stories published separately, which throw light upon the thinking of Jesse Stuart. There are presentations of opinions of leading critics, both pro and con, as well as of my own opinions, in the evaluation of Stuart.

The works have been presented by form of writing rather than chronology. Since Jesse Stuart is an intensely subjective writer, and in this respect greatly akin to his friend Thomas Wolfe, it is requisite that a study of his life be made along with a study of his works in order to determine prime conditions that have guided his writing. Because of the inherent part that Stuart's environment and early years have played in his literary achievement, I have made this subject the opening chapter.

Jesse Stuart

1

··

Jesse Stuart

Background and Environment

THE KENTUCKY HILLS AND THE PEOPLE

JESSE Stuart's rich literary vein lies in the region which produced
him. This is the region of Greenup County, Kentucky, in the
hitherto little-known mountainous section of America on the
northeastern border of the state, where, locked in by the mountains, the people have been living independent lives closely
resembling those of their pioneer English and Scottish ancestors.
Only in recent years has the isolation of the hills been pierced by
the building of roads into the remote areas, and the tempo of living there brought more into line with that of the outside world.

Here Jesse Stuart was born on August 8, 1907, and here he
has spent most of the years of his life, finding in his native region one of the most rewarding sources of material in American
literature, but, more important, in his personal credo—fulfilling
a mission of making his people known.

"It is a proud land; we are a proud people. It is a rugged and
individualistic and loving land; so are the people . . . We remain

3

the least changed—holdouts against an American mass culture—
with one of the most stable, sturdy, and stubborn peoples in the
nation. Our geographical, ancestral, and cultural roots bind us
together as a small, fiercely loyal country within a country. What
makes us this way?"[1]

As Thomas Hardy spoke for the inarticulate people of his
Wessex country, so Jesse Stuart has been the spokesman for his
people of the Kentucky hills. With bardic fervor, in poetry and
in poetic prose, he has created a literary microcosm with such
realism that, to an ever-widening group of readers, both in
America and in numerous foreign countries where his books
have been translated and published, Stuart's region has been accepted, like Faulkner's mythical Yoknapatawpha County Mississippi, as an authentic part of the contemporary literary scene.

Typical of the impact upon the reader when he gets a glimpse
into this alien world is the following excerpt by Thomas Burke,
the English critic, which appeared upon publication of *Head o'
W-Hollow* in 1936:

> In that part of Kentucky which is the setting of Mr.
> Stuart's *Head o' W-Hollow*, the material and characters of
> his twenty stories may be commonplace. But to one English
> reader they come more foreign than the material and char-
> acters of any translated stories of farming communities of
> Norway, Finland or Czechoslovakia. . . . Here is the old
> America, the vital, enduring America, of which current lit-
> erature takes little account: an America which uses the Eng-
> lish tongue but is otherwise remote from anything an English-
> man knows. Mr. Stuart has treated this strange region and
> its people lovingly but truthfully. His themes are varied, but
> whether they are grim or humorous or homely (even the
> humorous or homely themes of this primitive people have
> a grimness for the English reader), he handles them with
> the quiet power of the poet. . . . His book presents a little
> world, and though some of the stories are overlong for their
> material, when you have read a half dozen of them, you
> accept that world.

[1] Jesse Stuart, "Ascend the High Mountain," *Country Beautiful*, I
(February 1962), 10.

The very fault of slow-footed meandering helps to give the sense of great hills and great distances and vast skies. *What basis his episodes and characters may have in actual Kentucky life does not matter. They have the truth of art,* and they live with greater reality than the front pages of American papers . . . their method is obliquely narrative, and their matter is the every-day matter of strange, rough life, set down without expurgation or comment, but with illuminating vision. The result is work that is vital and new.[2]

Edgar Lee Masters wrote of Stuart's first novel, *Trees of Heaven,* in 1940:

This book is full of life, incident, human nature, comedy, tragedy. He got it out of living—not out of books—it is a rich book and, in so far as it is artless, better than any sophisticated stuff that you can find. His feet are on the earth, his head up where his eyes are level with the stars. I'm sure everything he writes will be true and beautiful. It will be a report of the life he knows.[3]

Here was recognition from the heart of a poet universally acclaimed, and one cognizant of the decision which the writer must face if he would endure—whether to write of the life he knows, or of the life he imagines.

From the beginning, Jesse Stuart's destiny has been with his region, and his writings have shown deep environmental influences. In presenting the life he knows, he has sought both to create his world of art and to immortalize his people.

"Human beings from deep out of the masses, people never written about, have been my subject," Stuart wrote recently, as he emphasized that, in delineating the inhabitants of his Kentucky hills, he has attempted not only to record a way of life, but in so doing to dramatize the joys and sorrows, the central passions of the human race.[4]

[2] Thomas Burke, "The Short Story in America," *American Mercury,* XXXIX (September 1936), 102-5.

[3] Edgar Lee Masters, "To Jesse Stuart," *News of Books and Authors* (New York: E. P. Dutton and Co., March-April 1940), 1.

This duality of purpose in Stuart would seem to be a counterpart of that for which T. S. Eliot commended Mark Twain and his writing of Mississippi life in a speech delivered in America in 1953. In Eliot's words Twain showed ". . . the two characteristics which must be found together, in any author whom I could single out as one of the landmarks of a national literature: the strong local flavour combined with unconscious universality."[5]

Regionalism, says Allen Tate, is something which develops as self-protection and produces a strong sense of group loyalty. "Regionalism is a conscious program, but turned in upon itself: a cultivation of the local color, the local characters, the local customs, of the community for their own sake."[6]

The region for which Jesse Stuart has been the authentic spokesman and colorful historian for the past quarter of a century,[7] through its period of emergence from a static area of pioneer American life to an area more and more encroached upon by modernity, was, of necessity, turned in upon itself within its natural mountain boundaries, from its earliest days of settlement.

Lying within Kentucky's famed "Dark and Bloody Ground," the area where Indians at last fell before the whites in the closing decades of the eighteenth century, Greenup County and bordering counties which comprise "the Jesse Stuart country" were settled by adventurous pioneers who pushed through Cumberland Gap and over the Wilderness Road or down the Ohio River. They maintained their foothold despite great danger from both men and wild animals. In self-protection, the men of the moun-

---

[4] Jesse Stuart, "I Have to Write or Die," *Christian Action*, XIV (December 1959), 20.

[5] T. S. Eliot, "American Literature and the American Language," an address delivered at Washington University on June 9, 1953. *Washington University Studies. New Series*, No. 23, p. 16.

[6] Allen Tate, "Regionalism and Sectionalism," *The New Republic*, LXIX (December 23, 1931), 158.

[7] Studies proving Jesse Stuart's authenticity for his region have been made by Mary Washington, "The Folklore of the Cumberlands as Reflected in the Writings of Jesse Stuart" (diss. University of Pa., 1960), and by Lee Ramey, "An Inquiry into the Life of Jesse Stuart" (M.A. thesis, University of Ohio, 1941).

tains, linked by similar European backgrounds and customs, banded together and suspiciously resisted the advent of strangers and attempts to bring them into wider communal living.

In *Kentuckie Country*, Willard Rouse Jillson describes the initial settlement of Kentucky during "one of the greatest human migrations in history" in the years between 1769 and 1792, as being made by some people of western and European strains, but, to a large degree, by those of Anglo-Saxon and Scotch-Irish ancestry.[8]

Kentucky, with its tall forests and rolling green hills, provided a welcome frontier especially for the English and Scottish pioneers from Virginia and North Carolina who pushed on there in search of land.

N. S. Shaler states:

> The thirst for land, which we find so strongly developed in the Elizabethan English, seems to have been transmitted to Virginia in an intenser form. Knowing that free lands were to be won by giving life for it [*sic*], the Virginia and North Carolina people were driven to desert their comfortable dwelling-places in the colonies for the battle in the West. There is no other case where this land-winning motive is so clearly seen as here. All our other Western immigration has been fostered by the protection of the government. These people could look to no protection but what they gave themselves.[9]

But, Shaler points out, the biggest exodus to the frontier came at the close of the Revolutionary War and the combative spirit that has characterized Jesse Stuart's Kentucky region, even as late as the days of his boyhood—the clan feuds, the fighting, the hard drinking, the hard living and boisterous playing, and proud assertion of rights — may be partially explained by the fact that disbanded soldiers made up the most important element of the Kentucky colonists. Shaler states also:

[8] Willard Rouse Jillson, *Kentuckie Country* (Washington: H. L. & J. B. McQueen, Inc., 1931), p 11.

[9] N. S. Shaler, *Kentucky—A Pioneer Commonwealth* (Boston: Houghton, Mifflin and Co., 1900), 111.

Kentucky alone is fairly to be called the child of another Commonwealth. She owes to Virginia the most of the people she received during the half century when her society was taking shape; her institutions, be they good or evil, her ideals of life, her place in the nation's history, are all as immediately derived from her great mother, Virginia, as are an individual man's from the mother who bore him.[1]

In Kentucky, however, the Virginia ideals of genteel living were transmuted to meet the exigencies of frontier life. In contrast to the settlers in New England, who were gregarious and banded into towns, Kentucky's colonists who came from Virginia preferred living in isolated farmhouses, as was the custom in rural England. Their absorbing passion was the possession of land, and this passion handed down through generations finds constant expression in the works of their spokesman, Jesse Stuart, particularly in Stuart's first poetry collection, *Man With a Bull-Tongue Plow*, in his first novel, *Trees of Heaven*, and in his book *God's Oddling*, his study of his father, an "earth poet" with a passion for owning land.

This beauty of the countryside, with its luxuriant greenery and fertile valleys, its poetry of changing seasons, did not obscure the fact that hillside farming, the business of wresting a living from the poor, flinty soil of the mountains, was hard and relentless labor from dawn to dusk, both for pioneer and the farmer of Stuart's day. In the Kentucky hills, the transplanted Highlanders found more than the scenery reminiscent of their homeland. "The Highlanders, for all their unearthly beauty, were hungry lands, often too hard and bitter for the plough or the pasture. The battle of life absorbed the people."[2]

But the pioneers of Stuart's region were for the most part a hardy lot who clung stubbornly to their small farms, and passed down the rigid doctrine of hard work from father to son. Of course, the hills had notable exceptions, such as the shiftless

[1] Ibid., 1.
[2] A. M. Maughan, "A Walk Through Scotland's History," *Holiday*, XXVII (May 1960), 74.

Tussies, depicted by Jesse Stuart in his humorous satire *Taps for Private Tussie*. Such lazy tribes of people, popularized by TV and movies as mountain types, give support to the "linchpin" theory of pioneer settlement in this Kentucky area.

As to the physical quality of the mountain people themselves, there is an old argument which continues to hang fire like a badly loaded and primed muzzle-loading rifle. Many have asked if the mountain people were of virile stock or if their forebears were shiftless men who failed to keep up the folk movement westward. One group of sociological students has said they were shiftless, unambitious people. They have held that the more virile of the pioneer settlers moved westward to find better land, and neither accident nor incident steered them aside. It is the old linchpin theory that stimulates this point of view. A wagon broke down, or a horse broke one of its legs, or a member of the party became ill and died, and the family stopped to bury him and never moved on to their primary destination.[3]

But shiftlessness is a characteristic treated with vigorous contempt by the great body of hill people of Jesse Stuart's region, as Stuart points out in his characterizations of such pestiferous clans as those of the Tussies, and of the Hammertights, who their neighbors decide, should be eliminated from the hills.[4]

Malcolm Cowley paid tribute to the pioneers of Stuart's region, at the time of publication of *Man With a Bull-Tongue Plow:*

There is an easy American myth which holds that the pioneers, after crossing Cumberland Gap with Daniel Boone, pushed westward—or rather their grandsons pushed westward —to dig for gold in California and later to become the ancestors of the great American industrialists. But the truth is that the great Western fortunes were made by men who crossed the mountains after the country was safely settled and the

[3] Thomas D. Clark, *The Kentucky* (New York: Rhinehart & Co., Inc., 1942, 122.

[4] Jesse Stuart, "Zeke Hammertight." *Ploughshare in Heaven* (New York: McGraw-Hill, 1958).

Indians herded away. The pioneers themselves were mostly poor men, driven onward by their poverty and never able to rise out of it. Today their children's great-grandchildren are digging coal in southern Indiana or share-cropping in the Arkansas river bottoms, or perhaps plowing a hill farm in eastern Kentucky. They have never seen anything but the underside of American business enterprise. Jesse Stuart himself, who paid for his education by digging ditches and mowing hay, says that he is "the first of my people to finish college." More important, he is the first spokesman that the pioneers of the Kentucky hills have found for themselves.[5]

"Regionalism implies fundamentally the cult of the primitive and unsophisticated, a return Antaeus-like to the earth-mother, for strength and inspiration," E. Glyn Lewis observes.[6]

Throughout his works, as Stuart has been hill spokesman, there has been always as guiding principle the close communion with nature, the affinity of the mountain men for their land, which has given them their solace and strength, along with the hard labor, from pioneer days.

Against his lyrical descriptions of the land in its cycle of seasons, however, he has filled his books with incidents and color contrasting the simple piety and childlike traditional folk humor of the people with the grotesqueries of life in the hills—the macabre humor of the Kentucky hangings, the horror of the clan killings, the perversions practiced by some of the people under pressure of isolation, the boisterous savagery, for instance, with which the men conduct their chase of the witless Zeke Hammertight. Paradoxes of life, in general—the juxtaposition of the gentle with the cruel, evil with good—seem shown in the exaggerated dimensions of caricature in this microcosm. But Jesse Stuart insists always from the lecture platform, in articles, interview stories, and in personal letters, that he does not exaggerate. He takes his stories from life as he has observed it—and much of it as he has lived it—in this pioneer pocket, "the back country" of one

[5] Malcolm Cowley, "Man With A Hoe," *The New Republic*, LXXX (October 31, 1934), 342.

[6] E. Glyn Lewis, "Modern British Writing," *Anglo-Welsh Literature*,

of Kentucky's oldest settlements.

Kentucky's northern border, as far east as West Virginia, is marked by the Ohio River. A few miles down from the point where the Big Sandy empties into the Ohio, the town of Greenup, county seat of Stuart's county, is situated. Greenup County was formed in 1803, and named for Sir Christopher Greenup, an early governor of the Commonwealth. The town was incorporated in 1818.

Lewis Collins, an early historian, described "Greenupsburg" (later called "Greenup") as having in 1874 a total population of 250, with "a large brick courthouse" as the center of the town life, and "one church, one school, three physicians, four lawyers, eight stores, six groceries and 16 mechanic shops . . ."[7]

In *Trees of Heaven*, Stuart refers to "Greenupsburg" when he quotes the last verse of the ballad "Down in the Valley," as sung in his region:

Write me a letter, send it by mail
Send it in care of Greenupsburg jail;
Greenupsburg jail, love, Greenupsburg jail,
Send it in care of the Greenupsburg jail.[8]

Ashland, a little to the east, outgrew Greenupsburg, becoming an iron and steel center during the Civil War, and building into a busy metropolis as increasing railroad and river traffic brought about new industries. It was in Ashland that Jesse Stuart had the experiences in a steel mill, of which he gives vivid account in *Beyond Dark Hills*.

But a few miles inland from Greenup, well into the days of Stuart's young manhood, there were stretches of wild forests, abounding with game much as they had in Daniel Boone's day. Stuart writes in *Beyond Dark Hills* of trapping wild animals for hides to sell to help with expenses for his high school attendance.

---

ed. Denys Val Baker (New York: Vanguard Press, Inc., 1947), 151.

[7] Lewis Collins, *History of Kentucky* (rev. Richard H. Collins, Louisville: John P. Morton & Co., Inc., 1924) II, 299-304.

[8] *Trees of Heaven* (New York: E. P. Dutton & Co., 1940), 61.

Today, Greenup is still a quiet little country town of less than two thousand population, with its life still centered about the courthouse square. This courthouse square has provided the nucleus for many of Jesse Stuart's works.

A certain repetitiveness that characterizes his writing has been pointed out as a weakness by some critics. Others praise it and say that, though it can grow tiresome, it is used artfully to provide in monologue form the style for stories that suggest an origin in the frontier "tall story," handed down by folk tradition, or for local stories of similar vein; or for the arguments in dialogue, dearly loved by the hill individualists, particularly on politics. The Kentuckians, with their Virginia heritage, have cared less for the religious disputations of New England than for the fire of politics. They love arguments.

Sitting around the square with "the boys," listening to the stories and the exchange of opinions—and contributing his own, as well—Jesse Stuart has absorbed the color for his poems and tales that reflect the mores of his people—the fox hunting, fist and gun fighting, square dancing, hard drinking such as occurs at dances when the long white jugs with their brown necks suddenly become a prominent part of the scene (this is vividly recorded in one of his early short stories, "Kentucky Hill Dance"), the following of primitive religious customs such as that of snake worship, and the nursing of an inherent suspicion of education and new ideas.

This suspicion of education, which has been a bête noire for Stuart throughout his own struggle for an education and his school-teaching days, is in the hills an instinctive attitude left over from the frontiersman.

In discussing the Frontier Mind, Arthur K. Moore says of the early Kentuckians, "The lower classes especially, but the upper somewhat, too, appear for one or more reasons to have regarded learning with varying degrees of suspicion, mixed in some cases with obvious hostility."[9]

When Jesse went away to college his family came under the

[9] Arthur K. Moore, *The Frontier Mind* (Lexington: University of Kentucky Press 1957), 218.

heavy disapproval of the local hill preacher. In *Beyond Dark Hills,* Brother Tobbie, one of Stuart's most vivid characters, stands foursquare against education. Jesse Stuart's mother says: "Say, Jesse, I didn't tell you about Brother Tobbie preaching the other night against education, did I? Well, don't you know, he got up and preached a sermon on mothers sending their children away to college where they would be educated right for hell. He looked right at me when he said it . . . Oh, he just made me so mad."[1]

The camp meetings, with their violent emotional displays, are inherent in the life of the hills. Through the years, Stuart has gone along with the family and his neighbors when they flock to the camp meetings, and there he has listened to the exhortations of Brother Tobbie and his counterparts.

> The big revivals would be held in the springtime. Men and women would get saved over and over again each year. "There is a great rejoicing in Heaven tonight. A sinner here at Plum Grove has repented. This ain't no mourner's bench call—this is a funeral. Sing the last stanza of 'Nearer My God to Thee!' O won't you come? The Lord and the Devil are waiting to see how this meeting is a-comin' out. That's right, Sister, come right up. God may let a tree fall on you before morning. O won't you come?" They would fall at the altar. They would cry and jerk.[2]

In their square-dancing and their other folk customs carried on for communal amusement, the people's emotions are given an equally active display, but here a joyous Elizabethan note is reflected, as Stuart describes in his story of young Tarvin and Subrinea in *Trees of Heaven,* and their celebration at "molasses-making time." Thomas C. Clark, in *The Kentucky,* tells of this pioneer custom: "When molasses-making time comes, the people of the community gather for "stir-offs." Courting couples pair off, and dip paddles into the boiling syrup which they lick somewhat after the fashion of lollypop sticks. Stir-offs are the scenes of a great deal of practical joking. Molasses-making season is like-

---

[1] *Beyond Dark Hills* (New York: E. P. Dutton & Co., 1938), 207.
[2] Ibid., 86

wise a dancing season."[3]

In Jesse Stuart's works, which cover his region's transition from a remote area, repository of early Anglo-Saxon customs and language, to an area now responding to the influences of good roads, scientific farming, better schools and television,[4] and falling into the pattern of modern life, there is careful attention to use of vestigial words and expressions, as well as to use of the current vernacular. "The language reflects sweeping social and economic changes. It is full of inconsistencies and anarchronisms, expressions Chaucer would have recognized often keeping company with coinages as new as last night's newscast . . . Its most significant characteristic is its flexibility and variability in the language pattern of any given individual living there."[5]

At the turn of the twentieth century, the vernacular of the Kentucky hill people still showed a strong flavor of Chaucerian and seventeenth and eighteenth century usage, so that historian Shaler emphasized: "In Kentucky, we shall find nearly pure English blood, mainly derived through the Old Dominion, and altogether from districts that shared the Virginian conditions. It is, moreover, the largest body of pure English folk that has, speaking generally, been separated from the mother country for two hundred years."[6] The Southern Highlanders, in their isolation, were strongly reminiscent of the rural Elizabethans, and their language, found in Stuart's earlier works, contains such sound Elizabethianisms used by Shakespeare as the strong preterits, "clum" for climbed, "drug" for dragged, "wropped" for wrapped, "fotch" for fetched, and "holp" for helped. Among Scottish words and expressions still surviving in "the Stuart Country" today and used in Stuart's writing are "drap" for drop of water or to give birth to; "hoove," to swell; "line out," to be straightened out; and "strath" for river valley.[7]

[3] Clark, *Kentucky*, 388.

[4] Jesse Stuart's leadership in effecting these changes will be discussed later in this work.

[5] Mary Washington, Folklore of the Cumberlands, 85.

[6] Shaler, *Kentucky*, 23.

[7] Blair Dickinson, "A Lexicographical Study of the Vocabulary of

In a letter to the writer, dated May 7, 1953, Jesse Stuart said:

> Such words as "liefer" for "rather," which you find in Chaucer, are in use here, and my mother used to say, "fornenst" meaning "against." "Liefer" was more in use by the people of my father's and mother's generation. I believe it's dying out now. I do use exact expressions in my books and stories. But so many of these will not be accepted. So I have toned them down. Use less and less dialect and less idiom. My early stories will show more of the exactness They do not exaggerate. I love colorful incidents, colorful people . . . those who are different . . . but I'm trying now to tone them down.[8]

Mark Van Doren says: "It is rather by manipulations of word order, grammar and syntax than by apostrophes and misspellings that he [Stuart] succeeds in giving the flavor of a remote and special speech."[9]

The late Carl Woods, an education professor, and Mrs. Woods, natives of Prestonsburg, Kentucky, near Stuart's home, paraphrased the first paragraph of Stuart's novel *Trees of Heaven* for the writer, using the exact vernacular of their area. Fronnie says in the paragraph as it appears in *Trees of Heaven:*

> Tarvin, you ain't taking that gun out agin. I'm gittin tired of seein that gun out this house every time your Pa gits away. You take the gun and go. You never bring back any game. What is the matter? Has your eyes failed you? Don't you know your Pa comes to the house and furses with me every time you go out with the gun?

Greenup County, Kentucky, Set Forth in Jesse Stuart's *Beyond Dark Hills*" (Unpublished Master's Thesis, Department of English, University of Virginia, 1941), 3.

[8] The Clerk of Oxenford, "For him was lever have at his beddes heed, Twenty bokes, clad in blak or reed"—Geoffrey Chaucer, *The Canterbury Tales*, ed. Rev. Walter W. Skeat (New York: Random House, 1929), 14.

[9] Mark Van Doren, "Good Speech of a Kentucky Hollow," *New York Herald Tribune Books*, XII (May 3, 1936), 7.

The Woods' paraphrase:

> Tarvin, you hain't a-taking that gun out again. I'm a-gettin
> sick and tard uv seein that gun tuk outa here ever time yore
> Paw steps off'n this place. You take that gun and lay off the
> blessed day. You never bring back nuthin. What's the matter?
> Has yore eyes failed you? Don't you know yore Paw come
> to the house and fussed with me every time you go out with
> the gun?

This paraphrase would seem to confirm Stuart's statement that
he attempts to tone down many of the expressions he uses. In
others, in order to make them more colorful, he approximates
the vernacular.

Opposing views of Jesse Stuart's use of regionalism have been
expressed, particularly of his use of the vernacular. From *The
New York Times:* "Mr. Stuart's prose, which is colloquial, racy,
pungent, and wholly his own is almost miraculously suited to
the mood and atmosphere of his stories."[1]

From *The New Yorker:* "These short stories have unity of
place and atmosphere, distinction of theme, and great skill in the
telling."[2]

Robert Van Gelder, writing in *The New York Times*, sees it
differently: "Mr. Stuart is, as the critics have said, a 'discovery,'
and an 'authentic' writer, and an 'original.' He is sincere and honest in his works, he has talent. Yet . . . these stories are difficult
to read. His descriptions are tangled and often repetitiously
phrased . . . One puts this book down with fuzzy knowledge.
No character is rounded. They are done in flat caricature."[3]

The accusation of "caricature" is one which Jesse Stuart
vigorously denies. The writer, in an interview on March 27,
1953, questioned him about the shiftless Tussies, for instance,
who figure in several of his books. He said:

I see characters like that around me every day. Usually,

---

[1] Anon., "Jesse Stuart's Kentucky Tales," *New York Times Book
Review,* April 26, 1936, 6.

[2] Anon, *The New Yorker,* "Books," March 22, 1941, 70.

[3] Robert Van Gelder, *The New York Times,* March 23, 1941, 70.

I don't use real names, but the Tussies are real. They've always fascinated me as story material because they don't work, won't work, and I've always been used to hard work. One day, I saw a fellow named "Tussie" standing in front of the drug store window at home, where there was a display of my novel, *Taps for Private Tussie.* I walked up by him. He didn't know me. He turned to me and laughed and said, "Ain't it a sight what some folks will do to make a livin!"[4]

Aversion to work is not a general characteristic of the people who form the source material for Stuart's writing, but aversion to reading definitely is. They are extroverts, and like most people of the agricultural South, prefer hunting, fishing, and hard playing in their spare time. Stuart says:

So many peope here haven't read my books, so they don't know whether they are in them or not. I never tell anybody who is or isn't. I let people find out for themselves. I always say that if it is favorable, he comments on it and loves it. If it isn't favorable, he doesn't mention it. There are a few exceptions, of course. I did get one letter from a man, a real mean one, telling me to stay off his property. But that's an exception. Most of the people mentioned in *The Thread That Runs So True,* either with their own or different names, have made it a point to get up at public meetings and say how proud they are to be in it. Teachers here in my county are a hundred per cent back of that book, I'm happy to say.[5]

He points out that he uses his material and the figures in it with no personal motives involved. "I'd like to make it clear that I have never tried to hurt people in my writing. I love people, and I love writing. Sometimes I laugh with my characters, sometimes I cry with them, but I've always loved writing about them."[6]

Critic Harry Hansen, of the *New York World-Telegram,* confirms, from the reader's viewpoint, Stuart's affection for his story subjects: "There is no argument about it, Jesse Stuart, the Kentucky story-teller, loves life and love, and the hills and

[4] Jesse Stuart, interview with the writer, Spartanburg, S. C., March 27, 1953.
[5] Ibid.
[6] Ibid.

valleys of the land where he was born, and from which he draws
his inspiration to write. This is a robust vitality that keeps stirring
among the flora and fauna of Kentucky, and Jesse Stuart is the
animated, eager and melodious reporter of it."[7]

In showing exuberant affection for his state, Jesse Stuart ex-
hibits a characteristic which is inbred in Kentuckians, as it is in
Texans, and in people from other states where there is strong
frontier flavor of pride of place. Historian Clark says: "A pro-
nounced state character has lent glamour and distinction to Kentuckians. Their home state, with its history and tradition, is their
cherished possession. It matters little whether the tradition is of
polite society, sheltered in Blue Grass or city mansions, or of dis-
tilling, horse racing, or bloody personal feuds. To a native son,
there is no more musical name in the English language than Kentucky."[8]

For those readers who may not particularly share Jesse
Stuart's enchantment with his native state, his poetry collection
Kentucky Is My Land might be considered exaggeration, a strong
piece of chauvinism. But Stuart's deep identification with his land
and with his people is instinctive, as he writes with his poet's
fervid conviction:

> I didn't have any choice as to where I was born,
> But if I had had my choice,
> I would have chosen Kentucky.
> And if I could have chosen wind to breathe,
> I would have chosen a Kentucky wind
> With the scent of cedar, pinetree needles,
> Green tobacco leaves, pawpaw, persimmon and sassafras.
> I would have chosen too,
> Wind from the sawbriar and greenbriar blossoms.
>
> If I could have chosen the spot in Kentucky,
> I would have chosen W-Hollow,

[7] Harry Hansen, *New York World Telegram*, Book Review, April
16, 1936.
[8] Clark, *Kentucky*, 401.

The place where I was born,
Where four generations of my people have lived,
And where they still live.
Here, too, I have always lived where
The hills form a semicircle barrier against roads
And there is only one way to get out.
This way is to follow the stream.
Here, I first saw Kentucky light.
Here, I first breathed Kentucky air.
And here I grew from childhood to manhood.
Before I had been away to see what lay beyond
The rim of hills that closed my world.[9]

He left his native region for a few years to see the outside world and to work his way through college. He spent two years abroad on a Guggenheim fellowship, saw two years' service in the Navy during World War II, and in the summer of 1960, went to Egypt to spend a year teaching at the American University in Cairo. With the exception of those absences, Jesse Stuart has lived and written and taught school in the area of his birth—and even when he has been away, just as Burns carried Scotland with him, Stuart has carried along Kentucky:

I take with me Kentucky embedded in my brain and heart,
In my flesh and bone and blood
Since I am of Kentucky and Kentucky is part of me.

As the bard of his people, he wrote, in *Beyond Dark Hills:*

No one has sung for us and may I sing
As one of us, for all of us, my songs,
Though futile as the mountain winds that fling
Their fluffy silver bellies on these throngs
Of jutted hills oak-crowned against the skies.
I sing of mountain men, their lives and loves,
And mountain waters and the wild-bird cries,

[9] *Kentucky Is My Land* (New York: E. P. Dutton & Co., 1952), 11.

And percoon blooming in the late March coves.
It's fun to run on iron legs and shout
Songs to the wind my blood has left unsung,
The tunes at home they never thought about,
Too busy living life while they are young.
I'll keep on singing long as this blood flows
And brain keeps active in this living head;
I'd like eternal spring when this blood goes
To sing among ghosts of the mountain dead.[1]

THE EARLY YEARS

The strong environmental influence on Jesse Stuart's work is exceeded only by the conditioning which he received early in life, both at home and at school, to an existence of bitter poverty and back-breaking labor. This hard conditioning forced his thoughts inward. Seeking expression for emotions that clamored for an outlet, he produced intense, personal writing, born of introspection in long hours spent in the field or in his lonely W-Hollow cabin at night. Fortunately, his despair was mitigated by his ability to see things through the eyes of an embryo poet, to see with the awareness of the spirit attuned to nature. A lyrical quality was the result, even in his prose descriptions of the life about him. This poetic awareness is evidenced from the first in *Beyond Dark Hills*, as he writes of his boyhood home (p. 26):

> In a place where miners come to dig coal in the high hills of Greenup County, Kentucky, I was born. The log house had, at that time, a huge single log room. . . . This house is five miles from Riverton, Kentucky, the nearest post office. The spot is a lonely one. The Little Sandy River runs near and the waters can be heard going over the stony riffles on silent nights. But when the wind is blowing through the pine trees the water cannot be heard. And in the days when we lived there, we could hear the foxes barking from the lonely hilltops. Squirrels played in the tall walnut trees near our home. We could hear the leafy branches of a tree shaking on the

[1] *Beyond Dark Hills*, 379.

early autumn mornings and that would mean a squirrel. All we had to do to kill a squirrel, take the gun when we went after the cows. The rabbits played around the house, ate the bark off the apple trees during the winter, and cleaned the cabbage out of the garden during the summer. And snakes often writhed through the tall weeds not far from our door. . . . Dogs for us were not something to be kept as luxuries. They were essential things. We could not do without good dogs.

Here, the construction is loose, but not rambling. He maintains the single line. Step by step he pictures the details of his life. By the use of such devices as the repetition of the words "log" and "lonely," he gives the reader the feel of his primitive, isolated home.

We had only one book in our shack. That was the Bible. We kept it out on a little table for everybody to see. And above the Bible, with the trigger guard hanging over one spike nail that was driven into a joist, the end of the long barrel resting on another spike nail, was our shotgun, which my father kept hanging ready to protect his family. . . . My mother was the educated one in our family. She had finished the second grade and she wrote the letters we had to write, read the few we received.[2]

Jesse Stuart's mother was from an English family by the name of Hilton (original spelling, Hylton) which pushed northwestward from North Carolina to Kentucky. The Hiltons were characterized in the story of his life as being lovers of color, lovers of their home and small hill farms, but, most of all, lovers of books. Martha Hilton Stuart, Jesse's mother, was strong, loved the feel of the soil, worked in the fields beside her husband and sons in spite of their protests. At home at night, beside the fireplace, she encouraged Jesse's reading, smoked her clay pipe, and dreamed about when her son would be educated and would find a world beyond the rim of their W-Hollow home.

Her influence appears throughout Stuart's writing, as does

[2] Stuart, "What America Means to Me," *American Magazine*, May 1951, 10.

that of his father. From both parents he inherited a strong love
of the land and the ability to appreciate the world of nature
about him. Deep family ties which are characteristic of the people
of his isolated region have colored much of Stuart's writing. Although his father could not read or write, he is the subject of
some of Stuart's more poignant works, for example, his short
story, "My Father is an Educated Man," and *God's Oddling,*
which he wrote as a tribute to his father.

From his father's side, Jesse Stuart is the descendant of Raphy
Stuart, one of six tall Scottish Highland brothers who left Perth-
shire and the Firth of Forth area to come to America. These
brothers settled in Burkes Gardens, Virginia, for a while; then the
clan broke up. Six-foot-six Raphy, Stuart's great-grandfather,
went in search of land. He pushed into Kentucky and established
claim on a spot on the Big Sandy River. The Stuarts were fighters,
stubborn and independent.

Mitchell Stuart, Jesse's grandfather, a soldier in the Civil
War, and later a Kentucky hill feudist, is representative of his
clan.[3] He is described graphically in one of Stuart's first poems
"Elegy for Mitch Stuart," which is quoted here in part.[4]

> I. O clansmen, weep!
>   Mitch Stuart's dead!
>   Old age took him
>   At home in bed.
>   No Van Horn put
>   A bullet through
>   Mitch Stuart's head.
>
>   One war was not enough for him.
>   He gathered in his clan;
>   And warring in the black-oak hills,
>   They fought it man to man.

[3] Stuart, at Vanderbilt in 1959, told the writer and Dr. Hensley Woodbridge that the Stuarts had been part of the McCoy clan, in the Hat-
field-McCoy feud.
[4] *Kentucky Is My Land,* 30.

And old gin-drinking Mitch
He thinned the Van Horn clan.

.   .   .   .

VI. If on his slab were carved
Something beside his name
And dates and regiment,

I know old Mitch would want
His epitaph to be:
Here lies old Mitch Stuart
With a bottle and a gun;
He's a-drinkin' and a-fightin' still
He's got them on the run.
His feet are to the west...
No Van Horn's left to hit
The heart in his clay breast.

Old Mitch's a-fightin' still,
He's got 'em on the run . . .
One hand is on his bottle,
The other on his gun.

Stuart calls his father's people "figures of earth," and they
are colorful source material for much of his work. They appear
in stories as the Powderjays. His father, another Mitchell Stuart,
is "Mick," and often Jesse himself is in the stories as "Shan" and
his brother James, as "Finn."

His mother's people, the bookish Hiltons, were just the opposite of the Stuarts. It was no wonder that Grandfather Hilton
cried out frantically, "My heavens, my daughter is marrying an
outlaw!" when she married Mitchell Stuart.[5]

But Jesse Stuart's father was not in the fighting tradition like
Grandfather Stuart. He was on the quiet side, a hard-working
miner in a nearby coal mine. He came home at night to work on
his plot of land, and later became a railroad section hand. The

[5] *Beyond Dark Hillls*, 14.

young writer learned early in life the creed of his father, which he reiterates today: "I don't care what it is you want in life—if you want it, you've got to work for it."[6] Work that began with morning chores before sunrise, followed by a five-mile walk to and from the little one-room Plum Grove School, and ending with hard labor in the fields after school hours—work was the keynote of existence for Jesse Stuart.

If there was hard work, there was, too, the exciting, elemental life of the hunt at night. Jesse Stuart's love of his dogs and of the hunting in which he was always quick to join, and other pastimes of his boyhood life are told nostalgically in *Hie to the Hunters*, which will be discussed later in this work. The square dances; "funeralizin'," in which groups of people would sit around graves singing primitive, antiphonal chants; camp meetings, and superstitious tale-tellings of his people made up the life of the young Stuart.

In his secret heart, however, he was living another life. He was feeling even then the relentless urge to write, to express himself. He read Robert Burns and Edgar Allan Poe, and, during moments snatched from work in the fields, he wrote verses on scraps of paper, on poplar leaves, on anything he could find. He was not mastering poetry, poetry was mastering him, he said in *Beyond Dark Hills*.

"I thought I had never heard words more beautiful than those in 'Flow Gently, Sweet Afton.'. . . It was sung in school once or twice each week. The sentiment of that song choked me, for I loved it deeply. . . . I feasted on the poetry of Robert Burns. It seemed as if something big in life had taken hold of me. I wanted to write poetry like Robert Burns. He was a Scottish plowboy. . . . And my prayer, if I ever prayed one then, was to write poetry that would endure like the poetry of Robert Burns."[7]

Throughout his poetic career, Jesse Stuart has had Burns as his

---

[6] Stuart, interview with the writer, Spartanburg, S. C., March 27, 1953.
[7] *Beyond Dark Hills*, 58.

lodestar.[8] Stuart's first poetry collection, *Man With a Bull-Tongue Plow*, was a book of sonnets of the soil for which many critics called him "the Burns of America." Those poems can be traced back directly to his early years, to the long hours when he worked close to the land, and when for comfort and inspiration he turned to Robert Burns.

[8] Criticisms of *Man With a Bull-Tongue Plow* will be given in "Poetry" chapter. The Burns influence is pointed out a number of times in this work, in statements of Stuart, and in lines and spirit of both his poetry and his prose.

2

Poetry: A Survey

WHEN Jesse Stuart emerged upon the literary scene in 1934 with a prodigious volume of poetry—*Man With a Bull-Tongue Plow*, 703 sonnets, rooted in his native Kentucky region, expressing with insistence and abandon the poet's deep love of the land and a determined creed to be himself in defiance to all rules—he was an anachronism. He was a romanticist in a "cerebralist" world.

Stuart's poetry was a great, compulsive flow of words, with scant attention to form, characterized by a strong subjectiveness, lyrical quality, and intensity of emotion.

His amorphous poetry sprang naturally from a genius nurtured by powerful environmental influences—the isolation and beauty of the hills. It might be called the antithesis of the New School poetry as exemplified by Eliot, Auden, and Spender in such poems as *The Waste Land*, "Musée des Beaux Arts," and "Not Palaces, An Era's Crown," poems in which "aesthetic distance," objectivity, and density are the guiding principles, requiring infinite study for unraveling references and allusions.

No gloss was needed for the study of Jesse Stuart's poetry, except for an occasional clarification of an idiomatic word or phrase purely Kentuckian. He had written not only from deep inner experience, but also with a sharp, probing observation of the life about him which had given him the overwhelming urge for communication. Stuart was the poet in the old bardic tradition which placed upon the poet the necessity for expressing not only his own emotions in heightened, dramatic form, but also those of his people, in a way that would establish immediate identification. As Robert Burns, in speaking for the Scotsmen of his region, had only to examine his own mind and heart, so did Jesse Stuart speak from an equally indigenous intuition for the people of his Kentucky hills—"No one has sung for us and may I sing, as one of us, for all of us, my song. . . . ."[1]

Man With a Bull-Tongue Plow drew instant attention from the literary world—delight from critics who hailed it as a refreshing innovation upon the scene, unequivocal rejection from those who judged it from the accepted standards of analysis and interpretation.

Mark Van Doren was one of the first critics to attest to the Burnsian affinity in Stuart's strong sonnets, expressing love of the land and the poet's reiterated vow to be himself. He wrote, of the collection: "It ought to be interesting, even to those who think they cannot read poetry. They can read Jesse Stuart, if they please, as autobiography, and find themselves in the company of a modern Robert Burns. . . . It is rich in imagery and helps to explain the dimension possessed by Mr. Stuart's persons, and his place."[2]

One reviewer accused Stuart of "raggedness of rhyme" and "loose arrangements," but stated: ". . . Poetry is there, impressive in steady flow and refusal to abide by classic rules — startling volume, remarkable for its scope and power and beauty."[3]

[1] *Beyond Dark Hills*, 379.
[2] Mark Van Doren, *New York Herald-Tribune*, Books, XII (June 12, 1934), 31.
[3] Anon., *The Chicago Tribune*, Book Review, June 12, 1934, 3.

Another reviewer, writing anonymously in *The Cleveland Press*, on June 19, 1934, hailed Stuart's volume as a new American classic, rich and robust. Jesse Stuart's poems are the essential pulse of America, grown from the soil as much as the oaks and elms of the American earth. Structurally, they are related to the Shakespearian [sic] sonnet, although the author likes loose arrangements. In spirit, in preoccupation with the simple, homely things of life, these poems are strongly reminiscent of Burns."

Years later, Stuart recalled the thrill which such comparisons to his boyhood idol brought to him. He said to the writer, in an interview held on March 27, 1953: "Robert Burns certainly was a source of inspiration for *Man With a Bull-Tongue Plow*, but I don't think that I can, or that any other American can, ever equal Burns in the love lyric and in some of the other types of poems which he wrote in his short life in Scotland. What a great poet he was. . . . I can sit down yet and read him, and get tremendous inspiration from Burns."

The first volume of Stuart's poetry, in spite of faults, won for him, along with his short stories that had been published in literary magazines, the John Simon Guggenheim Literary Award in 1937 "for the universal appeal of his poetry and prose."

Adverse criticism of *Man With a Bull-Tongue Plow*, however, was merciless in its assailment of the poet's lack of form, the carelessness of construction, and "monotony." One of the most ruthless critics was John Gould Fletcher, the Imagist poet.

> Stuart's poetry cannot for a moment sustain the comparison with Burns . . . for Burns, to do him justice, realized what a wealth of folk song, old minstrelsy, rough ballad-making, lay behind him in his path. . . . Stuart has apparently no models to go on, has poured out all his feelings and experiences in mould of a single seven-hundred-times repeated form. The result is monotony and blind confusion. The book lacks all cohesion of plot, structure or "story," suffers from the same defect, but in a greater degree, as that which made "Spoon River Anthology" almost unendurable, and which defeated, in the end, Vachel Lindsay. It is all too much in the same key, in the same mood; all or nearly all, on the

same level. Great poetry, or even good minor poetry, cannot be written thus. There must be heights and depths, lights and shadings. There can be no doubt that Mr. Stuart is a poet. But he does not know the first word of his craft.[4]

Small wonder that the poet of conciseness, of the sharp, immediate word for the carrying of imagery, the poet of a school which adhered to the containment of thought within rigid bounds of form, should flay the Kentucky hill man who poured out his feelings in such an unrestrained, adjectival way. It was the old antipathy of the poet of restraint, the metaphysician, for the intensely subjective poet, the romanticist, for whom feeling was of more importance than form or conscious intellectualism.

Devastating, also, yet encouraging, was the critic Malcolm Cowley, who appraised *Man With a Bull-Tongue Plow* for *The New Republic*. He said of the book's 703 poems:

> Jesse Stuart calls them sonnets, but they are not sonnets by way rules that Petrarch or Shakespeare would recognize: rather they are short lyrics, sometimes with refrains, often with repetitions that take the place of rhymes. MWBTP is approximately seven times as long as an ordinary collection of verse, yet I should judge that it contains no more than half the poems written by this young man of twenty-seven; I have seen many others in manuscript, and some of them are better than any of those included here. He writes entirely too much for his own good or the reader's. At least half the time, he is careless, trite or perfunctory; but always he is speaking in his own words about his own people, and he doesn't know how to lie.[5]

Cowley conceded that it was "a new sort of book," that Jesse Stuart was a writer, not from the outside, but "a poet who lives inside the cabin and writes about the life he knows best." He stated further:

[4] John Gould Fletcher, "Kentucky Georgics," *Poetry: A Magazine of Verse*, XLV (January 1935), 217.

[5] Malcolm Cowley, "Man With a Hoe," *The New Republic*, LXXX (October 31, 1934), 342.

He writes about sidehill farmers, moonshiners and log-
gers, not because they are picturesque but because they are
his own people. More often, he writes about the land itself,
because it is his own land, because he knows the smell of it
when his plow turns it over, and the feel of it. . . .

At their best, his poems have the springtime freshness of
medieval ballads. Their worst fault is that they are written
without effort or economy. Jesse Stuart says everything at
least twice. The lines come to him quickly and he sets them
down as they come, without seeming to know the difference
between the good and the bad ones, between the thoughts that
are his own and those that have been expressed not once before but ten thousand times, by every poetaster since the first
bastard children of Homer. It is true that by using new images
he can sometimes lend new color to a very old conceit. Thus,
when he describes the beauty of his lady (whom the medieval
poets endowed with skin white as snow, lips red as blood, hair
black as the raven's wing), he invents a whole set of fresh
comparisons:

> Her teeth were bloodroot white—her hair was black
> As thick rain clouds—her lips were soft as new
> Bark peeled from a slippery elm and her back
> Was straight as a horseweed upon the shore.
> Her legs were brown as the buff-colored corn.

He can even dress the moon in a new epithet—"the sliced
muskmelon moon"—but there are times when he simply par-
rots what other poets have said. . . . The book as a whole
would be vastly improved if it were arranged in some simple
and coherent theme—the life of a hillsman, for example, or
the cycle of the Kentucky seasons. As it is, the poems are
tossed at us helter-skelter until they end by beating down our
enthusiasm . . . but even if we saved only twenty of the best
poems out of seven hundred, we should still be left with a
considerable body of fresh and honest writing.

Here the writer is constrained to observe that Cowley's criticism of the organization of *Man With a Bull-Tongue Plow* and
the suggestion that it should be arranged in a coherent theme is
unfair. Stuart's theme is the recurrent seasons in the Kentucky
hills and their effect upon the lives of the people. This was his

theme, too, for *Album of Destiny*, as he stated to the writer in the tape-recorded interview at Greenup, Kentucky, July 1, 1960. Each collection was to be considered *in toto* as a "rivulet," and not in terms of individual poems.

William Rose Benét, in *Saturday Review of Literature*, saw the poems in their proper perspective, as did Mark Van Doren, as an "autobiography," or "native journal," which had its "merits," though Benét pointed out that "considered as sonnets the poems are bad, indeed, monotonous and repetitive—and his emphasis often jars."[6]

Horace Gregory, writing in *The New York Tribune*, said, "It is quite unfair to subject his verse to close analysis or jot down annotations on his abuse of the sonnet form. His emotion is fluid, and his words are glib and careless; he tells you what he is about to say, and less often finds the time to say it." But Gregory overlooked faults of form, to hail Jesse Stuart's poems as an innovation. ". . . A document of this kind is seldom found between the covers of a book. . . . Reacting against the so-called 'intellectual' poetry of the last ten years in America, many will read Jesse Stuart's 'sonnets' with genuine relief, will say that here is something that the average man can understand."[7]

Structurally, *Man With a Bull-Tongue Plow* has four divisions, which correspond, generally, to the seasons. They are: "Leaves From a Plum Grove Oak," "Blades From a Field of Corn," "The Enriched Resignations," and "Preface for After Death." Sonnet 7 illustrates the strong individualism, expression of deep love of the land, and feeling of close kinship with nature, which mark all the sonnets:

My land is fair for any eyes to see—
Now, look, my friends—look to the east and west!
You see the purple hills far in the west—
Hills lined with pine and gum and black-oak tree—

[6] William Rose Benét, "Round About Parnassus," *Saturday Review of Literature*, XI (September 22, 1934), 129.

[7] Horace Gregory, "A Farmer Singing Behind His Plow," *New York Herald Tribune Books*, October 14, 1934, 128.

Now to the east you see the fertile valley!
This land is mine, I sing of it to you—
My land beneath the skies of white and blue.
This land is mine, for I am part of it.
I am the land, for it is part of me—
We are akin and thus our kinship be!
It would make me a brother to the tree!
And far as eyes can see this land is mine.
Not for one foot of it I have a deed—
To own this land I do not need a deed—
They all belong to me—gum, oak and pine.

Although the verses in *Man With a Bull-Tongue Plow* are constructed generally upon the framework of the Shakespearean sonnet, Sonnet 7 is a departure from the traditional verse form. With its fifteen lines, this verse is one of Stuart's "variations on the sonnet" admired by poet-critic Robert Hillyer.[8] Rhythm and the theme of the poem are accentuated by the repetition of phrases and clauses referring to the land—for example, "My land is fair," "This land is mine," "My land beneath the skies," "To own this land."

Sonnet 125 has the conventional fourteen lines, and is even more lyrical, with its play upon the word, "April," and with its ecstatic picture of the mountain spring:

April is here, without a doubt in mind.
April is here—look in the cool fresh wind!
See how the buds begin to burst again!
So fresh they burst after this April rain!
The dogwoods spread their white sails on the hill.
They are the sails of many thousand ships.
When winds are still the dogwood sails are still.
When the wind blows, the white sails toss about.

      [8] Robert Hillyer, Undated clipping of publicity release from E. P. Dutton & Co., "Announcing a Major Work by one of America's Most Gifted Writers," Scrapbook 15, p. 2, in Stuart Room, Murray State College, Murray, Kentucky.

These sails move up and down—move in and out!
Pine trees are sailors with green-bearded lips.
They stand beneath and help to shift about
These great white dogwood ships with flapping sails.
The high green hills are rough waves on the sea,
An ocean of green water beckoning me!

The line "Pine trees are sailors with green-bearded lips" and
the reference to "those great white dogwood ships with flapping
sails" are characteristic of the whimsical and fresh imagery employed by Jesse Stuart.

Many of his sonnets are devoted to his friends in the mountains, and to descriptions of square dances, foxhunting and other
mountain customs. In this homespun vein is Sonnet 429, quoted
here, in part:

"Son," said my father, "take you a strong wife;
Take you a mountain girl strong as a tree—
It takes a tree to meet the winds of life.
Your Ma, she was the kind that suited me.
Get you a wife with eyes bright as a star
And teeth white as a thunder-cloud's white head;
Get one with cheeks red as the wild plums are
And ankles thin as runners on a sled."

Sharply opposed in mood is Sonnet 277:

Civilization has a bed-rock stand.
His ears are heavy with the mammon-gongs;
His eyes blood-shot to beauty of the land;
His brains are stunned to any wind-grass songs.
And what is he but trial to bones of men:
What is he but a weariness to human flesh:
Better for us to go quail-wild again.

Sonnets 291 and 292 are illustrative of the intensity of feeling
and the violence which is recurrent throughout Stuart's writing:

When I am gone, have some respect for me.
Have some respect for me when I am dirt.
Don't read my rugged poetry at your tea.
Don't make those sweet comments upon my work.
If there are any comments to be made
Above the pretty stories folks will tell,
Just say I lived and felt both sun and shade.
I saw some heaven and I saw some hell.

If there is malice in this stubborn heart,
Remove it, blackness of this mountain night.
This man's an oak tree that will play a part.
Oh, night, don't let him stand to kill and fight.

One of the most powerful groups of poems written by Jesse
Stuart is the section entitled "Preface for After Death" in *Man
With a Bull-Tongue Plow.* This writing underlines the strong
subjective and dramatic qualities which characterize his work.
Many of the sonnets in this section are addressed to Donald
Davidson, professor at Vanderbilt University, who, more than
anyone else, encouraged Stuart to write.[9] Sonnet 578, quoted
here in part, is an example of those verses dedicated to Davidson:

Don Davidson, I walked on top of earth.
My guts went empty and my flesh went bare.
I wrote of sadness and I wrote of mirth,
I was a poet and I did not care.
I was not greedy for small things in life;
Don Davidson, you know I write the truth.
It is all right if poets come and look;
My earth is six feet long and two feet wide.

As was the seventeenth-century poet John Donne, as Shakespeare, and poets through the ages, Jesse Stuart is preoccupied
with the subject of death. The sonnet variation above expresses
his strong feeling of frustration, the fear of the young poet that

[9] Stuart, interview with the writer, March 27, 1953.

death will find him unread and unsung. Most of his death sonnets, however, are naturalistic, unsparing in detail descriptive of the process of dying, and of the physical aspects of death. Like Donne, he broods upon the horror of bodily change. Sonnet 374 is a case in point:

> Someday I shall return to dirt and stone,
> And grass and briars and trees and growing things;
> And over me night winds shall make their moan,
> And over me white dogwoods bloom in Spring—
> And rats will leave their footprints over me;
> An epitaph for only rats to read
> When I am rotting in eternity,
> When I am sleeping soundly with the dead.
> Only the rats and wind and briars will know
> I was a poet—and the place I sleep;
> Only the roots of grass and briars will know
> About the ringed worms that writhe and creep
> And feast upon the matter of my brain;
> They will go down and know—they shall remain.

The death sonnet sequences of *Man With a Bull-Tongue Plow,* "Preface for After Death," are presaged by the section "The Enriched Resignations." In this section the poems are sometimes given titles, named for people who have died. These persons are analyzed, given voice, and treated objectively in a manner reminiscent of Edgar Lee Masters' *Spoon River Anthology.*

In this section, too, there are highly subjective poems dominated by the personality and the thoughts of the writer. Such a poem of the subjective is Sonnet 444, "Easter Sunday, April 16th:"

> Why do you come to us this Easter morning
> And slowly walk among our narrow beds?
> Poet, I ask, why do you come this morning
> Where yucca blades are wet in mourning,
> Wet with cool white tears of April rain?

Lines from Sonnet 589, with their play upon the word, "fare-well," have a ballad-like repetitiveness which accentuates the tonal note of mourning, and makes this sonnet the epitome of his sequences on death:

Farewell to highland pink and Scottish thistle;
Farewell to purple blossoms of iron weeds;
Farewell to woods rain-washed clean as a whistle
And shoe-make leaves now red enough to bleed.
Farewell to the sweet smell of autumn woods—
The rich sweet smell of golden leaves and flowers.
The days that did excite poetic moods
When I with gun and book did waste the hours.

Striking contrasts in diction may be noted in the two sonnets given above, which illustrate Stuart's versatility in choice of metaphors. Sonnet 668 has vivid lines ". . . woods rain-washed clean as a whistle/And shoe-make leaves now red enough to bleed." It has also the picture of autumn, with its "brown stacks of grain, and fields of frosted weeds where rabbits nest," which portrays Stuart the farmer, the down-to-earth Stuart. This rich imagery, with its mixture of the fanciful and the matter-of-fact, is one of the characteristics of Stuart's writing which distinguishes it from the ordinary, in the opinion of critic Mark Van Doren.[1]

A persistent theme in Stuart is reverence for the past, in particular, for the spirit and hard labor of the pioneers who built the nation from the wilderness. Reminiscent of Carl Sandburg's tribute to amalgamated America, "The People, Yes," is the sonnet sequence on the "Blue Dreamers"—the pioneer dead—in the section "The Enriched Resignations."

Of special eloquence are the excerpts from the following sonnets:

Number 478

"America, we sleep—Blue Dreamers now,
We sleep, America—the dust of you.

[1] Van Doren, *New York Herald-Tribune.*

We are men from the foundry and the plow,
Men from ore mines, coal mines and hilly farms;
We are men builders of railroads and cities—
American and builders of the nation. . . ."

Number 479

"America, why don't you speak for us!
America, why don't you speak to us!
Above our beds the leaves hang tremulous
And gossip to the silver sheets of wind.
Now, speak to us, for we are left behind
And you push on, America—and on.
Speak out for us—let poets rise and sing,
But not of butterflies and white-moth wing;
But let them sing of earth and men of power,
And let them sing of seasons and the flower. . . ."

Number 482

What do you say, pioneers—who speaks for you?
Blue-bellied lizards speak for you. I see
Them crawl above you on the cedar tree
And they sun on your gray stones in the grass;
They seem to try to tell men when they pass
Some one lies here. The blacksnake speaks for you;
He writes your epitaph across your graves
Where sawbriars cluster and the thin grass waves.

Again there is repetitiveness here, but it serves to underscore a theme, as in a musical composition. Throughout *Man With a Bull-Tongue Plow*, the thematic variations harmonizing with the seasons emphasize the poet's intent of making this collection a "rivulet of poetry," with the stanzas flowing into one another, instead of standing individually, in the composition.

It is interesting to note here that Jesse Stuart seems to have

answered the pioneers' plea in Sonnet 479 to "Give us a singer
that will sing for us" in his stanzas in this section of "The Enriched Resignations," and later in *Album of Destiny*. And, in a
dramatic way, he paid tribute to the ideals of the settlers of America in "Freedom Lanes," a poem written after his return from
a year spent in Europe and the Middle East.

> In my America, I drive my car
> On Freedom lanes at sixty miles an hour;
> A speed at which I see both near and far
> With mind alert and fingertips of power.
> Over the surface of this mighty land
> Where Freedom rides the currents of the air,
> Since Freedom is a word I understand
> And where it is one can expect me there.
> Ten thousand miles will never satiate
> My freedom hunger, for I've been away
> Experiencing of late the haters' hate
> American, in their diseased decay.
> For added pleasure, I can turn my dial,
> Hear news uncensored on this continent,
> And I can hear unbridled music while
> I ride on Freedom lanes in my content.
> And I, you may be able to discern,
> Buzzing ten thousand miles around this nation,
> Wearing American pride without concern,
> A pride this time will not know deflation.

This poem, printed first in *American Forests* magazine, for
January, 1962, then reprinted in *Daughters of the American Revolution Magazine* for November, 1962, was hailed by James B.
Craig, editor of *American Forest*, as "a solid patriotic statement,
made all too infrequently today by our poets and other writers."[2]

Though a poem such as this runs the risk today of being
termed "ritualistic" and a piece of "rhetoric," in dealing with "the

[2] *American Forests*, ed. James Craig (January 1960), 10.

national pieties naively and directly," as Robert Penn Warren pointed out in a letter to the writer,[3] I believe that its sincerity may be accepted as a continuation of Stuart's early reverence, shown in *Man With a Bull-Tongue Plow*, for his native land, its pioneers and their ideal of freedom. He is still singing for the "Blue Dreamers."

In reading the "Preface for After Death" group of *Man With a Bull-Tongue Plow*, one experiences a feeling of kinship between Stuart and Thomas Wolfe. There are very much the same qualities of nostalgia, of personalization, in the writing of the two men. In both, there is strong identification of the writer with his material, and there is morbid contemplation of the future. The stream-of-consciousness technique is a favored device of Jesse Stuart's as it was with Wolfe.

Strangely enough, when the writer mentioned to Mr. Stuart that his "Preface for After Death" poems reminded her of Thomas Wolfe, he said that those death sonnets had been great favorites of Wolfe's.[4]

This first volume of poetry won for Jesse Stuart, besides the Guggenheim Literary Award of 1937, the Jeannette Sewal Davis Poetry prize in 1934, and a place on Dr. Henry Seidel Canby's list of *The Best One Hundred Books Written in America*.

Not only did Jesse Stuart's verve and originality in the writing of these first sonnets, and of his earlier short stories and first novel, catch the imagination of the literary world, but also the young poet's personality seems to have made him a favorite in top New York writing circles when he found time to visit the

---

[3] Robert Penn Warren, letter to the writer, July 13, 1959.

[4] "I was standing in front of Scribner's building in New York one day," he said, "when Thomas Wolfe came out." He said to me, 'Jesse, I've just read your book, *Man With a Bull-Tongue Plow*. I think it's one of the greatest books that ever came out of America.' How did I feel? I wondered if he was kidding me. I knew him well. He was older than I and, of course, I looked up to Tom in two ways, in height and in writing. I thought he was the greatest writer that I had ever met—in fact, I knew it. He liked the death sections of *Man With a Bull-Tongue Plow*—and he would. Tom should have been a poet. He was, really, a poet." Jesse Stuart, interview with the writer, March 27, 1953.

city. The best personal picture of the Stuart of that era was given by three outstanding literary figures of the day who responded enthusiastically when they were asked by the poet's publishers, E. P. Dutton and Company, for their opinions of the Kentucky writer. Edgar Lee Masters, William Saroyan, and Whit Burnett, editor of *Story* magazine, described their impressions of Stuart and of his work for Dutton's *News of Books and Authors,* the March-April 1940 issue. Edgar Lee Masters said:

> Jesse Stuart blew in on me last fall, and he was like a breeze from the hills. He is as full of life as a young colt, and as normal as earth. . . . I have such confidence in him that I would turn him loose in Boston for the rest of his life without any fear that Boston would ruin him. I'd say the same thing of New York. But if I knew him he will not leave his Kentucky hills. He is living in a day when there is no magic lure in the city. In Howells' time, Emerson and others were in or near Boston, and Howells went there. It is unfortunate when a young writer gets the idea that famous men have something to offer him beyond what they have put in their books. Howells got nothing except more book learning. He became an editor, and for one reason or another grew more timorous and restrained. Jesse Stuart does not need to be told that there is nothing in the Metaphysical poets of this day; he is not interested in theories, in gropings after the recondite, the vague thistle-wanderings of the imagination. By knowing life, and by devoted interest in it, he has all the criticism he needs.
>
> I can't see anything that will turn him aside, blow him up, corrupt him. His feet are so firmly planted on nature that he is safe from all literary perils. His sense of humor is a help to salvation. He loves the hills there in Kentucky; he loves his mules; he loves to work with his hands. You can't beat such a man. He will write a good novel, and *Trees of Heaven* will be it. His short stories are fresh, original, and rich in human nature.
>
> I had many fine talks with him last fall, full of fun, banter, story-telling and comment on writers. I didn't offer him a word of criticism. He is a good tree and should be allowed to grow the way that nature wants him to. His own sap and roots will take care of the apples.

Whit Burnett had this to say of Stuart: "Jesse Stuart, like John Gunther and Thomas Wolfe, is one of those huge fellows. He stands well over six feet and is built of muscle. He never does anything by halves. He doesn't, like Gunther, take a continent for his subject matter, nor rhapsodize for reams about a railroad journey; but there is a vastness and a spaciousness in this Kentuckian's stuff which makes him, standing in his fields in Kentucky, seem as elemental as a hound dog baying at the cosmos."

William Saroyan's estimate of Jesse Stuart is, perhaps, the most perceptive of those given. Saroyan wrote:

> As I see it, Jesse Stuart is a natural. A natural is somebody who could be nobody very gracefully, but happens to have genius, and is therefore *somebody* very gracefully. He is anonymous and a personage at the same time. Any person capable of genius and anonymity simultaneously is a person who is truly great. In his greatness is no element of stress, and in Stuart's greatness there is no stress. It is a casual, easy-going greatness. Such a greatness in a writer means better, simpler and more durable writing. It means naturalness. Stuart is one of the most natural writers in the country. I think of him as an American Robert Burns. He is not a city-made writer, and in him is none of the irritation and confusion of the city-made writer. He is, and the people of his writing are, real, against a natural, not an artificial, background.
>
> When I met Stuart, I was delighted with his simplicity and directness. He talks easily and sincerely and in his speech there is no straining for wit (which is characteristic of city writers and a thing which soon becomes monotonous), although there is a great deal of homely comedy in it. Stuart writes swiftly and abundantly, but he is not out of time with nature, so that among the younger writers of America, he stands out as one who is certain to stay, to work steadily, and to grow.

Album of Destiny, Stuart's second volume of poetry, did not appear until 1944. Taking heed of the critics, who had accused him of having loose arrangements and raggedness of rhyme, he wrote and revised meticulously before releasing the second collection to his publishers.

"I worked eleven years on *Album of Destiny*," Stuart said, in a letter to the writer. "It came out in war time and not too much was said about it. It almost went by unnoticed. Robert Hillyer wrote one of the finest letters I've ever received regarding this book—but the work I did on it! I have made the comment that *Album* is the best book I've written."[5]

Album of Destiny is a series of sonnets built around seasonal themes, concerning protagonists who have lived the seasons. Kathaleen and John Sutton are the central figures, and, in their place, the reader of the sonnets can easily substitute the poet, Jesse Stuart, and his wife, Naomi Deane.

Like Whitman's *Leaves of Grass*, *Album of Destiny* has been given a cosmic, or universal effect through the unifying instrument of the grass, as it is given voice through the various seasons. The theme is set in the Prologue, quoted here, in part:

> Speaks the Whispering Grass:
> See young John Sutton with his Kathaleen
> In love with life, alive to kiss and dreams;
> A fairer couple I have never seen
> Through April eyes of my green liquid stems;
> Now let them love while spring is in their blood,
> Know joy of living, ecstasy, and pain;
> And let them know each coming season's mood,
> Let them know life that will not come again.
> Snakes, lizards, scorpions, boast eternal spring
> But I shall drink their cold blood through my tendrils;
> Fair Kathaleen and John who laugh and sing
> Will give me their portion for my petals!

The iambic pentameter line is followed most uniformly throughout the book, but, as in line ten above—"But I shall drink their cold blood through my tendrils"—a feminine ending may appear in some lines.

In diction and architectonics, again through repetitious use of

⁵ Jesse Stuart, letter to the writer, April 18, 1953.

words that build the mood, through onomatopoeia, the lines from the following sonnet in the winter cycle of the *Album* are memorable:

A Winter Dirge of René Madden Crump

So drips, drips, drips the winter rain for her;
So drips, drips, drips the winter's cooling rain
A-splitting bitter wind again, again. . . .
Rain drip, drip, dripping from the winter fern,
Rain drip, drip, dripping with its soft cool spear
That wailing bitter winter winds discern
The touch of tears that have been shed for her.

Such verses as the one just cited show Jesse Stuart's strong sensitiveness to rhythm and sound. Along with the lyrical quality projected, the dirge for René Madden Crump conveys a strong characterization of the town woman who lived for love, and loved too well.

A characterization from life, and with diction indicative of the salty humor of Jesse Stuart's region, is that of Lonnie Biggers. In the first section of the book, entitled "Our Rights to Spring," young Lonnie Biggers speaks:

I'll tell you what I'll do when I'm a man
And get broad shoulders and big muscled arms,
I'll have my teeth all gold-crowned if I can,
I'll work and buy me six or seven farms.
Men will walk up and say: "There's Lonnie Biggers
Got seven farms and he's got money lent!
He cannot read nor write nor don't know figures
But Lonnie's got enough to be content. . . ."

In later life, under the section "Winter's Wan Cocoons," Lonnie Biggers looks back on the years broodingly and says, with regret:

The grave is such a dark and gloomy place
For eyeless dark-rimmed sockets to discern;

I know one never sees a lovely face,
I know one's lips are slivered by the worm.
Where worms are guests and love and life are dead;
I know that spiders fortify the skull
With geometric patterns of white thread.
Had I but known the end would come to this,
I would have lived my life without regrets;
I would have been excessive with the kiss
To many loves, drunk heady wines, made debts
Instead of banking cash I can't use here
Where life and love and dreams return to dust.
If I were man alive, I would not fear
To drink and spend and satisfy my lust.

The lovers, John and Kathaleen, the grass, snakes, lizards,
scorpions, and such village personalities as René and Lonnie,
speak throughout the different seasons that are portrayed in the
Album of Destiny. But the character analyses never overshadow
the central theme, which is the mutability of time. In the Epi-
logue, "The Wind's Finale" summarizes the argument of the sonnet sequences:

I told the boys and girls of yesterday
When April trees were white with blooming spray
To love while spring was in them with their might,
To love before they met their final night.
I warned them of the seasons left behind.
That left bare traces on the earth's cold rind.
To John I whispered and to Kathaleen
To love while they were on the April green. . . .

The publication of *Album of Destiny* brought some of Jesse
Stuart's most enthusiastic and rewarding reviews from the literary
critics, but it brought, inescapably, the suggestion by some of the
reviewers that Stuart's book was based on Edgar Lee Masters's
Spoon River Anthology.[6] To this comment, Stuart replies, "I

---

[6] Henry Nash Smith, *New York Herald-Tribune*, June 5, 1944.

knew and admired Mr. Masters deeply. But my idea for *Album of Destiny* came from a little verse inscribed on a tombstone in the grave yard of the Plum Grove Church, where I used to browse around a great deal of the time. The verse went as follows:

Remember me as you pass by;
As you are now, so once was I.
As I am now, so will you be;
Therefore, prepare to follow me."[7]

Plum Grove churchyard, near Jesse Stuart's W-Hollow home, thus provided the source for some of his most highly acclaimed poetry writing, as did the Plum Grove School when his writing turned to reminiscences of his early educational life. One need never look beyond the rim of Stuart's hill region for the sources of his work. If there are some critics who find in his works suggestions of Edgar Lee Masters, Hardy, Burns, or the other poets who figured so deeply in the lonely reading of Jesse Stuart, these suggestions come, the author insists, from his subconscious.

"I have never strived to imitate anyone," Mr. Stuart says. "The writing just comes out of me. I have never tried to develop a style. I just feel the compulsion to write, and I write."[8]

That he must be classed as a "natural-born" writer and that his work has a distinct stamp of originality has been the opinion of many critics, in particular, of those critics who reviewed *Album of Destiny*. Poet-critic Robert Hillyer wrote, in *Saturday Review of Literature*: "*Album of Destiny* is obviously a fine piece of work and something that will last. He [Stuart] controls the single line, which few moderns know how to do. One does not forget a line like 'Each has gone to take his garnered dream.' "[9]

A note less enthusiastic than that sounded in most of the criticisms was given by Henry Nash Smith:

[7] Letter to the writer, August 13, 1953.

[8] Interview with the writer, March 17, 1953.

[9] Robert Hillyer, in section, "Letters to the Editor," *News and Views About Dutton Books and Authors*, Scrapbook 15, p. 25, in the Stuart Room, Murray State College, Murray, Kentucky.

The plan of *Album of Destiny* seems to derive remotely from the *Spoon River Anthology;* most of the poems have as their titles the names of characters and most of them are written in the first person. Stuart's characters are much less vividly distinguished from one another than those of Masters. It is difficult to keep the people straight. He attributes similar emotions to supposedly distinct characters. . . . Despite seeming diversity of themes and characters, the series has a certain monotony, although an exception should be made of the often charming poems uttered by snakes, scorpions, lizards, grass and wind which integrate the human dramas with the non-human forces of nature. One feels that Mr. Stuart has some fresh insights and structural ideas, but that he has allowed them to be smothered by cliches . . . and by the simple fact of too great prolixity.[1]

A reviewer in *The New York Sun* said of Stuart and *Album of Destiny:* "This book has the special qualities of *Man With a Bull-Tongue Plow,* but it is poetry which is at once of apparent greater skill, deeper understanding of his [Stuart's] characters and of the whole created world. The fresh genius of his early work persists, though now underlaid with a profounder note."[2]

These criticisms listed are indicative of the general acclaim and the constructive criticism which *Album of Destiny* received. Considering the book's reception, the highly favorable press given by some of the country's most discriminating critics, as, for instance, Robert Hillyer, it is to be wondered why some of the poems in this collection have not been included in anthologies of Southern literature, such as *Literature of the South,* edited by Richmond Croom Beatty, Floyd C. Watkins, and Thomas Daniel Young. Jesse Stuart is represented in that anthology by two short stories, "Another April" and "Uncle Jeff." No space is given to his poetry, not even to that of *Man With a Bull-Tongue Plow,* which has been previously described in this book as winning several of America's outstanding literary awards for its author.

"The well-tuned strings of his [Stuart's] instrument are

---

[1] *New York Herald-Tribune,* June 5, 1944.
[2] Anon. June 11, 1944.

strung between earth and heaven. Noble and loving poetry!" was the encomium given by Hillyer, in a re-examining of *Album of Destiny* in 1961.[3]

Album of Destiny is Jesse Stuart's most cohesive poetic work. It is a far cry from the spontaneous "unretouched" out-pourings of *Harvest of Youth*[4] and *Man With a Bull-Tongue Plow*, though, as has been shown, many critics (the writer among them), while admiring the beauty and finish of the stanzas of *Album of Destiny*, prefer the naturalness and vigor of the earlier collections.

Stuart himself was keenly disappointed over the lack of attention gained by *Album of Destiny*, which, he said, he had spent eleven years in producing. In 1956, he wrote a poignant article for the literary magazine *The Prairie Schooner*, entitled, "Why I think *Album* is my best." "*Album*," he said, "was a different brain child."

He described the inception of his idea for the book. In late 1932, as he was turning through an old family album of yellow-ing photographs, pictures of his father and mother, and of others, made when they were very young, he was struck more deeply than ever by one of his recurrent themes: the evanescence of time. Time had changed these people, and they would soon fade from the earth. He thought that it would be a dramatic idea for a book, to take fifty people and write portraits of them in verse, dividing their lifetimes into four parts, to represent the four seasons.[5]

In the beginning of *Album of Destiny*, he used a young cou-ple, Kathaleen and John, to narrate this story. It was they who turned the pages of the album of each season, and their children, who spoke out for America.

> My whole panorama of life, beginning with symbols of
> Time's beginning, reptiles, waterdogs, lizards, terrapins, wind,

[3] Robert Hillyer, letter to the writer, April 15, 1961.
[4] *Harvest of Youth* actually preceded *Man With a Bull-Tongue Plow*, but was unpublicized.
[5] *The Prairie Schooner*, **XXX** (Spring 1936), 32.

grass, and with the young handsome pair, John and Kathaleen
. . . impressed only a small minority of reviewers. I thought
the plot would make this book a novel in verse where colorful
characters poured from every page. I toyed with ideas of its
being a musical of people's fleeting days upon this earth, where
their joys, trials, tribulations, plots and counterplots were recorded with carefully chosen words. But my strong, healthy
brain-child grew weary shortly after birth. *Album* was so unknown, unnoticed, and neglected that it died of loneliness.

Stuart was particularly disappointed that none of the critics
mentioned the symbolism woven throughout this work, with the
black snake representing Good and the copperhead Evil.

Album, then, was a failure in gaining attention, except in elic-
iting the aforementioned glowing letter of praise from Robert
Hillyer. Eleven years of painstaking work had produced a big
disappointment. But, said Stuart, he did not regret the time spent
on his "short-lived" *Album:*

> For if a man's offspring, whether he be physical in his own
> image or a brain-child, is different from all others in the fam-
> ily, he singles him out as one to be handled with loving care.
> If the child, image, or dream, gives the parent plenty of trou-
> ble and unnecessary labor, he is remembered and often loved
> partially, over all others. And if his dream or image dies young,
> the bereaved parent has the right to wonder what he might
> have been. . . . My *Album* is not of the oddest odd that make
> up both the dead and the living societies in the over-populated
> world of poetry.

Stuart said that when he finished *Album*, eleven years after
beginning it, "There was some frost around my temples where
there'd never been frost before." He had written more than 2000
poems for the book, though only 423 were published. Critics had
scored him for carelessness in the spontaneous poems of *Man
With a Bull-Tongue Plow*, so for *Album* he wrote four or more
portraits in verse for each one used, revising meticulously.

The whole stands in unison like stones in the wall of a house.
Each part complements the others to make a near-perfect whole.
"To select a few poems might be like trying to pull stones from
the wall. But few poems were ever selected from this book, indi-

vidually, or collectively, until eleven years after publication when an anthologist in far-away Japan selected six from *Album* for his selective, slender, little volume *American Poetry: 1855-1955.*"

Album of Destiny was a *tour de force,* the work that was "different," the one for which Jesse Stuart still grieves as being neglected and misunderstood, as William Faulkner grieved for his most "misunderstood" book, *The Sound and the Fury,* he said, in a group interview with foreign correspondents in Japan in 1956, in which the writer participated.

Kentucky Is My Land, which was first published in 1952, then reissued in 1953, is Stuart's third collection of poetry. It was in 1954 that Jesse Stuart was named Poet Laureate of Kentucky a natural honor following publication of this bardic collection, *Kentucky Is My Land.* Of his four poetry volumes, this work is his most personal. *Man With a Bull-Tongue Plow* and *Album of Destiny* contain portraits of other people, but *Kentucky Is My Land* does not, with the exception of one poem. The exception is "The Ballad of Lonesome Waters," which tells the story of a man who gets a girl "in trouble," goes to war, and comes back to kill the older man she has married in the meantime. There is a legend in the hills that anybody who drops a dime in "the lonesome waters" will return. The man in the ballad cannot drive the idea of revenge from his mind, and so returns to his native hills, thus fulfilling the theme of the legend.

Kentucky Is My Land contains eighty-four poems, which are divided into seven sections: "Kentucky Is My Land" (one long poem); "The Ballad of Lonesome Waters," which has six poems, but is named for the first of them; "Songs for Naomi," Stuart's wife; "Poems For My Daughter," written for his small daughter Jane; "Songs of a Mountain Plowman," which are a group of sonnets reaffirming his affinity with the soil; "Great Lakes Naval Training Station," similar poems about his home, but written with great nostalgia, from his wartime station, and a long poem at the end, "The Builder and the Dream;" about a mountain boy who makes it his lifework to rebuild the forest which has been cut down in his region.

The scope and savor of this collection can be given only

through the quotation of some of its poems. The lead poem is one which, to quote its author, "has been loved all over Kentucky." That poem is now under glass and in frames, "hanging in many offices, schoolrooms and home walls in my state." He was very happy to have this collection of poems published, Mr. Stuart said, because of its significance for his fellow Kentuckians. He was interested, particularly, that members of the Armed Forces from Kentucky should receive copies of the book.[6] The lead poem of *Kentucky Is My Land,* is quoted in part:

Kentucky is my land.
It is a place beneath the wind and sun
In the very heart of America.
It is bounded on the east, north and west by rivers
And on the south by mountains.
Only one boundary line is not a natural one.
It is a portion of southern boundary
That runs westward from the mountains
Across the delta to the Mississippi.

. . . .

I followed the little streams
That flowed over rocks between the high hills to the rivers
And then somewhere into the unknown world
I hunted the wild game in the hunting seasons
Skillful as an Indian.
And I ran wild over the rock-ribbed hills
Enjoying this land of lonesome waters, sunlight,
Tobacco, pine, pawpaw, persimmon, sawbriar, greenbriar and
    sassafras.
I enjoyed the four seasons,
Sections of time my father used to divide his work for the
    year,
As much as any boy in America ever enjoyed them.

. . . .

[6] Jesse Stuart, letter to Lydia Creighton Marsh, E. P. Dutton & Company, New York, March 7, 1952.

I saw New York, a city so large it frightened me,
Cliff dwellings as high as Kentucky mountains,
The streets and avenues were deep gorges
Between high walls of multicolored stone.
And while it interested me
To see how fellow Americans lived,
I longed for Kentucky sunlight, sights and sounds
And for logshacks and the lonesome waters.
I was homesick for the land of the fox
And Spring's tender bud, bloom and leaf,
For white sails of the dogwood and the crabapple
And the flame of redbud in the sunset.
I knew that my Kentucky was different
And something there called me home.
The language too was different,
Not that it was softer
But is was more musical with the hard "g"s
Left automatically from the spoken word
And the prefix "a" supplemented . . .
I knew more than ever before my brain
Had been fashioned by the sights and sounds
And beauties of wildgrowth and life of the hills
That had nurtured my flesh from infancy to full growth.[7]

From the section "Songs for Naomi," which is dedicated to
his wife, there is this lyrical work:

WIND MUSIC

I'm thankful for a love who goes with me
When there is music in the wind at night
On mountains where boughs weave incessantly
Between us and the moon and pale starlight.

[7] During the Poetry Colloquim, which was a feature of the Vanderbilt University Literary Symposium, April 1959 (attended by the writer),
Jesse Stuart stated that the opening poem of *Kentucky Is My Land* was
first written as prose, but that his wife, after reading it, said, "Jesse this
is poetry!" She persuaded him to put it into free verse form.

Immortal symphonies are played by wind
Of destiny that sweeps the upland cone;
Night wind in pines is a crying violin,
Night wind in oaks is a tenor saxophone.

For his daughter there is a poem which shows Stuart in a different aspect from that of poet of nature and of rugged individuality:

I must be careful not to break her slumber
With brogan steps upon this knotty floor;
She must sleep through this storm night of November
Sleep soundly to the music of its roar.
Too soon she'll know of greater storms than this
When she must be awake to know of life;
She must sleep now, know warmth and love and kiss,
Before the days of work and dream and strife.

Jesse Stuart's father is a subject about which he can never finish writing. In *Kentucky Is My Land* there is the poignant "Prayer For My Father":

Be with him, Time, Extend his stay some longer,
He fights to live more than oaks fight to grow;
Be with him, Time, and make his body stronger
And give his heart more strength to make blood flow.
He's cheated Death for forty years and more
To walk upon the crust of earth he's known. . . .

From "Songs of a Mountain Plowman," two poems which appeared originally in the *Saturday Review of Literature*. "Hold to a Living Dream" and "I Cannot Write Tonight" are strongly expressive of his major themes—importance of the individual and his personal vision or dream, and intuitive awareness of nature and of nature's timelessness.

Hold To A Living Dream

Hold to a living dream if you have one
For dream is not akin to dirt and stone,

What is more precious here beneath the sun
Than human dream, this something that you own
Created by your heart and pulsing brain
At any hour, through death's throes of sleep,
Or when you wake and walk in white spring rain,
Or in your youth or when the late hours creep?

Stones will crumble, the poet sings, and buds in spring which
flower into fruit in summer will leave nothing for the winter.

Only your dream has value and can last,
This best your pulsing heart and brain did give
From your substantial or your shattered past
That flowered when you gave it breath to live.

Overlong, with its sixteen lines, this sonnet is illustrative of
Stuart's repetition of thought which might well have been ex-
cised, as the repetition is not made for musical effect, and as the
repetition, in this instance, does not give added strength. The
poem opens strongly, with a trochaic foot, "Hold to a living
dream if you have one." Since the origin of the dream in the
heart and pulsing brain is represented in the lines which follow
the opening, it would seem stronger to omit the repetitive sequence at the end, and to conclude with a line matching in
strength the opening one—such as this line, opening with a
trochaic foot, "Only your dream has value and can last."

"I Cannot Write Tonight" exemplifies Stuart's deep accord
with nature. It is a notable example, too, of his control of the
single line, and contains one of his typically indigenous similes,
". . . the moon is full/And large as a wagon-wheel."

I Cannot Write Tonight

I cannot write tonight for the moon is full
And large as a wagon-wheel above the timber;
I must go out for the world is beautiful,
Must leave the open fire and dying ember.
For what are words upon an ink-stained scroll

When magic moonlight floods this stubborn world,
When wary winds of ruthless winter roll
Over the knolls, and leaf and seed are hurled
Into illimitable starry space. . . .

"The Last Leave Home" contains nostalgic sonnets of farewell to his mountains, such as this one quoted in part:

Alien atolls I know will not have trees
Such as the blackgum, sassafras and beeches
That are tethered and as tough as these. . . .
They'll have pandanas, palms on their small reaches
They will not have red-raining of the leaves
From clouded tree-tops with a preening sound;
Nor will they have an autumn wind that grieves
Among sawbriars close to frosted ground.

Critic I. L. Saloman, reviewing the reissued edition of *Kentucky Is My Land* for *The Saturday Review*, had this to say:

    . . . *Kentucky Is My Land* offers remarkable surprises, a
handful of poems exceedingly choice, since they satisfy the
imagination, and an overweighted selection of personal sonnets, for the most part pedestrian in execution, if valiant, hum-
ble, and humane in subject matter.
Americana is considerably enriched by "Elegy for Mitch
Stuart," a gem of concision, and by "The Ballad of Lonesome
Waters," a folk myth, lusty, indigenous and veined rich with
images, flavored with provincialisms:

I am myself . . . I'll do as I durn
    please.
I'll churn no milk, black-flag no
    hound dog fleas.
I'll patch no pants, and stocking in
    the knees.
And from this yard I'll rake no
    blackoak leaves.

The title-poem in free verse, the lyric "By Sandy Waters," the third sonnet in "The Last Leave Home," and the narrative "The Builder and the Dream" contain excellences achieved with the sure touch of craftsmanship.[8]

"Elegy for Mitch Stuart" was Jesse Stuart's first published poem. He describes the arrival of the check for this poem, a milestone in his life, in *Beyond Dark Hills:*

> My father brings me a letter from the post office. It is a thin letter from the *American Mercury*. I open the letter. It is a $25-check for a poem! The first poem I've ever sold for money! Donald Davidson told me to send this poem to the *American Mercury* when I was in Vanderbilt University. I'd even forgotten about sending it . . . "Elegy for Mitch Stuart" . . . a check with H. L. Mencken's name on it! Just a short time ago didn't I see where H. L. Mencken had said there wasn't any worthwhile poetry written in America? What was he doing buying a poem from me? [p. 340]

Some thirty years have elapsed since the publishing of that first poem by Stuart, and the poem has received recognition today just as it did in its first printing. Perhaps it may be said that Americana is permanently enriched by "Elegy for Mitch Stuart." This poem highlights the singular versatility of the author, who achieved initial fame through the intensely personal and songlike sonnets of *Man With A Bull-Tongue Plow.* Interspersed with the lyrical verses of that collection, as has been seen, there were the tough-minded and penetrating sonnets which characterize Jesse Stuart's realistic approach to life, the lines alive with bold metaphors and defiance of traditional forms, and the subject matter strikingly original.

Two poems in *Kentucky Is My Land* seem, in particular, to show that Stuart writes in the spirit of Burns. "May I Be Dead" reflects the strong individualist and the social critic. "By Sandy Waters" is akin to the Burns lyric.

May I Be Dead

May I be dead when all the
    woods are old

[8] XXXVI (December 26, 1953), 21.

And shaped to patterns of the
    planners' minds,
When great unnatural rows of
    trees unfold
Their tender foliage to the April
    winds,
May I be dead when Sandy is not
    free,
And transferred to a channel not
    its own,
Water through years that sang for
    her and me
Over the precipice and soft
    sandstone . . .
Let wild rose be an epitaph for me
When redbirds go and helpless
    shikepokes must,
And red beans on the honey-locust
    tree
Are long-forgotten banners turned
    to dust . . .
I weep to think these hills where
    I awoke,
Saw God's great beauty, wonderful
    and strange,
Will be destroyed, stem and flower
    and oak,
And I would rather die than see
    the change.

By SANDY WATERS

Much have I roved by Sandy River
Among the spring-bloomed thyme,
Where love and life go on forever
And where I've spun my rhyme.
Much have I loved by Sandy River

Girls with the light brown hair;
I thought love would go on forever
Spring be forever fair.
The Spring for mountains goes forever
But not for us who fade
In love and life by Sandy River
Before our dreams are made. . . .
Before our dust goes back forever
To mountain earth we've known;
Before the sweet thyme blossoms hither
Among the gray sandstone.
I pray the music from this river
Will sing for them and me;
Will sing for us, for us forever,
In our eternity.

Burns wrote in "Halloween":

Whyles owre a linn the burnie plays,
    As thro' the glen it wimpl't;
Whyles round a rocky scaur it strays,
    Whyles in a wiel it dimpl't;
Whyles glitter'd to the nightly rays,
    Wi' bickerin, dancin dazzle;
Whyles cookit underneath the braes,
    Below the spreading hazel
            Unseen that night.

Stuart does not adopt the Burns stanza, but, the occasional dimeter and trimeter lines in the verse have a suggestion of the fillip of the Burns end-rhymes.

It is interesting to note that "Sandy" recurs in Stuart's later volume of poetry *Hold April* (1962), in an even more songlike Burnsian mood, as "Sandy Will Flow Forever."

Sandy will flow forever to the sea
Beneath the clouds of green leaves on the willows;

Sandy will flow as long as winds are free
And ironweeds purple on the summer meadows.
Now I shall catch a breath of wind tonight,
Walk down this twisted road beneath the moon;
And I will surely find one song to write
Where whippoorwills and cornfield insects croon.
And Sandy River mad with April showers
Flows headlong down spring's corridors of green,
Her grassy banks whitewashed with April flowers
As pretty as this mortal eye has seen.

In discussing the modern poet and his tradition, Cleanth Brooks says of the tendency today to substitute new and unworked material for old:

> The tendency merges . . . with a certain kind of regionalism to produce a poetry of local color, as Jesse Stuart's *Man With a Bull-Tongue Plow*. The question of regionalism and traditionalism is raised in acute form by all American poetry. It is bound up with the technique of inclusion, the welding of the past with the present. The Southern poet who is unwilling to sentimentalize the past or to limit himself to objective descriptions of local color of the present must, of necessity, mediate his account of the Old South through a consciousness of the present, that is, of its present non-existence. To sum up, his experience will include both positive and negative elements and his real test as poet is his ability to bring the two sorts into unity.[9]

A structure of inclusion may be said to underlie the poetry of Jesse Stuart. Stuart, in deep fidelity to his Kentucky region, to his native South, relates the past with the stirring challenge of the present and brings to his empathic readers a sense of identification with the protagonists in the drama of life portrayed.

"The critics whose habits were formed a generation ago feel that they (the modern poets) are obscure, difficult, and willfully

---

[9] *Modern Poetry and the Tradition* (Chapel Hill: The University of North Carolina Press, 1939), 75.

perverse," says Cleanth Brooks. "Certainly every one-volume history of English literature still conceives of the Romantic period
as the one, far-off, divine event toward which the whole course
of English poetry moves. The modern poetry of our time is the
first to call that view seriously in question."[1]

In the sense that the modern poet is "obscure, difficult, and
willfully perverse," Jesse Stuart is not, it would seem, a modern
poet, although he is writing today, and is achieving recognition
for his poetry. The inspiration for his work goes back to Wordsworth, Robert Burns, Edgar Allan Poe, and, in form, he rarely
strays far from the traditional Shakespearean sonnet. Occasionally,
as in the lead poem of *Kentucky Is My Land*, he uses free verse
reminiscent of that of Whitman, Sandburg, and Edgar Lee Masters. But, generally speaking, Stuart may be found on the side
of the Romantics, his poems revealing a fervor of mind that was
characteristic of the Romantic poets. This fervor was established
as a dictum for poets by Plato in *Ion:* "For all good poets . . .
compose their beautiful poems not as works of art, but because
they are inspired and possessed. And as the Corybantian revellers
when they dance are not in their right mind, so the lyric poets
are not in their right mind when they are composing their beautiful strains. . . ."[2]

Archibald MacLeish, in lecturing to a contemporary literature
class at Peabody College, said: "The kind of knowledge which
poetry is capable of giving, the kind of knowledge of which poetry is an instrument, is not the kind of knowledge which abstracts
general truths and expresses them by symbols and images or in the
logic of the syntactical statement. The kind of knowledge of
which poetry is capable is the thing you have always known was
true, yet never knew until you saw it in those words."[3]

That Jesse Stuart has always felt it the function of the poet

[1] Ibid., 8.

[2] Plato, *Ion, tr.* W. R. M. Lamb (New York: G. P. Putnam's Sons,
1925), 421.

[3] "The Reading and Teaching of Modern Poetry," *The Peabody Reflector,* XXVI (1953), 6.

to transmit the immediate knowledge of experience rather than to attempt its expression to the elect "in the logic of the syntactical statement" is recorded in his autobiographical novel *Beyond Dark Hills:*

> I take long walks over the old pathways. Yes, back to Plum Grove at night. Didn't I have a thought once that the dead would like to speak from their Plum Grove graves?. . . Why not let all these speak? All the dead I'd seen hauled here and buried. That is what I would do. . . . I go among these graves at night. It is lonely here among these departed ghosts. I let them speak. The whippoorwills sing in the moonlight from the drowsy Kentucky fresh-leafed hills. I write and write and write for them. On Sundays I come here and write. I let them speak for themselves. . . . The people have passed through the pages of a book, all kinds of people, and they have spoken. Even the worst of them had something good in them when they spoke what was in their heart. I put myself honestly into their places and spoke for them [p. 374]

Not for Jesse Stuart is the Wordsworthian idea of poetry as emotion recollected in tranquility. His is a more dramatic and mystical approach, which seeks to convey the exact feeling, or emotion, at the time of the poet's experience of it, and does not await the reflection or analytical moment. Thus, Stuart visited the graveyard at Plum Grove Church at night, and wrote his death sonnets for *Man With a Bull-Tongue Plow* while on the actual scene, writing by lantern light or bright moonlight, to capture reality as he put himself "in the places" of his characters and "spoke for them."[4]

Again, he stresses his practice of writing at the moment of experience in order to put exact sensation and impressions into his poetry, as in this passage in *The Thread That Runs So True,*

---

[4] When the writer visited the Stuarts at W-Hollow in July, 1960, they took her to Plum Grove Church yard, and there, in that quiet and most peaceful setting, Jesse Stuart showed her the graves where he had copied long-dead names from the tombstones—including the grave, which had the little verse "Remember me as you pass by" which had inspired him to write his death sonnets—and described for her his writ-

which describes his five-mile walk from his home in the hills to his office in the town of Greenwood (Greenup) as Superintendent of the Greenwood County Schools:

Often I walked to my office with ice frozen in my hair, for I went bareheaded regardless of rain, snow and sleet. When I reached my office in the morning, I would have a sheaf of almost indecipherable poems I had written in the winter rain so I could catch the exact sounds of the water hitting oak leaves. When I saw something along the way that excited my brain to poetic moods, I sat down on a stump, log, or rock, and jotted down the ideas that came to me, just as I had done when I worked on the farm the summer I was elected Superintendent of Greenwood County Schools. This was the only time I had now. I could not write these moods in my office. But after my day in the office—after the city was blanketed in darkness—I would remain in the office, and use the county typewriter and the county's minute-book stationery, and type these poems.[5]

Jesse Stuart's philosophy of meeting the challenge of life, which he follows even today when he might well withdraw to the restful seclusion of his hills, was early expressed in this sonnet, "Batter Me Down, Life," which appeared in his very first poetry collection, *Harvest of Youth*, published in 1930, and again in 1938 in *Beyond Dark Hills*:

Batter me down, you who are strong, I plead.
I who am weak, in the little ways I know
will learn to battle young and soon take heed.
Batter me down, as rain beats grasses low!
I know when cherry buds learn to obey

---

ing at night in the graveyard, to get realism for his poetic characterizations. These sonnets were published actually as he wrote them, he said, in natural, spontaneous moods—in contrast to the carefully polished lines of his next collection, *Album of Destiny*, which took him eleven years in the writing.

[5] *The Thread That Runs So True* (New York: Charles Scribner's Sons, 1949), 211, 212.

The gusty April rain drops' stern command;
I know that night will usher into day
Sun gems the lark will rise in afterglow
Of storm . . . . proud wings above the scarlet lea;
And a river young will wear a way to go
Until it cuts a channel to the sea.
Batter me down, Life! Give me blow for blow!
I'll take the bleeding lips and liberty!

In 1962, in stanza IX of his long free-verse tribute to earth, "Dawn," in *Hold April*, he was still welcoming and defying challenge:

This earth, a mighty living giant,
Cannot throw me off his back
For I am man.
I will have my say before the end
When he has hidden me,
If in my game of hide and seek with him,
Like a wild hare with the hounds,
I can dodge him long enough.
The little I have borrowed from him,
I shall return with interest.

But the most dramatic and revealing of Stuart's fighting sonnets is No. 365 in *Man With a Bull-Tongue Plow*, in which, characteristically, he gives the abstraction Defeat personification and defies it with youthful belligerence, as quoted here in part:

I've met you many times before, Defeat.
Not everytime we fought you blacked my eyes,
For many times I've staggered to my feet
And hit you hard enough to break your ribs.
You know, Defeat, I whipped you at the plow.
I fought you at hot furnaces of steel.
You whipped me at the circus, made a show of me—
Of me for men to see—and now I feel

That when we meet again, one man must kill.

The diction of this poem is conversational, direct, and the use of five-stress iambic lines containing ten monosyllables contributes to its hard-hitting effect, its blunt summation of a lifelong Stuart creed.

In *Lyrics from Lincoln Memorial University*, a small volume dedicated "To Chancellor John Wesley Hill, who has wrought mightily for the highland boys and girls," published in 1928 and edited by Jesse Stuart, the young poet includes two of his works which show his earliest affinity for the conversational style.[6] The two poems are sharply opposed in tone. "Things I Have Loved" is quiet, reflective, and puts Stuart's native rustic construction upon Rupert Brooke's famous lines:

> I have loved cool walnut groves, wide-mirroring streams;
> The many beetling rocks with soft impressive seams
> Of clinging moss, and old houses with patched window panes.
> . . . And I have loved wind-waves of grass,
> Plush carpets, and silver rims on china-ware and glass.

"Six Hickories," in a free-verse narrative style that is more poetic prose than poetry, is brusque and dramatic, reminiscent of Sandburg:

> Listen: we were running a water sawmill, somewhere at Six
> Hickories . . . [sic] seven men, broad-shouldered, husky,
> stormy, and brawling. We chewed tobacco and flapped
> broadrimmed and dusky felt hats.
> Six Hickories, a town of seven families, crouched in the sha-
> dow of Big Horn Mountain . . . empty and gaunt. . . .

In *Harvest of Youth* "Six Hickories" becomes "Steel Gang," and the first lines, "Listen, we were dogging steel, somewhere Between Six Hickories and Muldraugh Hill. . . ."

[6] *Lyrics from Lincoln Memorial University* (Harrogate Tenn: Lincoln Memorial Press, 1928).

Although *Man With a Bull-Tongue Plow* was hailed as Stuart's first collection of poetry, *Harvest of Youth,* published in 1930 by The Scroll Press, at Howe, Oklahoma, was actually his first collection to be in print. It is not listed with his other published works, but this *juvenilia* is of the greatest interest to the biographer of Jesse Stuart. It shows his early preoccupations and early experimentations with verse forms before settling upon the traditional Shakespearean sonnet and its variations.

The dedication of *Harvest of Youth* is to the professor who was a great influence upon Stuart at Lincoln Memorial University: "To Harry Harrison Kroll—Genius, Novelist and Southern Realist, These Artless Poems of My Youth Are Dedicated With All Good Reasons." Acknowledgements, which show the Kentuckian's early success in publication, include *Kentucky Folklore and Poetry Magazine, International Poetry Magazine, Poetry (Bristol Courier), The Stratford Magazine, The American Poet, Poetry Quarterly, The Echo, Braithwaite, The Spring Anthology* (England, 1929).

A long poem from that first collection, entitled "Free God," is written in quatrains which give it the swing of a ballad, but the subject is an awesome one for the lilting ballad rhythm. It reveals the superstition of the hill people toward the Almighty and the conscience-stricken state of the young poet who is away from his mountain home. Some of the verses of "Free God" are as follows:

> While I was yet a young child
>   I heard an old man pray
> For his Saviour to come down
>   And bear our souls away.

> He told us his Saviour wore
>   A halo round his head;
> He told us that Judas' beard
>   Was of deceitful red.

And when we got to Heaven,
　　How we would understand
How the Saviour went walking
　　With a cane in his hand.

Then the eyes of the people
　　Were lit with fiery glow,
When he pointed his finger
　　Each brother nodded, "So."

I believed I heard God's word;
　　I formed my belief
From the prelude of wind words
　　From the crisp dry leaf.

I surrendered to the God
　　That the old man knew;
I dared risk my own thought
　　And read the Bible through.

Then for thirteen stanzas, the poet lives with youthful sin, forgets the God he has accepted—until "one stark terror night, I left
my bed-fellow. . . ."

I read my dusty Bible
　　From cover to cover;
I found one God and one God
　　Was a jealous Lover.
　. . . . .
He was a jealous Lover;
　　And I a fool for Love;
When I read into His word
　　My heart grew full thereof
　. . . . .
I found him in the rising sap
　　In a March sapling tree;
I found him in the winter wind,
　　Blowing wildly and free.

I found him in the water;
 I found him in the air,
I found him in Sinful Flesh;
 I found him everywhere.

He had a tremendous soul
 Of all under the sun.
And the bloods of his people
 Were to him as one.

And I make my vows for his love
 And from sin to recover
And to calm rebellious flesh
 Of any sinful lover.

This poem, with its transcendental overtones, shows Jesse Stuart's deep conviction from his earliest writing that God is as much in Nature as in a church, that he is a "Free God."

A section devoted to "Epitaphs" has quatrains, also, and is characteristic of Stuart's preoccupation with death as a subject for poetry:

Poet

If there is life beyond the grave,
 He lives in future bliss.
If there is not another world,
 He made the most of this.

My Landlord

He had the gold and three estates;
 But when he had to pass
Life's finished line, he did not leave
 His shadow on the grass.

For J. Y.

They hauled her here from West Birmingham
 But the neighbors did not know

When they earthed her down upon her grave
   A tree with tongues would grow.

Carelessness of rhyme shows in these early verses, but this section contains, also, two of Stuart's finest elegiac poems—"Mountain Funeral," which appeared later in the collection *Kentucky Is My Land*, and was reprinted in the "Poet's Corner" of *The New York Times*, and "*For Warriors Dead*." "Mountain Funeral" puts into poetic form the atmospheric impressions of a funeral such as that of Battle Keaton in "Battle Keaton Dies," an early short story.

Mountain Funeral

We could not stay about the house
   Where so many were crying;
We pushed on through the sobbing crowd
   From where the corpse was lying.

We walked the path behind the house
   Among his blooming trees
And wondered if he dreamed again
   Of gathering fruit from these.
. . . .
The bees he loved were working on
The tall wind-waves of clover;
The evening winds he loved to hear
Were softly blowing over.

"For Warriors Dead" is an elegy not only for the Indian, but for nameless pioneers and soldiers whose dust is mingled with that of the later hill generations.

If warriors' bones should rise from forlorn hills,
Assume colorful flesh and brittle blood,
Forget the death dance, the fife's whirring shrills,
Forget thin, cool wrappers of writhing mud,
They would find cloistered houses rich in change,

Treeless hills bent in tawny sun-down flames;
They would find new kin, defiant, proud, yet strange—
But not one cross bearing their long-lost names.

The young Stuart experimented lavishly with verse forms with results that were interesting and sometimes dramatic. "Undulated Season," with its sharp imagist word-pictures, shows a touch of T. S. Eliot and e.e. cummings influence:

  1
i met her a tiny flame
in a tiny town that hath not understanding
when March tree sap
was turbulent young blood
in young arteries
when prophetic March winds sang
through the white plum leaves

 . . . .

  2
copper August
myriads of grass
with tawny arms clutching
dry concrete breasts for nourishment
papers and the wind hither and thither
down monuments
dark alley ways
called time

  3
a tiny flame in a tiny town
lies limb to limb with any lover
  the world is young
  and you are young
  feast while you may

  4
nassal Autumn
tweaking winds in bare twigs

plum leaves in a golden shower
rustle with the wind
down alleyways
called time
    birds fly to bare plum twigs
    to chat of love
    one by one they come
    remembering the glossy green
    of their season
    mating

    5

now the old men talk
where is she now
gone is she
who was so beautiful
we knew her
but she is gone
we dare not speak of her
we dare not speak for her
since she is gone

    6

yellow the winds drift
the winds drift yellow
time is strewn yellow with plum leaves
footprints of school children
innocent metallic imprints
are buried under
for the old to see

    7

winter of life
an undulated season
for storms age sap
but winter has drunk
the sap from summer's warm sweet body
    there was a season

when the world was young
God planned it
not i

Following, there is the refrain about "a tiny flame in a tiny
town," and the form becomes even more irregular and the language even more epigrammatic.

In contrast to this lengthy and labored exercise is an exquisite
little stanza, with great depth of feeling:

Hurt Not the Proud

Hurt not the proud for they shall live
   Enduring strangely quiet alone;
They who were proud words in flesh
   Shall surely carve proud words in stone.

This brief poem might well be called a Jesse Stuart credo. It
was included in W. S. Braithwaite's *Anthology of Magazine Verse
for* 1929 (New York: Sully, 1929).

In defiant mood is "Saint or Sinner":

You tell me with two eyes like stone
That I am a rugged sinner;
That I shall know by bending bones
When you pass me by the winner.

Since we are fruit of a human tree
And death frost blights our common lot,
To cling or fail is same to me
When saints dry up, when sinners rot.

A recurrent Stuart theme, the ephemeral quality of life, appears in "One Life":

One life
Is a wisp of fog
Between eternities . . .

No second choice for Death wipes the
Slate clean.

Though reluctant to leave his friends, the poet shows great
nostalgia for home in the poems "My City," and "My People's
Prayers." "My City," a long poem, is much in the free-verse style
of the opening stanzas of *Kentucky Is My Land,* and could well
be poetic prose:

My City

Riverton, my city of two hundred houses
Was built when the Ohio Valley was young,
In the dawn change of clean sky mists
By new men of a new West
Who had a dream to build a city.

My People's Prayers

I always go to Plum Grove Church
To hear my peoples' prayers
I know here is religious air

For the mood of God is theirs.
Even the side lamps' dingy flames
Are low red moons on the wall;
Without, the dreary dark expanse
Covers the trees, the field and all.

. . . .

Stuart's penchant for creating atmospheric lines in the settings
for his poems with metaphors that are original and stirring of the
imagination, is seen here in the picturing of the old church's side
lamps, whose ". . . dingy flames Are low red moons on the wall."
The low red moon is a bizarre moon whose image arouses wonder, like the phenomenon of Nature, the strange and "scary light"
which illumined the evening sky in his *Foretaste of Glory,* seeming to portend the end of the world. The red moons of the

church lamps are portents of Judgment for the young poet in his erring ways, to which he alludes later in the poem.

Though most of the early poems show unevenness of style and crudities, some of them adumbrate the sonnet forms and thought patterns characteristic of Stuart's later poetry collections which achieved distinction. "Harvard or the Sea" has the conventional fourteen lines of the sonnet; but the meter is iambic hexameter, instead of pentameter. The rhyme scheme of the octave is regular for the Petrarchan sonnet, but the sestet is irregular, ending with a couplet.

> I have lived my youth in one unsettled state
> And months of barren earth is life too much for me.
> The glorious close will bring me Harvard or the sea.
> Nine months earth prisoned! How can I bear to wait?
> Since I was twelve, I have been foot-free to the soil;
> Pocketless a dime, I've rambled through many a town
> When the winter moon and silver stars slanted down;
> Bunked with toughs; did with them a tremendous toil;
> Met pals, forgot; stopped and took my school life stay.
> Now within Harvard's Halls there is one life for me.
> Another life is on waste water's blue immensity
> That will make me turn my back on home, forget the day
> My feet were bound to earth. Then Great Seducer Sea,
> Be last to pant and lick your wet lips over me.

Four years later, in *Poetry—A Magazine of Verse*, there was eloquent testimony to the success with which Jesse Stuart had toned down his early flamboyance of style and had achieved richer depths of meaning. This sophisticated magazine, edited by Harriet Monroe, in Chicago, so influential in the early days of Imagist poets, had the following tribute for Jesse Stuart in its November 1934 issue:

> The Jeanette Sewal Davis Prize of one hundred dollars for a poem or group of poems by a young poet, offered this year for the first time through two friends of *Poetry*, is awarded to Jesse Stuart of Fullerton, Kentucky, printed in *Poetry* for May

1934, and now reprinted in his recent book, *Man With a Bull-Tongue Plow*. Among "Honorable Mention" for poems appearing in Poetry this year are "Canto XXXVII," by Ezra Pound, "That's the American Style," by William Carlos Williams, "Elegy as Epithalamium," by John Gould Fletcher and "New Times On the Plains," by Paul Engle.

In the same issue of *Poetry*, two sonnets from Stuart's prize group were reprinted:

No. 3 in the sequence *Young Kentucky:*

The August sassafras leaves are turning red;
The black-oak leaves are getting tough and thick;
The corn is dying and the beans are dead;
The pasture grass is short, and cattle pick
The leaves from sprouts and reach between the wires,
And crane their necks to gather tall grass there.
The yellow leaves are dropping from green briars
Like drops of water fall on the field stones.
The summer blood is dripping from the trees;
The trees are in a windy autumn mood
To give their blood in drops of flying leaves—
It must hurt them to lose their summer blood.
The trees are drunk till Spring gives them new birth;
Their blood is whiskey for the thirsty earth.

No. 7 in the sequence *Young Kentucky:*

The winds are kind to white bones on a hill—
The black snake loves to coil among white bones.
White bones are foot-rest for the whippoorwill;
White bones are a clean kind of pretty stones
And dust of one is quick growth for the weeds,
For round a pile of bones the weeds grow tall;
They get the kind of nourishment they need—
These barricades wherein the snakes may crawl.
Then let my bones lie open to the wind;
My dust give quick growth to the roots of weeds;

Let my eyes' socket-rims turn to the skies;
Let wind and weeds play the sweet violin.
This is the mountain requiem my dust needs
When on the surface of some hill it lies.

The diction is concrete and colloquial, but there is a ballad-like quality throughout, a repetition of words and sounds for musical effect, which overlies the commonplace and gives universal meaning.

In *Enjoying Poetry*, Mark Van Doren stresses the importance of music in poetry. In the analyzing of poems in the volume, Van Doren says, "I have considered nothing but what a poem says and how it says it. It says it with music, and so I have emphasized the contribution in each case of rhythm and sound."[7]

As stated earlier in this chapter, Mark Van Doren was the critic who first termed Jesse Stuart an "American Robert Burns," pointing out, among other similarities, the affinity of the two poets for the use of rhythm and of sound.

Stuart's books of poetry *Kentucky Is My Land* and *Hold April* do not have a plot and characters who appear and reappear throughout the work, are made up of highly subjective sonnets reflecting the life and ideas of the poet himself. These personal sonnets and nature sonnets, written usually in iambic pentameter, are typical of the individual poems of Stuart's which have been published in magazines in recent years. A surprising, highly dramatic exception to the usual pattern was "Colorado," a long Whitmanesque tribute to Colorado, in stanzas of varying lengths, with verisification ranging from free verse and blank verse in iambic pentameter, to quatrains in dimeter and trimeter. The effect is interesting, and the tone intense and incantational.

Colorado

The Great Plains

Accept Us Colorado: We who

[7] Mark Van Doren, *Enjoying Poetry* (New York: William Sloane Associates, Inc., 1951), X.

Are strangers to your fascinating land,
We who have driven across your plains,
Encountering winds we never faced before,
We loved their open mouths and white-spike teeth,
Voluminous, light-silvered with a special moan.
Accept your curious strangers who seek,
Like ancient Greeks, beauty wherever found.
Grat Plains, the jutted, snow-capped peaks
And seas of golden wheat from darkling ground.[8]

This long poem has been selected by W. S. Braithwaite to be featured in his forthcoming *Anthology of Magazine Verse*. "Kitty-Hawk," by Robert Frost, was featured in the 1960 one.

Early in 1961, there came for Jesse Stuart, at long last, the important recognition for his poetry for which he had hoped ever since the stir over *Man With a Bull-Tongue Plow* had died. He was awarded the 1960 Fellowship of the Academy of American Poets, the highest award in America for poetry. He was in the middle of his year of teaching at the American University in Cairo, Egypt, when news of the award reached him. His wife and daughter Jane were with him there. He was tremendously moved by his unexpected honor, and among the first persons he notified about it were his former professor and mentor, Donald Davidson, and the writer. The writer received an excited letter from Cairo, dated February 5, 1961:

> This might be out in America, if not now, by the time you get this letter. Anyway, its big! It's what you've said, hoped for, and said you believed would happen. But, can you honestly believe, Eve, I've been given the 1960 Fellowship Poetry Award of $5,000 by th Academy of American Poets? Can you? You know the story. Twenty-seven years ago, I got the Jeanette Sewal Davis prize of $100, and 1957 or '58, the Lyric Magazine prize of $50. Never dreamed such as this would happen to me! Well it has! Over 1600 poems, and I've never budged from what I believed about poetry—that

[8] Stuart, "Colorado," *Best Articles and Stories*, III (October 1959), 50-52. Jesse Stuart told this writer that he would continue to experiment with form rather than keep to his usual sonnet stanza.

it should *communicate*—I wouldn't become a part of a school. I never gave an inch from what I believed. . . . Well, now, this—God has let me live for something!

Writing to the Academy of American Poets for a list of the chancellors who had awarded Jesse Stuart the fellowship, the writer learned that Stuart's longtime friend, Robert Hillyer, the noted poet-critic, was a member of the group. Hillyer, whom Stuart had never met, had written admiring and encouraging letters to the Kentuckian ever since the publication of *Album of Destiny* in 1944, which he had praised so highly. Responding to a letter from the writer, Hillyer wrote enthusiastically about Stuart's award, saying that he and Robert Nathan, who was also one of the Academy's Chancellors, and other members who felt that Jesse Stuart had never received just recognition for his poetry, had sparked a drive to give him the 1960 fellowship.[9]

Other members of the Board of Chancellors of the Academy (Edwin Arlington Robinson was among its founders in 1934) were W. H. Auden, J. Donald Adams, Witter Bynner, Dr. Henry Seidel Canby (now deceased), Max Eastman, Randall Jarrell, Marianne Moore, John G. Neihardt, Frederick A. Pottle, and John Hall Wheelock.

It was an unforgettable moment in life for the writer to be present, with Naomi Deane Stuart and Jane Stuart, for the Award ceremony which was staged by the Academy of American Poets in November of 1961 for Jesse Stuart at the New York Apartment of Mr. Eli Whitney Debevoise, a director of the Academy. Following the presentation of the award by Mrs. Hugh Bullock, president, a scroll which cited Stuart for "distinguished poetic achievement" in the whole body of his works of poetry, Jesse Stuart, the pastoral poet, read "Hold To a Living Dream," "I Cannot Write Tonight," from *Kentucky Is My Land*, and the lead sonnet from his *Man With a Bull-Tongue Plow*, "I Am a Farmer Singing at the Plow."

[9] Robert Hillyer, letter to the writer from Newark, Delaware, March 3, 1961.

He read these poems in an emotion-choked voice, to some of New York's most sophisticated intellectuals, who gave him their utmost attention. So must Robert Burns have held his listeners in the salons of Edinburgh!

The remark afterward of John Hall Wheelock seemed to represent the view of the Academy members present.

"A great poet, a great poet," Mr. Wheelock exclaimed. "A fine, sensitive poet! Jesse Stuart has an almost mystical union with the infinite."

Wheelock continued that he felt that the day of the romantic poet, the "natural" poet, who can "communicate" with the people, the bardic type such as Stuart represents is, indeed, on its way again.

Hold April is Stuart's latest volume of poetry, a collection of poems, which might be called the summation of his lifetime of poetic thought.

Hold on to April; never let her pass!
Another year before she comes again
To bring us wind as clean as polished glass
And apple blossoms in soft, silver rain.[1]

Jesse Stuart begins the title poem of his new collection with these typical dynamic lines for a fragmented world. Be ever aware of nature and its beauties, and hold fleeting springtime in the heart, the poet of the Kentucky hills adjures his readers in this summation of his lifetime of poetic expression.

Be in a joyful mood and walk with me
Into beginning Spring's cool solitude. . . .

"Be in a Joyful Mood," opening with the above lines, is indicative of the intensely subjective poetry of Jesse Stuart's "mood poetry," ranging through alternating periods of happiness, deep

[1] Stuart, *Hold April* (New York: McGraw-Hill Book Co., Inc., 1962), 87.

sadness, protest, and affiirmation. There is, however, an overall philosophy of optimism that is Stuart's particular contribution to today's world.

In "Light and Shadow," one of the most beautiful of the sonnets, "light over darkness has a final power." The poet writes of the "dispersing" of the darkness night has sown. The "Baby-handed moles" are sent back to their holes deep underground, and

> Invisible hands are now dispersing dew
> On morning-glory bell and buttercup—
> Long, unseen arms extend across wind-blue
> To gather all the jewel dewdrops up.

Love of life permeates *Hold April*. It is especially apparent in the deeply religious poem "Back Where I Belong," in which Jesse Stuart thanks God for his return to life, following his near-fatal heart attack in 1954—his return to his valley, to his garden, to the land where he belongs:

> I'll stand beneath the gray-barked sycamore
> And with soft hands I'll feel its scaly bark,
> Not any man will ever love life more.

Naomi Deane Stuart, who has been such a vital influence upon her husband's career and a central figure throughout his writing in both poetry and prose, receives even deeper tribute in "Love Song After Forty," the lead poem in *Hold April*. Deane, still "neatly-patterned as a willow tree," as he referred to her lyrically in an early poem, is seen in strong romantic aura as the poet looks back on their twenty-four years of marriage, averring that "the second ledge has views that are sublime." Autumn contains a nostalgia for spring, but has its own deeply significant meaning:

> Higher and higher
> Where the dim path goes.

By a late primrose.
There is more to admire
Where the late leaf goes.

"Autumn Sequence" is a group of six sonnets, which explores in greater depths of awareness the significance of late middle life approaching the metamorphosis into the winter of older age. Stuart follows scrupulously in this group the Shakesperean rhyme scheme and the fourteen-line stanza. "Autumn Sequence" belies the impression too often given by Stuart in his poetry that he is a careless craftsman.

The tone of this group varies from melancholia to exaltation:

There is no need for one to say the bee
Has come to gather honey from the clover
And honeydew from leaves of sweetgum tree,
It is too late because the summer's over
With frosted petals of late flowers dying.

Autumn beauty has a special poignancy for the poet:

Never was night as wind-swept beautiful!
Blow by them winds, in deep poetic mood!
Go whine among the sedge where cidia lull,
But do not chill poor circulating blood[2]

The fifth sonnet increases to incantational intensity:

Autumn is not forever for the land,
It brings new beauty and a change of season;
Life in declension follows death's command,
Then sleeps and knows rebirth for valid reason.
Life is linked with the Sun from birth to death.
O, mighty Sun! Let us now thank the Sun!

[2] The writer asked Jesse Stuart if the word "cidia" in this sonnet were a colloquialism for "cicada." He replied that it is, and he said "Our word is softer, prettier than 'cicada' so I used it."

. . . .
O, mighty Sun, above our ancient gods!
O, mighty Sun, above our autumn earth!

. . . .
Our gift, O mighty Sun, are plants from you!
We lift, O, mighty Sun, a chant to you!

In contrast to these heightened lines are the conversational ones of two poems which are Burns-like in theme—"The Day I Drove My Truck," an episode of the killing of a mole by Stuart's dog, describes the poet's dismay and his subsequent carrying home of baby moles for feeding; and "Free Ride," the only humorous poem in this collection. "Free Ride" is the result of Stuart's idle speculation about a fly which enplaned with the passengers on a flight from Dallas, and left with them in Chicago, greeting a fly that met the plane there.

"The Ballad of the Bride," does not have the quatrain form, but it is written in alternate four-stress and three-stress lines, giving it the traditional rhythm of the folk ballad. "House in the Wind," written in rhyming couplets, is an early Stuart experimentation in form, having been published in the *Yale Review* in 1934. These poems are notable departures from Stuart's usual sonnet stanza.

The varied poems for Jesse Stuart's *Hold April* were selected by Robert Hillyer, at Stuart's request in 1961 when he was still in Cairo. Hillyer did not live to enjoy the collection in its published form. His critical comment, quoted on the book's jacket, takes on, then, the significance of a valedictory from a distinguished figure on the contemporary literary scene to a younger poet in whom he had recognized and encouraged the strong spirit of optimism so much in harmony with his own.

Hillyer said of *Hold April:* "A beautiful book, a rare book, with its own golden place in our too-often shadowy literature."

This summation of Stuart's latest poetry volume, a book which is in itself autobiographical, and a summation of Stuart's creeds, seems particularly apt. Incisively, it places into proper perspective Jesse Stuart, the poet who sees both light and shadow, but for whom, as *Hold April* states lyrically, "light over darkness has a final power."

3

....

The Short Story

Balladry and exaggerated humor characteristic of Jesse Stuart's mountain region are natural elements of the oral tale, or folk tale, and, as the short story as we know it today developed out of the oral tale,[1] Stuart's material is singularly rich as a source for works in this literary genre.

Combining as it does both the narrative objective tale and the subjective essay of character, the short story provides a happy medium for Stuart to bring into sharp, swift focus an indigenous personality of the hills through description and through the drama of the "told tale," which, in the selection of subject matter, makes its subtle but potent comment about the narrator.

Jesse Stuart's forte, then, might be said to be the short story, since it is in this field that he has achieved recognition most consistently. Edward J. O'Brien, original editor of the *Best American Short Stories* anthologies, and Martha Foley, successor to O'Brien,

[1] Donald Davidson, *American Composition and Rhetoric* (New York: Charles Scribner's Sons, 1953), 365.

have included some seventy Stuart stories in their collections, beginning in the year 1936. O'Brien's anthology of the best American stories for a quarter of a century, 1915-1939, includes "Hair," by Jesse Stuart, along with "My Old Man," by Ernest Hemingway, "The Return," by Sherwood Anderson, "Haircut," by Ring Lardner, "The Half-Pint Flask," by DuBose Heyward, "That Evening Sun," by William Faulkner, "Babylon Revisited," by F. Scott Fitzgerald, "The Chrysanthemums," by John Steinbeck, and "Only the Dead Know Brooklyn," by Thomas Wolfe. A number of Stuart's short stories have been included in college-level and in secondary-school-level textbooks.

In the introduction to the 1915-1939 anthology, O'Brien states that the progress made by the American short story in that period in finding subject matter rooted deeply in American earth and in American life had been reflected in the revolutionary change made by the short story in form.

Twenty-five years ago the American short story was written with elaborate artificial hauteur. Rules for its correct structure abounded and the form was as artificial and cramping as the eighteenth-century rhymed couplet. Inside this rigid framework, nothing was left to chance . . . nothing was left to life. It seemed as if all American writers were afraid of life. Then little by little life began to creep in and take charge. The rigid inorganic structure collapsed. The critics complained that the American short story had become formless.[2]

Actually, the American short story had not become formless, O'Brien concluded, but had begun to shape its own pattern. It had begun to find a satisfactory American subject matter, rooted deeply in American life. Good writers, he said, had come to look more closely at themselves and their environment, and, thus, had begun to write realistically. These writers had come to know that "the short story, like life, can seldom be shocked into a sudden surprise ending."

[2] Edward J. O'Brien, "Introduction," *50 Best American Short Stories 1915-1939* (New York: The Literary Guild of America, Inc., 1939), ix.

Jesse Stuart's rise as a short story writer began in this quarter-century period covered by O'Brien's anthology, the period when the importance of realism in writing gained recognition, and when the use of the contrived plot in building a story lost in favor of the use of a series of impressionistic scenes taken directly from life, or to the use of a plot which falls naturally into place.

A number of Stuart's stories will be discussed in this chapter. Most of them will be seen to be plotless, or to be based upon so slender a framework as to appear to have no plot at all. Yet this absence of formal plot does not preclude the presence of a structure of careful craftsmanship which Jesse Stuart employs in his stories, in order to give the feel and flavor and the true picture of life in his region.

"I have always felt that there is considerable artistic calculation in his [Stuart's] fiction," Robert Penn Warren, who was one of Jesse Stuart's professors in graduate studies at Vanderbilt University, commented in 1959. "He very early struck on his characteristic style and way of telling a story. And I don't think that this is naive."[3]

In contrast to Warren's tribute to the artfulness of Stuart's fiction is the judgment by Dayton Kohler, in 1942, that "After five books, his [Stuart's] writing remains a frontier talent for anecdote and character drawing, and the chief impression from his work is one of much power poorly-controlled. He is by turn a reporter, an atmosphere man, a poet, and a racy fabulist."[4]

Significant comment upon Stuart as a short story writer was made by W. S. Wabnitz, who discussed Stuart as "one of the prominent revolutionary writers who write the new informal commentary short story with a certain 'exuberance' or 'rhapsody' rather than the conventional kind of story with practically all action and plot."[5]

[3] Robert Penn Warren, letter to the writer, July 13, 1959.

[4] Dayton Kohler, "James Still and Jesse Stuart, Mountain Regionalists," *College English*, III (March 1942), 528.

[5] W. S. Wabnitz, "Jesse Stuart and the Old and New in Short Stories," *New Mexico Quarterly Review*, VII (August 1937), 183-8.

Stuart writes of rural life in the same informal, intuitive style as does Saroyan about city life, Howard Baker observed:

> It seems to me that the same dangers beset Jesse Stuart. Like Saroyan, Stuart tends to be lax, disordered, repetitious, and directionless. It is true that up to a certain point, he presents people and scenes that are convincing; but I wonder whether or not, in trying to gorge his reader on extravagant dialect, on the tremendously quaint orations which serve for dialogue, on elaborate, homely similes, on the crudest, and, it seems to me, most meaningless sort of action, on the sheer youthful gusto which makes him comparable with Saroyan—whether he is not catering to the same taste that likes hillbilly programs on the radio. Stuart is better than this, of course; but his gusto and his dialect point in the direction. He is sensitive—"Fire runs through W-Hollow," he writes: ". . . and I have seen the copperheads white whips of ashes on the new ground." The question is what to do with this sensitivity.[6]

But sensitivity and the lyricism of language found in Stuart's writing often pales in significance beside the powerful social commentary achieved indirectly by his selection of characters and situations around which to build a short story. This fact is commented upon in *Kentucky, A Guide to the Bluegrass State:*

> Stuart resorts to poetry to celebrate the beauties of nature and an ancestral way of life that he finds good, but uses prose to tell about the people of the foothills of eastern Kentucky. Something of their angularity is portrayed in some of the casually grim or profanely humorous stories in *Head O'W-Hollow* (1936). In these stories, with their odd characters and episodes of frustration and tragedy, Stuart achieves a form of implicit criticism not often found in his poetry.[7]

His selection of bizarre characters and exaggeration of treat-

---

[6] Howard Baker, "The Contemporary Short Story," *The Southern Review*, III (Winter, 1938), 590.

[7] *Kentucky, A Guide to the Bluegrass State*, comp. Federal Writers' Project, WPA of the State of Kentucky, sponsored by the University of Kentucky (New York: Harcourt, Brace and Co., (1939), XXVII, No. 5, 124.

ment which frequently borders upon grotesquerie and makes comment upon the futility of life is an attribute of his short stories, in the main. In his autobiographical writing, Stuart gives "an understanding account of the more representative folk of his region—the hill farmers who have wrestled with a tough, stingy soil for generations, and faced sickness, hardship, isolation and death with equanimity."[8]

Critics in the early years of Stuart's writing were as sharply divided, then, as to the merits of his style—artful writer or careless craftsman?—as critics are today. Among favorable estimates given was that of William L. Chenery, critic and editor *Collier's Magazine.* He mentioned Jesse Stuart, with Stephen Vincent Benét, John Steinbeck, Elizabeth Madox Roberts, and others as among "those skillful craftsmen who produce well-wrought short stories."[9]

Pointing out that fiction reflects changes, the economic and social upheavals of the era in which it is written, and that, at that gloomy period (the thirties), 'fun" was demanded in literature, Chenery placed Jesse Stuart among the writers who had succeeded in entertaining.

> Those who support themselves by writing tend, as in the cases of Stephen Vincent Benét, Jesse Stuart, John Steinbeck, Elizabeth Madox Roberts, Morley Callaghan and Manuel Komroff—all of whom are represented in Mr. O'Brien's current volume—also to write for the popular magazines. These skillful craftsmen and others likewise produce well-wrought short stories intrinsically designed for small rather than the large audiences. Mr. O'Brien rates their stories aimed at the few as better than more popular efforts. This is a matter of taste. . . . The business of the story writer is to interest and interest is the result of artistic achievement.

"Hair," Stuart's story which appears in O'Brien's anthology, is a "told tale," a narrative told in the first person, which has more plot substance than have most of his stories. The banality of the

[8] Ibid.
[9] William L. Chenery, "Picking Popular Fiction," *The Saturday Re-*

"surprise twist" in the tale is avoided, however, through the author's use of the word, "hair," as the title, and through his description at the outset of the story of two remarkable heads of hair. The title and these descriptions foreshadow the events to follow in the story.[1]

Rister James, a leading figure in the story, has "the prettiest head of black curly hair you ever saw on a boy's head." The narrator, one of the 'Harkreader boys," has thick curly hair, unruly, and of a funny gold color that "ain't pretty. . . . It's just about the color of a weaned Jersey calf's hair." People even called him Jersey. Rister is beloved by the girls in his neighborhood, but one girl, Lima Whitehall, claims him for herself. Lima is the girl whom the narrator loves, and he suffers intensely while she is courting with Rister. One night, the narrator watches while Rister climbs a ladder and goes through a window of Lima's bedroom, after giving a weird catcall. Jersey masters the catcall, and gives it himself under Lima's window a few nights later. He climbs the ladder and keeps a rendezvous with his love. Lima does not discover the change in suitors until Jersey's hat falls off as he starts down the ladder, and she sees his funny-colored hair in the bright moonlight outside. She screams, but does not betray her knowledge, although subsequent events place her in the position of the "ruint girl," when the philandering Rister, whom she still loves, refuses to marry her. The narrator calculates the time and waits. The baby is born. It has the funny-colored Harkreader hair, Jersey hair, and two crowns on its head. Jersey is overjoyed. He lifts up the baby, and it's "like lifting forty farms in my arms." He marries Lima, and "everything comes out just fine." Occasionally, when he and Lima are walking to church with Rister James and the "Widder Ollie," who captured Rister for a

---

view of Literature, XVIII (June 18, 1838), 15.

[1] Mary Washington, on page 405 of her unpublished Ph.D dissertation "The Folklore of the Cumberlands As Reflected in the Writings of Jesse Stuart," puts this in the tradition of stories of *deception* as a strong facet of folklore humor. She quotes Stith Thompson, *Motif-Index of Folk Literature,* rev. edn. (Bloomington: Indiana University Press, 1955), 248-65.

husband, Jersey will throw back his head and give the strange catcall. Lima understands, all right. Rister has a wondering look.

"Hair," is related to the ribald medieval fabliau, particularly in the seduction scene. The story is filled with graphic descriptions of the land and its changes through the seasons. It has such colloquialisms as the description of the Widder Ollie's family— "one of those proud families, think they're better'n everybody else in the whole wide world—have to watch about getting rain in their noses." They were "kindly rich people with heads so high you couldn't reach them with a ten-foot pole." "Ground will ball up in your hand" is a colloquialism used to describe the wet ground in a tobacco patch.

The isolation of the community is noted in the lines about churchgoing: "I just up and go to see and to be seen—that's what we all go for. It is a place to go and about the only place we got to go." Then in "Hair" there is noted the cruel custom of gossip, with the "ruint girl" as the topic: "The talk was all over the neighborhood. Everybody in the district knew about Lima. It is too bad when a girl gets in trouble and everybody knows about it. Around home she can never get a man. She's never respected again. For the man it don't matter much. He can go right back to the church choir and sing when they play the organ. Nothing is ever said about the man."

"Hair" was copyrighted by the American Mercury Publishing Company in 1936. In selecting this story for his 1915-1939 anthology, Edward O'Brien said of Jesse Stuart that all his short stories were "rich in drama and comedy, and full of a native poetry which is unusual among American short story writers."[2]

In 1936, the first of Jesse Stuart's collection of short stories was published. That collection was *Head o' W-Hollow*.[3]

[2] O'Brien, *Best Stories*, 867.

[3] Since then four additional collections of his short stories have been published: *Men of the Mountains* (1941), *Tales from the Plum Grove Hills* (1946), *Clearing in the Sky* (1951), and *Ploughshare in Heaven* (1958). The earlier collections were published by E. P. Dutton and Company, New York. *Clearing in the Sky* and *Ploughshare in Heaven* were published by McGraw-Hill, Incorporated, New York.

When *Head o' W-Hollow* made its appearance, Ralph Thompson, of *The New York Times*, wrote: "What Brete Harte was to the outcasts of Poker Flat, and Joel Chandler Harris to the plantation negro, Jesse Stuart is to the folk of the Kentucky mountains. There aren't many originals among American writers of the past few years; it is hard to think of one who can beat Stuart at his best.[4]

Lewis Gannett was equally enthusiastic in his estimate of the Stuart collection. He said: "There is music of the American tongue in his stories. He is an authentic writer, worth a hundred city slicker products.[5]

"Battle Keaton Dies," a story which is included in the *Head o' W-Hollow* collection, is one of Stuart's most dramatic and moving short stories. This story was his first. He tells about its sale in *Beyond Dark Hills*:

> A letter comes to me. It is from *Story* magazine. It says: "We are accepting your 'Battle Keaton Dies.' Enclosed is our check for $25." Strange, the first story I ever wrote! Strange It got the same money that I did for my first poem. Sold a story! It didn't have a plot. Just a man died and wanted to be buried in his shirt-tail. But it was not the same kind of money the poetry money was. It was fun-money. Poetry was blood money. [p. 387]

"Battle Keaton Dies" is a striking example of Jesse Stuart's distinctive treatment of the short story. Instead of a plot the story has a powerful, impressionistic summary of the life and incidents surrounding a single theme, the death and burial of a rugged old mountain man. No detail is left out which will portray the elementary, almost primitive folkways of the region concerning the treatment of death. The realism with which Stuart invests his story produces the calculated effect of placing the reader in the presence of death in its simplest, most unadorned state. Stuart

[4] Ralph Thompson, *New York Times Book Review* (March 21, 1936), 2.

[5] Lewis Gannett, *New York Herald-Tribune Books* (March 21, 1936), 3.

spares the reader nothing in presenting his picture of Battle's death, with the result that the brutally frank, the naturalistic descriptions throughout the story may easily turn away the faint hearted.

Battle Keaton's last hours are shown through the use of stream-of-consciousness technique to show the old man's dying thoughts. His unending monologue is interspersed with the "sip-sip-sip," as he quenches a burning thirst from water brought in answer to his constant demands by his grieving daughter, Fronnie. Battle is obsessed by the sight of a spider on the ceiling above him:

> Well, I lay here and I think I can reach up there and get that old she-striped-back spider sometimes. I want to cut its guts out with a knife. I want to crush that spider between my thumb and my index finger so bad I can taste it. God knows I ain't got no use for no damn fly, but I can't stand to see them lay up there in them webs and have to die by degrees. I have to lay here on this bed and I can't lift my arm sometimes to reach for that spider. . . . And I think of Old Tid Coons who used to run a sawmill and work his men eleven hours for a dollar and ten cents a day. He was a striped-back spider like that one up there on the wall . . . old Tid took the blood out'n twelve men instead of twelve flies [p. 152].

The old man admonishes his daughter for weeping, "I want you to quit actin like you are actin. Don't you know this is goin to come to you like it is comin to me and it is goin to come to everybody else that's born in this world." Then, he gives her specific instructions for his burial:

> See that I'm put in my coffin just like I go to bed—that I have my shirt on and no necktie—my shirt and my long underwear. I don't want any shoes 'r' socks on my feet neither. I want to lay down in my coffin just like I lay down in my bed—to bed is where this old clay temple is goin, Fronnie. To bed. Yes. I don't want no hat on me neither, for no one ever goes to bed with a hat on. I want a blue work shirt on and my long heavy drawers—I want my clothes clean and no smell of sweat in them or smell of brush smoke. I want to be laid over there on the Runyan Hill by Daid near them old cornfields

where we used to work together, from sunrise till sunset together [p. 162].

When Battle dies, his last breath is:

. . . a sharp sizzle of wind and it goes like wind pressed in a vise, if wind could be pressed in a vise. It is wind come out where the walls fall in . . . wind that if it could speak would say, "Wind has come in here and gone out for the last eighty-four years—but now the wind time is over and past."

There follows the description of the care and preparation of the corpse by the daughter, son-in-law, and neighbors who come to the rude little cabin to help. The mood of the world outside is depicted: "The sun is red behind the mountain. The wind stirs the green July corn . . . and now time would slowly disintegrate his [Battle's] burned-out clay to mix forever with the elements."

Recollections of Battle are recounted by the people at his "settin-up." There is a wail of guitar music in the night, and religious songs are sung by the group surrounding the corpse. "Holy-Joe Madden" speaks words over Battle, with a lot of "Thee's, Thou's and Thy's," but Fronnie is not comforted. She cries, "Poor Pa . . . Dead . . . Dead . . .Dead as a beef. Over there— See!" The coffin is constructed with a half-lid, so people will not see that Battle has on only his work shirt and drawers. His daughter and son-in-law see to it, in spite of the neighbors' protests, that the old man's dying wish is carried out. On the night of his burial, people from far and near come over the hills to pay their respects to an old friend. The welcoming speech of Sweetbird, the son-in-law, is indicative of the hill custom of making a funeral a social event. His words, too, show the spirit of feuding which characterized that area.[6]

Come on in, folks—just set any place you can find a seat. Anybody is welcome in my house but a person that has the

[6] Jesse Stuart said in an interview with the writer on March 27, 1953, that there is no longer any feuding in his native Greenup County.

last name of Turner. No Turner is welcome in my house. If a Turner is here now I want that Turner to get out before I put him out. I mean business, too. If a Turner goes to Heaven I don't want to go there. If one goes to Hell I don't want to go there. I hate a Turner and Dad didn't allow none here when he was livin and by hell Sweetbird Bradberry ain't goin to allow none here this night when poor old Dad Keaton lays a corpse. No, Dad is too near and too dear to me. Dad got on the Lord's side of the fence, but he could never forget the Turners [p. 191].

The story ends on a note that is reminiscent of the lyricism which is found in Stuart's poetry:

Out on the wind there are words floating among the leaves —floating on the wind. There are stars in the sky. There is wind in the corn. There is a red-oak-chip-colored moon riding in a pretty color-of-pond sky. See it all—See Battle too. He is in his coffin—if Battle could only see this night [p. 192].

Man's life ends and Nature continues in endless cycle of day and night. But, in the old mountain man's wish to be buried in his usual garment for sleeping there is the feeling that, though his life on earth is to be ended, Battle will merge his life with that of Nature and that he will continue through infinity to arise to meet the day. Jesse Stuart emphasizes the two time levels with his dramatic use of the present tense, directing the reader to observe Battle dead while Nature, ungrieving, and in timeless pattern, provides a canopy for him brilliant with red moon and with starlight. Death is natural. "I want you to stop grievin," the old man had said to his daughter. The symbolism of the story is that of acceptance. In the sympathetic tone which Stuart achieves throughout the story, there is shown the author's identification with Battle, giving insight to his belief of acceptance. "Battle Keaton Dies," with its implicit moral of affirmation, is in direct contrast to such sonnets of protest over the briefness of life as Sonnet 27, "Man's Life Is Like the Season of a Flower," in *Man With a Bull-Tongue Plow*, and "Why Ever Grieve," in *Hold April*.

Head o' W-Hollow contains a number of stories which dwell

on the theme of death as it is met by hardy hill characters like Battle Keaton. Among such stories is "Uncle Jeff," a simple recounting of a visit to a city hospital of a mountain man and his two sons to see their brother and uncle, an old railroad man, as he lies dying. "Battle Keaton Dies" might be said to be somewhat diffuse with its prodigious amount of detail. "Uncle Jeff" is tautly told. Although, it, too, has a wealth of atmospheric description, in action "Uncle Jeff" maintains the straight narrative line, achieving notable unity in plot. "Uncle Jeff" is included in the aforementioned college textbook, *The Literature of the South*.[7]

"The Bellin' of the Bride" is a story of a very different mood from the death stories of *Head o' W-Hollow*. This sketch shows the custom of serenading a couple who have just married. The couple in the story, T. J. Lester and Daisy Bee Redfern, hide behind the big chimney, which is built onto the lower half of their cabin where the fireplace is, and which leans away from the house enough to provide space for hiding. The "bellin party" probes behind the chimney with a clothesline pole, and the hapless couple come out. After the gunshooting and the cowbell-ringing which follow, the beating on washtubs and "plow pints," a sixty gallon barrel of hard cider is opened, and there are cider, food, candy, and square-dancing for everybody.

This collection has such varied stories as "Snake Teeth," which describes the religious primitivism of the people who believe in "the Unknown Tongue"; "The Governor of Kentucky," a hilarious account of a bus trip to Chicago by a man who is known as "the Herb King of Kentucky." The man resembles the Governor of Kentucky, Governor Randall Spoon, so he and his friends decide that he shall pose as the Governor on this pleasure trip into the city. Everywhere the bus stops, the "Herb King" is presented as Governor Spoon, and this practice is continued at a ball game which he and his party attend in Chicago. His attendants have been sampling generously the "herbs" which they have brought along for the trip, and when they say "We have Governor Ran-

---

[7] A more detailed study of "Uncle Jeff" will be made later in this chapter.

dall Spoon of Kentucky with us" to the world at large, the results constitute a high point of humor in Jesse Stuart's writing. "The Governor" enjoys his role tremendously. The climax of his adventure comes when he reaches home and hurries out to his barn to keep an early-morning date with a flirtatious widow. His wife has gone to the barn early to attend to the chickens. In the dark, he mistakes her for the widow, and grabs her in his arms. The wife, who hasn't spoken to her husband in two months, is thrilled to think that he still loves her. They make up then and there. The "Governor of Kentucky" is elated. This story, in its exaggeration of character, is in the "tall story" tradition.

Men of the Mountains, Stuart's second collection of short stories, was published in 1941. This book has such stories as that of "old Flem," who looks ahead to dying, digs his own grave, and tries it out for size. The grave's a good place to be when a man's tired, Flem theorizes. There's no worrying there about getting bread, or having land to tend. He savors his mountaintop restingplace, with the wind blowing through the chestnut oaks and the sound of foxhorns in the distance.

"For the Love of Brass" is a fascinating yarn about a little "bird-necked man" who says "just call me Bud," who came to stay overnight at Thorny Kirk's farm. He stays, to become a valued handyman on the farm. Thorny and his wife wonder about "Bud," who tells them nothing of himself, just attends to his work, and seems to love being with them. One day the Sheriff comes to pick up Bud, to take him back to the penitentiary. The Sheriff tells them that Bud is making his fourth trip to the "pen" for stealing brass. Bud has committed no other offense. His weakness is for stealing brass. Years later, Thorny gets a package of clothes. "I don't like my old home nigh as well as I liked my home with you. I'm 42 years old next month. Have spent 21 of my 42 here. Take care and keep the farm going." Thorny keeps Bud's big hoe hanging in the barn. Bud was a good corn hoer. He could outhoe Thorny. Some day, Thorny and his wife hope, they will look down the road and see Bud returning.

The *New York Herald-Tribune* book reviewer, Milton Rugoff, in writing about *Men of the Mountains* and Jesse Stuart, has this to say: "There is, in sum, nothing slick or tricky in Stuart's work, nothing even sophisticated. And yet, neither is there the rawness of the Southland etchings of Erskine Caldwell nor the horrifying decadence of Faulkner. Next to Caldwell, Stuart seems lyrical and classic and next to Faulkner, wholesome and conventional."[8]

Once or twice, this reviewer observed, Stuart dropped into the "feuding" and "moonshinin' " themes of the caricature hillbillies of radio and vaudeville, but the percentage of stories below standard in *Men of the Mountains* was very slight.

The Stuart short story collection entitled *Tales From the Plum Grove Hills* (1946), contains "Another April," a story thought by many critics to be Jesse Stuart's finest. "Another April" is included in *The Literature of the South.* It appears in Donald Davidson's college textook, *American Composition and Rhetoric.* Davidson uses only three stories for illustration of style in the short story—one from Thomas Hardy, one from James Joyce, and Jesse Stuart's "Another April."

The World of Endless Horizons, a textbook for secondary-level schools, has "Another April" in its section headed "The World of Human Kinship, Currents of Understanding in Families." Under the "Twentieth Century" division in this textbook's section listing writers "Across the Ages," W. Somerset Maugham and Jesse Stuart lead the list.

This association of the names of Maugham and Stuart seems a happy one when Maugham's introduction to his book *Maugham's Choice of Kipling's Best* is read. Maugham says in that introduction:

> One of the most absurd charges brought against him [Kipling] was that his stories were anecdotes, which the critics who made it thought was to condemn him (as they sometimes still do); but, if they had troubled to consult the *Oxford Dictionary* they would have seen that a meaning it

[8] Milton Rugoff, *New York Herald-Tribune Books* (March 16, 1941), 2.

gives the word is: "The narration of a detached incident, or of a single event, told as being in itself interesting or striking." That is a perfect definition of a short story.[9]

Jesse Stuart, in his writing of anecdotal or "plotless," short stories, would seem to be championed, along with Kipling, by Somerset Maugham.

"Another April" has the *tenderness* which is one of the outstanding qualities of Jesse Stuart's writing. There is no action in the story except the development in the mind of a little boy of the meaning of old age. The boy's grandfather, who is ninety-one, is allowed out of the house for the first time after a long winter. Grandpa's daughter, the boy's mother, fusses over the old man to see that he is clothed warmly enough. The boy laughs at his grandfather's ludicrous, bundled-up appearance. Grandpa goes out eagerly to enjoy "another April," and to greet an old friend. The friend is a terrapin who has spent fifteen years under the smokehouse. He has 1847 cut on his shell. He's ninety-five years old, Mom tells the little boy, maybe older. Grandpa calls the turtle "my old friend." He says to him, "Old fellow, it's been a hard winter. How have you fared under the smokehouse floor?" The boy is amazed, but sees that the terrapin seems to understand Grandpa. Grandpa stops to examine very carefully the blossoms from a dogwood and a redwood tree. He tells the terrapin that he is "a-gettin' a little chilly; I'll be gettin' back to the house," and he says good-bye to his old friend. The little boy watches, as Grandpa takes his cane and hobbles slowly toward the house. The reader understands that the boy has come to a realization that the terrapin will outlive humanity, but that Grandpa is spiritually unconquered.

Skillfully, Stuart has interwoven the levels of time. The past is represented in Mom's recitals of Grandpa's exploits and in the boy's memories, and the present fuses dramatically with the relentless future as Grandpa completes his last walk, still "enjoying April." The emphasis upon Grandpa as a physical creature, at one

[9] W. Somerset Maugham, *Maugham's Choice of Kipling's Best* (New

with Nature, is subtly felt in the brief, symbolic, almost nebulous action.

Jesse Stuart's stories are not consciously didactic. Stuart presents his incidents or sketches from life in photographic detail for the building of a mood or of a judgment. The morals drawn from them are created in the mind of the reader; rarely are they stated by the author. "Another April," with is unity and conciseness, might be called Jesse Stuart's most distinguished short story.

Tales from the Plum Grove Hills contains another of Stuart's most poignant stories, "My Father is an Educated Man." The author's father could not read or write his name, but he knew the land, he knew railroading, mining, and buildings, his son writes here. He has "raised food for his family to eat." He has given them a roof over their heads. He has encouraged his children to go to school. "And as I think of my father's autumn-colored face, of this small hickory-tough figure of the earth, I think of the many men in America still like him. And I say they are educated men" (p. 53).[1]

Jesse Stuart's father, dressed in his overalls, clean blue work shirt, and overall jacket, would go to town every Saturday to join the men grouped on the courthouse square. A simple figure of earth, he is one of Stuart's greatest creations from life. He recurs throughout his son's writing, but is never given more sincere tribute than in the story, "My Father is an Educated Man."

"The Storm" tells of domestic troubles that vie with the gloom of the elements. A storm is brewing outside, but Mom has decided to leave her husband and go home to "Pap." She has had enough, she says. She and her husband are different, that's all. Mick, the husband, tries to talk Mom into staying. She is determined to go this time. The storm hits the clapboards of the little cabin, with a fury of wind and rain, and plays the dramatic role of mediator. Mom weakens, decides not to go. She cannot leave her husband, and the homely, everyday things that have

---

York: Doubleday & Co., Inc., 1953), XXVI.

[1] Jesse Stuart's father died in 1954.

meant their life together. As the storm subsides, Mick puts his pipe in his pocket, pulls his wife outside happily for a walk, to look over their sweet potato bed.

A story with more substance than "Storm" is "Nest Egg," which is also found in *Tales from the Plum Grove Hills*. "Nest Egg," like "Another April," is one of Jesse Stuart's more famous stories. It was written when he was a high school student in 1924, then dug up and mailed to a magazine in 1944. *The Atlantic* published it. "Later, this story 'Nest Egg' was placed by Homer A. Watt and Oscar Cargill in their college textbook for English and American literature, *College Reader*, as an illustration of one of the better short stories." This textbook also includes short story illustrations from Jack London, Ring Lardner, Ernest Hemingway, Thomas Hardy, and Thomas Wolfe.

"Nest Egg" is a saga of a powerful "fightin' rooster," which was hatched from an egg that was supposed to have been destroyed. The nest egg had been guarded zealously by a stubborn "old Sebright hen," who had resisted all attempts to take it from her. When her chicken came, she took it to the woods and lived there with it. The chicken grew up to be a tall rooster, with big legs and little straight spurs that "looked like long locust thorns." When winter came, the Sebright hen brought the young rooster down to the corn crib for food, as there was none left in the woods. The fledging was dubbed "Nest Egg" by the boy who was supposed to have taken the egg from the Sebright hen. The boy knew the rooster to be the product of the egg he had failed to remove. Nest Egg was attacked by the five old roosters who ruled the barnyard, but he fought them off stoutly. When Nest Egg killed the veteran rooster, War Hawk, he became king of the lot. His fame spread, and the neighbors insisted on bringing their roosters around for matches with Nest Egg. Nest Egg was always the victor. The neighbors' chickens flocked to be with him. Hen's nests were found everywhere—under the ferns, under the rock-cliffs, under the smokehouse corncrib, in hollow logs and stumps. The neighbors accused the boy's father of being a chicken thief, but he maintained that "It's a good-lookin' rooster Nest

Egg that all the hens all take to; he tolls the hens here." The neighbors brought the father into court, but the judge threw the case out. The chickens continued to be charmed by Nest Egg. The whole community seemd turned against the boy's father. Then, fate stepped in and settled matters. A little screech owl flew into the chicken roost where Nest Egg was sleeping, lit on the mighty warrior's back, and killed him by pecking a hole in his head.

"Nest Egg" is an entertaining little animal fable, with a distinctly Chaucerian flavor. Nest Egg is given personification, as is Chantecleer of the Chaucer tale, but his human quality of overweening pride in his exploits is in contrast with that of the timidity of Chantecleer, who must always be bolstered by his wife, and who, in the end, saves himself through a craftiness born of sheer desperation. "Nest Egg" has an unmistakable moral, the moral being, of course, that the powerful, when taken unaware, can be destroyed by the weak. But the story is remembered chiefly for its humor of situation and for its characterization.

Among the remaining stories which appear in *Tales from the Plum Grove Hills*, "Weep No More, My Lady" is notable for its description of the custom of "funeralizing," the custom of having a funeral preached every year for the deceased. "Funeralizing" occasions the "norrating" of the news of a community gathering at the home of the departed one. The people who participate in the "funeralizing" enjoy festive meals and the contents of the gallon jugs that are brought out at the deceased's home. There is singing of hymns, accompanied by guitar music, and the giving of "testimonials" in the house. Afterward, the group moves to the graveside and continues the hymn singing and the drinking. The preacher delivers a long sermon, which consists mainly of eulogies for the departed neighbor. The Mountain Baptists are the people who practice "funeralizing." The Free-Will Baptists don't believe in it. The religious primitivism of the region is set forth graphically in "Weep No More, My Lady."

"Another Hanging" describes the custom of the region in making a social occasion of a hanging. This story, with its theme of a crass, almost unbelievable, mob brutality, is painful to read. "Another Hanging" is one of the best examples of naturalism in Stuart's works. "Naturalism" is employed in connection with the study of Stuart in the sense of the use of unsparing detail in the description of a scene from life, or in the delineation of character, with disregard for its effect of shock or of revulsion upon the reader. "Naturalism," in this study, does not refer to scientific determinism. Stuart is the opposite of the scientific determinist. His strong belief, which has been borne out in his own life story, is that one can rise above the restrictions and frustrations of an environment.

"Frog-Trouncin' Contest" shows the love of the people of Stuart's area for physical activities. The story contains exaggeration and the boisterous spirit of triumph in outwitting an opponent by fair means or foul, elements of broad frontier humor such as that found in Augustus B. Longstreet's "The Gander Pulling" in his *Georgia Scenes*. This sport of frog-trouncing was popular in Shakespeare's day, Stuart points out, and is, thus, another custom handed down directly from English forebears to the folk of his region.

"Dawn of Remembered Spring" is one of the most original Stuart's stories. The subject matter, that of snakes making love, comes as a surprise to the reader, in view of the highly poetic title of the story. Stuart says that he sent "Dawn of Remembered Spring" out to publications thirty-seven times. The thirty-eighth time he sent it out, it was accepted by *Harper's Bazaar*, and subsequently was included in a Martha Foley collection of *Best American Short Stories*. The history of this story, he says, provides a real lesson in perseverance for young writers who believe that their stories are doomed to receive only rejection slips.[2]

Tales from the Plum Grove Hills may be considered Stuart's most outstanding collection of short stories, since it contains his most diversified and best-known works in that field.

Clearing in the Sky, which was published in 1950, is Jesse Stuart's fourth and most studied book of short stories. This book

---

[2] Jesse Stuart, Riverton, Kentucky, June 22, 1953, letter to the writer.

is dedicated to his father, Mitchell Stuart. It is illustrated with beautiful woodcuts by Stanley Rice. On the whole, *Clearing in the Sky* seems more restrained in style and has fewer of the elemental themes than have the earlier story collections. There is less violence in the language and, it seems, a somewhat more limited use of localism. This would tend to bear out Stuart's previously mentioned statement that he is striving to "tone down" his use of the vernacular of the hills, and that his earlier stories show more of the "exactness" of his region. In this statement, he reiterated that those early stories "do not exaggerate."

One of the stories in *Clearing in the Sky* which is written in Stuart's earlier style is the lead story, "The Champion." This story is another rustic, frontier-type tale which Stuart insists is not exaggerated but is a true picture of his region. The story is featured in the section entitled "Enjoying Humour" in the secondary school textbook, *Adventure in Reading*.[3]

"The Champion" is included in *Story*, an anthology of "the fiction of the forties" which has appeared in that magazine. This anthology was published in 1949, with Whit and Hallie Burnett, the editors of Story, serving as editors of the collection. In this anthology, the editors, claim Jesse Stuart as "an early discovery of *Story*," since that magazine published his first story, "Battle Keaton Dies."[4]

"The Champion" recounts the adventure of a notorious glutton when, as "eatin' champion" of Raccoon Creek, he is pitted against a game rooster in a private eating contest. The instigator of the contest says that he will give his rooster a grain of corn every time he gives one to the glutton, Sam Whiteapple. Sam accepts the challenge. His "nail-keg stummick" rebels, however, after he has swallowed what " 'pears like . . . a bushel of shelled corn." Doc Hornbuckle is sent for; Sam is hauled away on a wagon to recuperate. The rooster walks away with his flock of hens.

"The Slipover Sweater" is among the numerous stories by

[3] *Adventures in Reading* (Chicago and New York: Harcourt, Brace and Company, 1952), 138-143.
[4] Whit Burnett and Hallie Burnett, *Story—The Fiction of the Forties*

Jesse Stuart which have been reprinted for their simplicity of
style and of theme. The theme emphasizes a common human desire, the desire to own something equal to or better than that
owned by another who is in competition with one. This Stuart
story has an autobiographical flavor.[5] The protagonist is a young
high-school football player who wants a slipover sweater to give
to his girl. The name of the boy is "Shan," a name often used
by Stuart to represent himself in stories. Shan is very resentful
of the fact that his girl is wearing a sweater that belongs to Roy
Tomlinson, his rival. Working his way through school, Shan
finds it difficult to meet daily expenses, and there is no money
for such luxuries as the sweater. He broods about the matter, and
finally gets up the courage to go to the town bank and ask for
a ten-dollar loan. Since Shan is a football star, the banker lends
him the money, after taking out twenty-five cents of the amount
for interest. Shan gets the sweater. It is the only one in school
with three stripes on the sleeve. Shan is elated when his girl
friend Jo-Ann accepts his sweater and gives Roy Tomlinson's
back. As time passes, however, he becomes despondent about
repaying the ten dollars to the bank. Jo-Anne tires of him and
humiliates him by returning his sweater to him publicly. A mountain girl, Grace, who has had a longing for Shan, comes to his
aid and helps him to gather roots and herbs for selling, so that
he can pay off his loan. The loan is repaid. Shan comes to recognize the difference between the loyal mountain girl and the
fickle Jo-Ann. He knows that one day Grace will wear his slipover sweater. He dreams of building a house for himself and
Grace on Seaton Ridge on the path that leads from her family's
house to his.

The most poignant story in *Clearing in the Sky* is that from
which the collection takes its title. Jesse Suart discusses this story

---

(New York: E. P. Dutton & Co., Inc., 1949), 618.
    [5] When the writer visited the Stuarts at Greenup in July 1960, she
asked them if Naomi Deane (Mrs. Stuart) was the girl who wore the
slipover sweater. Stuart said, "She was!" Mrs. Stuart smiled enigmatically,
but did not reply.

in an article entitled "Backgrounds and Results of Regional Writing," which he wrote for *The Peabody Reflector*, the alumni magazine for George Peabody College for Teachers.

> . . . I wrote an article, "Clearing in the Sky," which was a truthful account of my father and a garden he had hidden on a high hill top. It wouldn't go for an article, but an editor accepted it, didn't ask for a word to be changed, and published it as a short story. Since the publication of "Clearing in the Sky," it has been reprinted eight times. One of the reprints was in South Africa. The background was the center of our farm. The character in the story, one of the people on this earth I know best, is my father.[6]

"Clearing in the Sky" combines two of Jesse Stuart's most beloved themes, the land and his father. His father had been told that he had a bad heart, that he would have to take it easy, that he probably would not live long. Instead of "taking it easy," Jesse's father, Mitch Stuart, had followed a secret desire, and had planted a garden on "new ground" on the highest point of their native mountain. He had been climbing up to his small secret clearing on the top of the mountain, in defiance of the doctors' orders, to find the fresh, fertile soil that he had tilled as a young man. One day, Mitch Stuart shows his "clearing in the sky" to his amazed son. He tries to explain about it:

> . . . the doctors told me to sit still and take life easy. I couldn't do it. I had to work. I had to go back. I had to smell this rich loam again. This land is not like the land I had to build to grow alfalfa. This is real land. It's the land that God left. I had to come back and dig in it. I had to smell it, sift it through my fingers again. And I wanted to taste yams, tomatoes and potatoes grown in this land. [p. 40]

Jesse asks his father why he has so many paths coming from the flat up the steep second bluff. The father explains that the spring before, when the doctor had not given him a week to live, he had found that he could not climb the steep path. He had made a longer, easier path, then, so he would not have to do so much climbing. Then, as he got better, he made another, steeper path. He had continued this procedure, as the days went by. That was one way, he said, that he had had of knowing that he was getting better all the time!

The story ends with Jesse's following his father down the path that "wound this way and that, three times the length of the path we had climbed."

Jesse Stuart told the writer in the previously noted interview of March 27, 1953, that he enjoyed writing in the medium of the short story more than he did the writing in any other literary form, more even than the writing of poetry, his first love.

> I just love to write a short story. I can get ideas for short stories and put them right down on paper. Then I wonder why I don't go on and work them into novels. But the novel is too much longer. I can't sustain the mood. I can sustain a single mood in a short story, but I can't in a novel. This was pointed out to me by a critic, J. Donald Adams, of *The New York Times*. When he wrote about *Taps for Private Tussie*, he said that he could tell when I had written half of the book, and when I wrote the other half. He said that he knew they were written at different periods, and he was right. There were two weeks between the the two periods, and, in that time, little things had happened, not serious things, but little things in my life that had caused me to change moods in my writing. Adams picked that out in my book.

When Jesse Stuart's fifth volume of short stories, *Ploughshare in Heaven*, appeared in 1958, it seemed a happy omen to his public that the author had turned again to his favorite medium. The gusto and dramatic sweep, humor, realism, and tenderness displayed in this new collection was reminiscent of Stuart's younger days. Though some of the stories had been written in earlier days, others were new and seemed to signify an exuberant return to full, normal living for the man who had been so close to death as a result of the heart attack, in 1954, and who had fought his way back for two slow, agonizing years to a semblance of his former life.

Those years of recovery had produced *The Year of My Rebirth*, a quiet journal of Jesse Stuart's reawakening to the beauties of the world of Nature and of the life about him. *Ploughshare in Heaven* swung Stuart back into the orbit of his youth when his rugged mountain sonnets and stories caught the attention of the American literary world and won for him, from a number of critics, the accolade of being a new and vital force on the native scene.

Though *The New York Times* reviewer Charles Lee Snyder stated that Stuart would add much more to his reputation by writing another novel as amusing as *Taps for Private Tussie*, he hailed the new short story collection for its wide range and its general artistry, particularly for the poetic style.

> Mr. Stuart is a poet, and one of the secrets of his charm as a story-teller is a certain poetic touch in his description. Of the twenty-one tales in this collection, some deal with humorous or pathetic incidents in the lives of more or less ordinary hill people. Others deal in humorous or satirical fashion with odd and outlandish characters, rugged or ragged individuals from away back.[7]

To Borden Deal, writing in the *Saturday Review*, Stuart's stories were "mountain magic." He wrote, "He [Stuart] has, from the beginning, worked in an artful simplicity that has the solid, enduring shape of legend."[8]

"Walk in the Moon Shadows" is an example of this simplicity —a story, told in the first person from the viewpoint of a young boy (the young Stuart), centers about the pathetic loneliness of a mountain mother who takes her children for a walk in the moonlight to look for the ghosts of happier days as she is about to become a mother again. Atmospheric description throughout

---

[7] Charles Lee Snyder, "Kentucky Portraits," *New York Times Book Review* (September 21, 1958), 3.

[8] Borden Deal, "Mountain Magic," *Saturday Review*, XLI (September 20, 1958), 26-7.

"Walk in the Moon Shadows" deepens the symbolic meaning of loneliness and the wonder and fear of the children for their mother's withdrawal into a world beyond their understanding, as she takes them over the mountain paths to the deserted cabin of her friends of former years.

> There were a few dim stars in the sky but over the meadows, down where there were long moon shadows from the tall trees, thousands of lightning bugs lighted their ways, going here, there, and nowhere. Upon Press Moore's high hill where Pa had found a wild bee tree, and cut his initial on the bark, a whippoorwill began singing a lonesome song. [p. 29]

The whippoorwills' lonesome songs on the ridges, and the falling apple blossoms from the trees which encircle the old house form an imagery of death in the young boy's mind. He is frightened, and wishes to return home. There is no moon as the little party trudges back, after Mom has given up her vigil by the haunted house. It is dark, and the boy trembles with relief as his father, who has skeptically refused to go on the moonlight expedition, comes up the path to meet them and accompany them home. There is no plot here, only an incident related from the childhood memory of the narrator, an incident in which the protagonist, the mother, shows a primordial yearning for happiness and for assurance as her time of trial and of danger approaches. It is of interest in the study of Stuart to note that this story has a universality which caused it to be selected for featuring over the Danish Radio Network. It was read to a nationwide audience on Sunday, November 27, 1960, by Karin Nellemose, actress of the Royal Danish Theatre.[9]

"Alec's Cabin" in *Ploughshare in Heaven* has the same theme of loneliness as that of "Walk in the Moon Shadows." It portrays an individual who clings doggedly to a symbol of happier days, then destroys it when he leaves for new scenes.

Among stories to which Borden Deal gave special mention, along with those of serious mood, was "The Devil and Televi-

---

[9] This information, from Hensley C. Woodbridge, *Jesse Stuart News-*

sion," a story in a different vein. He noted its "funny and touching" conflict between the old Kentucky and the new.

Indeed, this story may be cited as an example of Stuart's realism in pointing up the changing attitudes of his region toward encroachment of the modern world. The tale concerns a man's mental struggle when he is threatened with being "churched" for owning a television set. Stubbornly, he decides in favor of the devil and TV.

"Whatever the story," Deal concluded in his review, "Stuart's prose and his people remain."

Even in his most ribald and wildly exaggerated tales, as in "The Governor of Kentucky," in *Head o' W-Hollow*, the story of a busload of drunken hill men on a trip to Chicago, or as in "Death and Decision," in this later collection, in which there is a donnybrook between two factions in a funeral party following the burial of a relative, it seems that Jesse Stuart can convey a poetic undertone. There is a feeling of the compelling force of the hills, of the lonely landlocked lives which find an outlet in actions grotesque, pathetic, or beautiful, according to the personalities of the protagonists.

Often it seems, however, that Jesse Stuart is overly preoccupied with the grotesque, the weird and distasteful in life, and seems to derive a sadistic pleasure in lending an eye to unsparing realistic detail that is like "the wielding of an axe"[1]—in centering his readers' attention on the ugly, instead of on the beautiful. This would seem to represent a dichotomy in the writer who is most often acclaimed for the air of optimism and of poetic beauty in his writing, yet it is really his way of accentuating the juxtaposition of good and evil in life.

In *Head o' W-Hollow* one of the most painful stories in the reading is "Sunday Afternoon Hanging," recalling "Another Hanging," of an earlier volume. The description of the event is

---

letter, I, No. 1 (July-December 1960), 2, states, also, that "more of Stuart's works have appeared in Danish than in any other foreign language."

[1] Lewis Gannett, *The New York Herald-Tribune*, June 23, 1938, 2.

bruising, told in the rugged vernacular of the frontier, yet there is dramatic poetry, an epic-like quality, in the narrative of this early Kentucky pastime of a people who sought amusement in such a way because of the restricted choice of diversions in the isolation of their lives.

A classic in the category of the grotesque is "Sylvania Is Dead," which is included in *Ploughshare in Heaven*. This unbelievably weird tale is a story from life, as most of his stories are, Mr. Stuart insists.

"Yes, 'Sylvania Is Dead' is based on facts," he wrote in a letter from Cairo, Egypt, dated June 5, 1961, in answer to the writer's query. "The story came from Hancock County in East Tennessee. Many people there will know about this story—which is quite a story. I wrote it in college."

Outlandish to the point of hyperbole, both in selection of subject and in descriptive details, the account of the life, death, and attendant difficulties of the burial of a 650-pound female bootlegger has an artistic unity for which Jesse Stuart has been commended by such previously noted critics as Robert Penn Warren and Edward J. O'Brien. With careful craftsmanship, Stuart approached the architectonics of his story with the selection of a name for his protagonist.

"Sylvania" is the incongruous poetic name evoking visions of willowy, ethereal heroine, which he gives to the mountain of flesh who is his central character. Having selected the name, he chooses the most dramatic title for the story, giving it the "spoken," the oral, flavor—not "Sylvania's Death," or "Sylvania's Burial," but "Sylvania Is Dead."

This sets the tone, and, from the first line, when Bert Pratt says, "it's too bad about Sylvania," as he pulls himself up another step of the mountain incline by catching a sassafras sprout, on his way with his fellow mourners to dig the bootlegger's grave, the story moves forward with dramatic pace, in the dialogue of the men, as well as in the concise but vivid account of the action. Sylvania had long enjoyed immunity from the law because officers could not drag the 650 pounds of her through the door-

way of her house. She had spent all of her life, from the days
of her young girlhood, in the house. To move her out would
have meant tearing down the house, so her parents moved out,
instead, when Sylvania married, leaving the house to the newly-
weds. In the vein of incongruity, Stuart naturally makes Sylvia's
husband "Skinny," a hundred-pound man who speaks with a pathetic formality of "my wife" at her burial.

As in all Stuart stories, the human action is given a harmonizing backdrop by the elements. Nature is in sympathy and takes
a symbolic part in the events, as in the scene when the men are
climbing the mountain towards the house of the deceased:

> September was here and the leaves were falling from the
> oaks and beeches. The backbone of the mountain was gray
> and hard as the bleached bone of a carcass. The buzzards
> floated in high circles and craned their necks. [p. 73]

The men reminisce about Sylvania, whose heart was as big as
her frame, who would trade moonshine for pistols, butter, tur-
nips, corn meal, or almost any commodity the men had on hand
if they did not have money. Now, they are increasingly disturbed
by the buzzards which swoop low toward the death shack. Lonnie
shoots into the swarm of scavengers. This brings Skinny out of
the shack in hysterical protest against "the boys'" bad manners,
yelling to them, "Shooting around here, and my wife a corpse!"

Crestfallen, the men explain that they are trying to scatter
the buzzards. They proceed to the spot where they are to dig the
graves, and again Nature plays an active part:

> The lazy wind blew over the mountaintop. Leaves
> swarmed in the wind. Leaves fell into the grave the men were
> digging for Sylvania. Buzzards flew above the shack while
> Flora Fitch and Vie Bostick worked in the shack and pre-
> pared Sylvania for burial. [p. 77]

The grave is dug, but there is the problem of getting Sylvania
out of the shack. In a quandary, the men consider taking up
the floor. But this might cause "disturbances," and they didn't

want "no disturbances" attributed to Sylvania, because "Sylvania's been a mother to all of us." Skinny might want "to jump the broom again," and he wouldn't want his first wife buried under the floor, they reason.

The expression "jump the broom," for "get married" is a colorful colloquialism which occurs throughout Stuart's writing. Stuart does not strive to be picturesque or intentionally regional, but he uses words and phrases to which he, as a man of his region, is accustomed in his simple, unaffected American-English. Thus his diction fits theme and tone of his subject matter, that of men living close to the soil whether in devout, superstitious or in crude and boisterous mood.

In these passages, some might question Jesse Stuart's use of the word "disturbance," along with his colloquialisms. Is it not "unnatural" to use the formal with the colloquial in this man's speech? Is such a word current in the ordinary conversation of the region and time? Would not the hill man have said "ruckus" or "trouble"? Certainly there were formal words used naturally in the hills as quaint relics of Chaucerian English or of seventeenth-century English, such as the word "oddling" for one who was different. But use of "disturbance" here and of "replenish" in the following sentence invites questioning. "All they [the revenuers] could do was pour out a barrel of good licker. It wasn't no time until Sylvania had the barrel replenished and we were going back again" (p. 76).

For another example of what might appear to be inattention to diction, there is this passage: "There never was a better woman than Sylvania. When she sold you a gallon of moonshine you got a gallon of unadulterated moonshine and not two quarts of moonshine with a quart of water and a quart of carbide all stirred up well and shook before drinking. I don't know what we'll do without her. We won't have no market fer our corn" (p. 76).

Would not the man of the region who said "stirred up well and shook," and "we won't have no market," have said "pure moonshine," instead of "unadulterated moonshine"? Is this a fault of diction, as some critic unfamiliar with the hill people might infer, or an instance of carelessness toward detail of treatment which, now and then, one finds in Stuart's works? At times, Jesse Stuart is reluctant to reread and revise his work after setting it down on paper when he is in the grip of mood. He is a spontaneous writer and an impatient editor of his own works. In this, he is closely allied in temperament to Thomas Wolfe.

The problem of getting Sylvania out of the shack is solved when it is decided to tear down the chimney which almost covers one end of the house. Placed in her coffin at last with great difficulty, Sylvania has an almost lifelike domination of the scene, as Skinny announces to the men her legacy to them: "It was my wife's dyin' request that she didn't have her funeral preached, nor no songs sung. . . . See that barrel over there! It's the last my wife made. It's all fer you, boys. There's the dipper over there. What you can't finish today you can finish Monday when you come back to hep me make my new chimney" (p. 81).

The "boys" gather around the barrel, and begin to carry out the dying request with alacrity. They look at Sylvania and weep.

"Just a lot of drunk men crying," is Rodney's tart observation in a short while, saying that they should have had the "licker" last. But Skinny says he is "conducting" the funeral, and he is doing what Sylvania requested.

Before the men are past walking, Bert, who has charge of the actual burying, gets them under way. Fourteen men lift the black-oak coffin and inch slowly out of the open end of the house where the chimney had been.

"Just like picking up a house with the family in it," Rodney groans, as they make their way laboriously to the pine tree under which Sylvania is to be buried. Here again is an example of Stuart's very apt and homely similes.[2]

The funeral fervor, characteristic of the hills, is evidenced in Skinny's hysterical scream, "I wish I was planted by 'er side!" Piety ingrained in these rough men, even in their inebriated state,

[2] However in the diction of this story, one might question Skinny's use of the word "conducting," in speaking of the funeral. Would he not have used a more informal, natural word in the vernacular, such as "running"?

is shown by Bert's words, "May God rest Sylvania's soul" after she has been lowered into her grave.

The conversation of the men during the process of the lowering of the coffin is staccato and graphic, like dramatic dialogue, as it forwards the action. Stuart is particularly adept at this stark, Greek-like technique of using sparse description in favor of de-development of theme by use of powerful dialogue, thus bringing a strong sense of reality through few words. In this, and in numerous other short stories, his treatment of narrative may be likened to Faulkner's taut, dramatic style in *As I Lay Dying*, as contrasted with Faulkner's usual convoluted, rhetorical and obscurantistic style.

In "Sylvania Is Dead" alternation between present and past is skillfully integrated—the present, constituting the action of getting the corpse of Sylvania from the house and burying it; the past, in the men's recollecting of Sylvania's role in their lives, and in their alcoholic celebration at her funeral, for which Sylvania, in character, her generosity following her to the grave, has provided.

The focus which Stuart maintains in this story is sharp and clear. Sylvania's character and personality dominate throughout, and the exaggerated dignity with which the bootlegger is treated in death, as though she were a leading citizen, is beneath its surface satire, indicative of a deep Stuart belief. Sylvania was one of Nature's freaks, but she had her place in life. She built a niche of immortality for herself in the heart of her husband and in the affections of her moonshine customers. The tone maintains the exaggerated, bizarre effect, yet underlying it is a tenderness of perception which is characteristically Stuart, in his belief that each individual, no matter how grotesque or useless in the eyes of the world, may still develop an innate dignity to give life meaning, no matter how small the periphery of influence.

In the category of the grotesque, "Zeke Hammertight" takes its place beside "Sylvania Is Dead," though its theme of violence differs drastically from the baroque note of sympathy interweaving theme and treatment of Sylvania's story.

Charles Snyder of *The New York Times* took special note of Zeke Hammertight as an "odd and outlandish character, patriarch of a pestiferous, prolific and pesky clan,"[3] who is shanghaied out of the way by his neighbors in a frighteningly brutal manner.

There is no tenderness of tone here. The subject matter, as in that of *Taps for Private Tussie*, is of a shiftless tribe of people who refuse to work, and who overrun the hills like the sassafras sprouts, leaving their destructive mark on everything they touch. The Hammertights, especially crazy old Zeke Hammertight, should be killed out, just like the sassafras, in the opinion of the other hill people. Objectively, in relentless detail, Stuart recounts the carrying out of the brutal plan for the elimination of old Zeke. He tells the story from the point of view of a young man who is a member of the posse that brings Zeke in. But there is nothing of the subjective Stuart in that youth. He is selected as narrator to point up the unwitting callousness of the hill mob which pursues its murderous objective with a sinister delight.

"The crazy, damned Hammertights and the sassafras sprouts are taking this country. They are taking Kentucky," is the flat statement of Cousin Milt, who has been the object of Zeke's hallucination that someone is "pizenin'" his cattle. Zeke, at least, "crazy as a bedbug," a useless member of the hill society, should be eliminated.

Milt enlists the unwilling aid of the sheriff, who in his election had bought the Hammertight vote from old Zeke for forty dollars. A posse is organized to clean out the hills of the Hammertights, beginning with bringing in the crazy head of the family. Around the barn in which Zeke has hidden himself, upon receiving the "noration" of the news via the mysterious hill grapevine, there is a whole ring of Hammertights, armed with gooseneck hoes, briar scythes, broadaxes, apple-butter stirs, clubs, and rocks. But they scatter into the brush when the sheriff's reinforcements storm the barn with their double-barreled shotguns, members of the posse screaming with glee as they charge up the hill after

[3] Snyder, *New York Times Book Review*.

them. In the words of the narrator, "Whooppee! Whooppee! . . . .
We are after the Hammertights."

Old Zeke is pulled out, "a-spitting and biting and fighting,"
and thrown into a big hog crate, and the men bring him triumph-
antly into town. "You ought to see us going to Greenbriar. Like
a big bunch of men been to the hills and caught a bear. Just that
away: a long line of men behind the wagon and Sheriff Watkins
up front, just riding as big with the bloodhounds with broken
noses strapped to the saddle" (p. 24).

Although this story is told objectively, two moralizing passages enter in. There is the sheriff's statement: "He's not safe
among civilized people. . . . He'll know where he is when he
wakes up in the asylum. He's lucky to get there. All this expense
on the county taking him over there. W'y he's not any more
good. He ought to be left out there among the sassafras sprouts.
Out there for the crows and the buzzards. Making us fight the
Battle o' Bunker Hill over again to get him" (p. 24).

And, in a rhythmic concluding paragraph, typical of Stuart
prose, which might often be free verse, there is the moralization
which reflects the feeling of the author as a man of Nature,
who thinks that Zeke should have been left to run free-crazy
or not. "Maybe the hills know we got old Zeke Hammertight.
Maybe the eternal rocks of Kentucky know it and the lizard
knows about it. The sassafras sprouts know that we got him. Like
the buzzard, the crow, the lizard, the snake, old Zeke would love
to get out of that hog crate and run wild over the hills that have
produced him and his generations thick as the hair on a dog's back,
thick as the sassafras sprouts on a Kentucky poor-clay bank and
under the Kentucky wind, and sun, and moon and stars" (p. 24).

This is one of the rare instances in which the moral is stated
in a Stuart story. Zeke Hammertight has been hunted by his
neighbors, with intent to murded him, has been caught and caged
like a wild animal. Even though contemptuous of the shiftless Hammertights, Stuart states his disapproval of the brutality
shown, a disapproval that would encompass all forcing of the
wild from their habitats.

Though it would be sheer loss to the reader to eliminate this concluding paragraph, with its poetic strength, it would seem to be in the interest of artistic unity to do so, for it weakens the effectiveness of the story as an unrelieved picture of naturalism. It is not artistically acceptable for the author to intrude at the end of the story, when he has been consciously out of it throughout the narration. He should maintain objectivity to the finish.

The author has shown in the story that the world of Nature is aware of what is taking place. As usual, Jesse Stuart gives the elements and birds and beasts a part in the action: "The wind lap-laps the poplar leaves about our heads. It is a lazy wind. The sun is hot and the lizards are sleepy on the rocks. They lift their heads when a green fly passes over and swallow the flies like a toad frog catching yellow jackets. The ground sparrows twitter in the seeding crab grass. The voices of the men are lazy as the wind" (p. 24).

As the victim is pursued, there is this passage which foreshadows Nature's awareness of the outcome: "We take over the hill, down the path, across the rocks, the stumps, the fallen trees, Cousin Milt in front with the pistol in his hand. . . . Maybe the lizard is watching us, maybe the rocks that have seen men kill before and men go crazy. Rocks that have seen stories they've no tongues to tell" (p. 24).

Here is the cosmic touch, the suggestion of Nature's endurance and indulgence for the wickedness and foibles of mankind. This passage makes sufficient moral comment, and in an expressionistic way, renders superfluous the author's intrusive didacticism at the close of the story, his preachment against the hill men's way of solving their problem concerning Zeke Hammertight— and against any such solving of the geriatrics problem.

In *Sunday Afternoon Hanging*, the moral is unstated, and the single effect is thus more artistically attained—that of a cruel, unsparing naturalism that often may be shocking in the reading, for Jesse Stuart in this vein of objective savagery is not for the timid reader. The story shows an artistic unity in construction—a unity that is weakened in "Zeke Hammertight" by statement of the moral.

Three of Jesse Stuart's short stories deserve special mention for their treatment of the theme of the strong hill man beaten by the machine—the natural man in conflict with civilization, defeated in the end by the rise of industrialization. These stories are "Uncle Jeff," "Huey, the Engineer," and "Tim." Uncle Jeff" is the best known of these stories.[4]

In "Uncle Jeff," the problem is stated in the beginning of the story: the uneducated versus the educated in life. Shan, who is young Jesse Stuart, asks his father, "What is the matter with Uncle Jeff?" Shan and his brother are walking with their father in the town of Ferton, West Virginia, on their way to the railroad hospital to see Uncle Jeff.

"He is a broke-down man," the father replies. "He is like I am. Look at me—I am a broke-down man. If you follow workin on a section long as your Uncle Jeff, then you would have one foot in the grave and the other ready to slide in, too. He's been on that Chatworth section for thirty-three years. Could have been a boss if he had the education. Can't read. Just like I am. Now you boys see that it pays to take education. I couldn't take it for there was none offered here in these Kentucky hills when I was a boy."[5]

In the ensuing conversation, the father explains Uncle Jeff's condition, and the similes used are sharp and homespun. Jeff and eighteen other men on a motor car had been hit by a Big Sandy train in a fog. Uncle Jeff had leaped "like a frog," or he would have been dead like some of the others, when part of the motor car and several of the men "flew through the air and lit on them like a bird. Brother Jeff was knocked cold as a icicle." When he woke up, he was in this railroad hospital in West Virginia. He hadn't been able to work since. "He is like a horse too old to plow but has to pull the plow just the same. I am a horse too broke-down to pull the plow, but I have to pull it just the same."

The boys are planning to take Pa to his first picture show

---

[4] It appeared in Stuart's short-story collection, *Head O' W-Hollow* (1936) and in two anthologies, R. C. Beatty's *Vanderbilt Miscellany* (1919-1944) and Beatty *The Literature of the South* (1952).

[5] "Uncle Jeff," *A Vanderbilt Miscellany*, ed. Richmond Croom Beatty (Nashville: Vanderbilt University Press 1944), 49.

after they leave the hospital, so they are walking to the hospital, to save money, instead of riding on a street car. Shan describes in detail the peculiar clothing that they are wearing, old clothes that do not fit, except for the new overcoat that Shan himself has on. Pa wears a big gray overcoat that strikes him around the ankles. It is a coat that Shan found in an old house and gave to him, but Shan says, "I believe he [Pa] sorty thinks I stole it." Pa resents the way "these damn big-headed people" of West Virginia hold their heads in disdain above the Kentuckians. He would like to tell those people about the time when he was sixteen years old and worked in the mines in West Virginia, and the place where he boarded had so many bedbugs he had to leave. "I'd like to tell these people about the bedbugs they got in this state—more than any State in the Union."

When they get to the hospital, at the reception desk, a woman "who looks mean out of a pair of glasses" tells them that they can not see Jeff Powderjay. Pa is ready to make a scene, when the boys grab his arm and take him to see the hospital doctor. The doctor says that it is good they have come to see Jeff. "None of his kin have come to see him and he will not get back to Kentucky alive." Pa is fascinated by the doctor's soft hands, contrasts them with his own work-worn ones. This descriptive aside to the story illustrates Jesse Stuart's eye to detail in making his characters and incidents realistic.

Pa goes first into the hospital room, greets Jeff and asks if he knows him.

"Know you? What do you think I am? I'd know you in hell, Mick. You are boy number eleven, and I am number ten. Ain't that right. . . . And you come up to see me kick the bucket."

Uncle Jeff wants the boys to come over "and say goodbye and old-Satan-bless-you Uncle Jeff." He has been praying to die, to get out of that place. The nurse, "that big-tailed thing they got waitin' on me" is trying to kill him too soon, he says. God won't have him. He wants to go some place, so he has been 'cussin and praying for the Devil to get me."

Here it is interesting to note that the Devil of the hill people is a real personality, as is the devil "Auld Nickie-ben," of Robert Burns, and is invested by the hill sinners, anyway, with human qualities of understanding and comradeship. The Devil will take in Uncle Jeff, the old man believes, since God would not have him.

While he is talking, Uncle Jeff has been holding tightly to Shan's hand. Shan does not like holding his uncle's hand.

"His hand is soft and warm and wrinkled like a thawed-out black snake. His lips have fallen down at the corners, beard is over his face—a white and red-sandy beard. His eyes are the color of faded slate."

Uncle Jeff asks for a chew of Red-Horse. "Give me a chew of Red-Horse, and I'll give you a cup of water in hell," he pleads, and Pa, with tears in his eyes, says he will give him a chew, even if the doctor throws him out of the hospital. Jeff wants to go back to the Big Sandy and die, "back where Pap and Ma died." He insists that he is going back. The nurse comes in to run the visitors out, saying that it is time for the patient to take his medicine. Uncle Jeff refuses.

"No, by God."

"Die then."

The doctor comes in and Jeff is more tractable. The visitors say good-bye.

"You boys don't work on no goddamn railroad," Uncle Jeff says, as they leave, and Pa, in grief, tells his sons, "Brother Jeff is a goner."

There follows a description of Pa's first trip to a picture show, which the boys have maneuvered him into making with them, while they wait for the bus that will take them back to Kentucky. They arrive home, they do their chores by lantern light and by starlight on their small rented farm. Pa lectures his sons throughout on getting an education so that they can stay away from working on a railroad section, where "you get the least wages in the world and do the hardest work."

The story ends with the arrival of the telegram announcing Uncle Jeff's death, and Pa's catching "Number 8" to ride up to the Big Sandy country to oversee Jeff's burial. Shan understands that Uncle Jeff will be hauled on a wagon over an old woods road, overgrown with weeds and brush, to the spot by a little peach tree "near Ma," which is the place he has specified for his last resting place. "It will be where the green peach tree leaves and the pink peach tree blossoms were crumbled down last year. There will not be the sound of a train whistle back there."

Thus ending his narrative with pungent words and with calculated artistic effect, Jesse Stuart evokes the symbolism of the peace and quiet of the woods where the man of nature has found his reunion with earth, in contrast to the cruel life of the machine age represented by the railroad—a sharp lesson which he desired in the mind of the reader. He does this without pointing a moral. He does not add the final paragraph which weakens some of his stories by a statement of that which has already been achieved by selection of theme and of protagonist, by colorful, incisive imagery and diction and by taut, dramatic treatment. For its embodiment of all of these essentials for attaining artistic unity, "Uncle Jeff" is rightfully considered a classic.

Its humor, which understates a larger theme of pathos, is typical of Jesse Stuart's attitude toward life, representing as it does a fatalistic acceptance of the triumph of industrialization, after salty individualism has gone down fighting. There are overtones of bitterness in the story for the poverty of men like "Uncle Jeff and "Pa," who lack an opportunity for acquiring an education, and who spend their lives in comparative slavery as a result. The note of social protest wherever it appears in Stuart's works is mainly concerned with this imbalance of educational opportunities, or, as in *Taps for Private Tussie*, with the government's paternalistic humoring of people who will not work but prefer to live on "relief."

Sharply opposed in tone to "Uncle Jeff" is a more recent story, evidencing Stuart's ability to turn easily from bawdy humor to poetic quietness.

"Angel in the Pasture," published in the June 1959 issue of

Esquire, is a perspicuous example of Jesse Stuart's sublimity of mind, as reflected in his writings, following his miraculous recovery from the heart attack which almost claimed his life.

Labeled a short story in the magazine, "Angel in the Pasture" is hardly more than a vignette of a mood. It is a dream sequence, an hallucination experienced under an oxygen tent, which might well have been taken from *The Year of My Rebirth,* Stuart's journal of his recovery and of his reunion with the natural world.

If "Angel in the Pasture" is a short story, it is a "short short," the briefest of Stuart's stories. Yet the insight which it gives into Jesse Stuart's thinking, his approach to life in his mature years, gives this story a real significance. It is important, also, as an example of the restrained style which is in marked contrast to the rugged "slice of life" style characteristic of Stuart's earlier works. Here experience is interpreted subjectively through the imagination of the writer and becomes a strong poetic expression through evocation of mood.

The theme of nostalgia, which embodies two time levels, the past and the present, and points up the ephemeral quality of life, is set in the opening paragraph: "Shan slowly closed his eyes and entered a beautiful world long past, with sun he could not hold in the sky, flowers he could not keep fresh on their stems and sumac leaves he could not keep from going into an autumn season, coloring and dying and blowing hither and thither in the autumn winds of 1916."[6]

The imagery is of a bright, sunlit world, the world of a nine-year-old boy, sent to find a cow in a pasture, as contrasted with the present world of gloom under an oxygen tent—"death-colored" (to use one of Stuart's favorite descriptive terms)—when the leaves of spring have darkened into autumn colors and are being scattered by autumn winds to their resting place on earth.

The young boy dawdles at his task, while he is alive to the natural world about him, seeing birds, animals, flowers, and trees through the perspective of the embryo poet. He goes first to the hollow where the tall beeches grow, to watch the squirrels return

[6] "Angel in the Pasture," *Esquire* LI (June 1959), 49-50.

from their early morning breakfast and play on the big, leafy branches of the trees where they have their holes. He watches the sudden flight of a pheasant which he has startled from a cluster of saw briers at his feet. He listens to young hawks and crows as they are fed in their nests, and visits again the nest of an old hummingbird which he had long tried to catch, "but he'd always fly off and whistle through the air like a bullet. Like the whine of a .22 rifle."

This simile of the bird's take-off as sounding like the whine of a bullet is an excellent example of Stuart's objective: always to find the exact descriptive words—as was the objective of the Imagist poets—to bring the sharp image, or correlative, which was in the mind of the writer, to the mind of the reader.

Similar sharp similes are to be found in this story:

> There were dewdrops on the pine-tree needles. These dew-drops weighted them like little lumps of polished silver until the sun lifted them skyward in white ribbons of mist. There were dewdrops on the red-tinted sand-brier leaves, on the hard stems of the sand briers, on the milkweed and silkweed leaves that were shaped like stiff hogs' ears, only they were green. And the bright wind above him was filled with streamers of mists. [p. 50]

Although only those familiar with farm life might appreciate the homely simile of the milkweed leaves as being "like stiff hogs' ears," any reader with vision can see the dewdrops on the pine-tree needles as "little lumps of polished silver" and the metaphoric "streamers" with which the mist laces the bright wind.

As stated, the name which Jesse Stuart gives to himself in much of his fictional writing is "Shan." Here we are in sympathy with young Shan as his revery is interrupted by the arrival of his mother in the pasture to speed up his search for Gypsy, the cow, so that she can milk her under the big white oak.

> He wouldn't have time now, since his mother had come, to talk to the birds, squirrels, hawks and crows, and pretend he was a brother to them. He didn't have a brother and he talked to everything when he was out in the woods alone. . . .

He wanted to be among the good wind, songs of the birds, beauty of flowers, leaf and brier forever.

If only I could command the sun to stop where it is in the sky and hold all the white mists where they are in the air, Shan thought. If I could only keep the birds singing like they are singing now, and keep the soft, warm June winds blowing. If I could keep the pasture daisies as white and the wild roses as pink as they are now. If I could keep the saw briers in clusters with red-tinted leaves and the little pines and sumacs the same size as they are now. If I could make this pasture and this world and time stand still I'd do it! [p. 50]

This wish for the immutability of time is followed by Shan's description of his mother, with more apt similes, as she suddenly appears before him in the pasture, "five feet eleven inches tall," her hair "black as the crows' wings," her eyes, "grey as the bark on the poplar tree" and her teeth "white as daisy petals."

Again, the similes come from Nature, from the world close to the soil which is Jesse Stuart's individual world, as it is the universal world. Again, in the wish for time to talk as to a brother with the birds, animals, flowers and trees, and to hold them forever in that perfect moment of communion, there is the strong feeling of transcendentalism which is evidenced throughout the life and works of Jesse Stuart.

But time will not hold still. Shan has found Gypsy under the sweet-apple tree, and he stretches out dreamily on the ground, to observe sky and earth, in close harmony with his mother, his "angel" in the pasture, as she milks Gypsy. But into his fantasy of an unchanging world steals the realization that he cannot keep it, this perfect world, from its degeneration and death.

He couldn't keep the pine seedlings from growing into saw-log timber. He couldn't stay the hunters' guns from pheasants, crows, hawks and squirrels. He couldn't hold the wild rose and the blooming daisy beyond their seasons. He couldn't keep the young spring wind blowing over him. He suddenly wanted his mother to finish milking. He listened to hear her say, "Shan, let's be goin'." For he was waking from this dream world he couldn't hold into a world of reality.

Instead of a warm, June wind and green leaves above him there was a clear, cool tent. That wasn't his mother standing there. It was a nurse. Reality. His mother no longer milked Gypsy under the white oak. She rested at Plum Grove. This wasn't 1916. This was 1956. Dream world or real world, there was one thing he was certain of: he had been with an angel in that pasture. [p. 50]

Despite the banality of the closing sentence, "Angel in the Pasture" remains a clear example of beauty of language and thought, of atmospheric feeling and of psychological depth. It is scarcely more than an etching, yet it is deserving of a unique place among the hundreds of Stuart short stories.

Since "Tim" is of short-story length, it is considered here in the study of the short story. Told from the point of view of a young boy, as are many of Stuart's most effective, most strongly intuitive stories (e. g.), "Another April,"[7] this narrative of a tramp is in the present tense, and the style employed is abrupt and dramatic. Jesse Stuart quickly brings into focus his protagonist, Tim, and by monologue and dialogue in the frontier oral tradition, probes deeply into his character, with a clinical detachment and disregard for the sensibility of the reader. Doubtless, the readers of *The Little Man*, a magazine for juveniles, were intrigued just as the young narrator of "Tim" was, by the vision of the tramp's stopping by a house to ask for shelter just after "straddling the back" of a polecat and killing it. Tim's fabulous story must have engaged their attention thoroughly, and Stuart's unsparing description of the appearance and odor of the tramp

---

[7] "Tim" made its first appearance as a part of the first issue of *The Little Man* magazine in Cincinnati in 1939, with Tim's picture on the cover drawn by illustrator Charles Atkinson. In 1958 Robert Lowry, of New York City, published in mimeographed form, a limited edition of twenty-five copies of Tim, which, he stated in a publisher's note in the back of the copy, was a reissuing of the pamphlet which he first published in 1939. The University of Kentucky has a copy of *Tim*, from the limited edition, in its Stuart collection. Murray State College, Murray, Kentucky, which has a "Jesse Stuart Room," housing Stuart's personal collection of his published works, manuscripts, and papers, includes a copy of *Tim*. And McKissick Library, University of South Carolina, has Number 16 of the 1958 edition of *Tim* in its complete collection of the works of Jesse Stuart.

would not, in all probability, have affected those young readers, whereas the reader of the 1959 edition of "Tim," an adult reader, might well be stopped at the outset, particularly the reader with a weak stomach! Along with this naturalism, however, this relentless, unpleasant detail, there are in "Tim" the inevitable poetic passages characteristic of Jesse Stuart, all skillfully combined to make a characterization and a story which sharply delineate the drama of the natural man in today's mechanized world.

The strong flavor of this story can best be conveyed by quoting from its beginning:

> "Rap-rap-rap," on the door. It is nine o'clock. The night is black. It is a night in December.
> "Open the door," says Pa, "and see who's there."
> I get up and open the door.
> "It is Tim," I say to Pa.
> I was tickled to see Tim. All of us boys liked Tim. He would give us apples, bring us candy, make us kites and show us how to fly them. He would show us how to hold rocks to make them curve in and out and drop.
> "Howdy do," says Tim. "How about a man sponging on you for the dark and stormy night?"
> "All right," says Pa, "just come right around and get you a chear."
> Tim walks around and gets the chair before the fire.
> "A bad night out for rambling," says Tim. . . . His clothes are raggedy and dirty. A great mop of brown weed-colored hair is almost dead-looking. His knuckles are dirty.
> " 'Pears like I smell something," says Mom, sniffing her nose. . . . "I've been thinking that all the time," says Pa.[8]

Tim says that he guesses they do smell something. He has been after a polecat. He tells his story of a Paul Bunyon-like fight with the animal, in which the cat showed an uncommon stubbornness and fought back so viciously it was able to use its weapon of scent before Tim could finish the beast with his knife. He tells his tale in such a realistic manner that the young boy listening dreams about the fight that night.

[8] *Tim* (New York: Robert Lowry, 1958), 1.

Tim continues to entertain with tall stories, bringing his hosts for the night up to date on the neighborhood news, and spinning a fascinating yarn about a ride he has had up in the cab of the engine of the Old Line Special. With a bribe of moonshine, he had been able to take the throttle from the engineer and fulfill his dream of running the engine, shouting his excitement the while and thrilling to the scream of the whistle. He says that he is "going to get me a job one of these days on a mainline somewhere running a big mallie. I'm going to show 'em how it's done."

Tim's brother, Gayheart, has been kicked by a mule, and he is content to stay on a farm, hauling coal in a jolt wagon. But Tim has dreams of hauling "a hundred cars of coal around the mountains and through the valleys to the big cities. Just sit up there and pull a big train. Do it, Mick, with your hand. Hell, I can run a engine."

Pa laughs and laughs, and, after Tim has washed his feet and gone to bed, Pa tells Mom that he could listen to "that fool" talk all night, but he wonders "what part of the tales he tells is the truth. Part of it is the truth. Part of it is the wind." But there was never anybody around like Tim. He likes Tim.

Thus Tim is pictured as the carefree man of nature, his stock in trade being tall stories and the genial, gossipy interest which he takes in people, in exchange for hospitality for the night. He is welcomed into the family circle.

Jesse Stuart's cheerful, gregarious tramp is in sharp contrast to the tramp in Robert Penn Warren's "Blackberry Winter," a dour individual who is antisocial, who carries "a mean knife," which he pulls against dogs, who resents his role of tramp. The world owes him a living. He leaves a deep impression of man's futility, in the mind of a young boy, whereas Tim is remembered with affection and pleasure by the families honored by him with a visit.

The youthful narrator of Tim's story (Jesse Stuart) is among Tim's many friends who anxiously await word of him during the days of World War I when he is serving in France. They exult when they hear the news that Tim is back and realizing his dream of "pulling a big Mallie on the C & O," out of Cincinnati. Tim salutes the town as he passes through, no longer a tramp, but still a happy traveler.

> We know Tim's train for he has the engine all decorated with shining brass. He holds the whistle down from the crossing above town to the one below while he passes near the Plum Grove hills. We know Tim's train. We remember Tim. We watch him pass. Tim waves his hand. His face is brown. He wears a bandanna around his neck and a cap on his head now. He waves from the cab at us until the big Mallie engine is out of sight—and the long train twists down the valley like a big black-snake crawling along the bed of a creek. [p. 13]

"Huey, the Engineer" is another of Stuart's short stories which has been given special publication as a book. The story appeared first in *Esquire*, in 1937, and in O'Brien's collection, *Best Short Stories of* 1938. In 1960, a devotee of the railroad, James E. Beard, seeing the work as a small epic and Huey, the protagonist, as a figure of legendary dimension in a fast-disappearing component of the American scene, the short-line railroad, published the story in a special 50-page edition numbering 585 copies. The epical nature of the work was given emphasis through wood cuts by Mallette Dean, which illustrate Jesse Stuart's tale in the oral tradition of a larger-than-life hero.

Beard's prefacing note in the small book mentions the origin of the work as a short story in 1937, and his reasons for wishing to perpetuate it.

> At that time there were yet many little short-line railroads meandering through the back country of America. One by one they are disappearing, leaving behind only their weed-grown roadbeds as reminders—traces that the hand of nature and the heavier hand of man are fast effacing. Those remaining are turning to the economy of diesel power for their last-ditch stand.
>
> . . . . . .

In "Huey, the Engineer," Jesse Stuart composed a sketch of a railroad that passed his door, yet in a sense he was writing about quaint backwoods railroads everywhere—their people, their freight, their passengers, and their times. As a fitting valedictory to a vanishing era it is printed now in a more enduring format for those for whom these things have had meaning.[9]

The saga of Huey is told in dramatic monologue. Stuart employs the high-humored rhetorical style of the frontier narrator for his story. From the opening lines, the reminiscent scenes are painted for the reader in strong, gusty words—lyrical prose which could easily be broken into free verse pattern:

> Can't you hear that whistle still—can't you hear it! Can't you hear the tee rails popping and the flat cars lumbering around the curves and the big-bear engine—flat as a bear— huffing and puffing like a tired horse up a hill with an overloaded express—that humpy-dumpy old E-K engine with her pistons screaking and the long line of black smoke laid back from the stack—following the way the wind was blowing— can't you see it all and the long train of seven cars—two for the passengers—two for logs and cattle—maybe I don't remember the two rusted streaks of tee rails running through the Plum Grove hills—two streaks of rust fastened to the decayed and cinder-buried crossties—rotted at the necks where the tee rails kissed the crossties. [p. 11]

Huey, the engineer, was an object of envy for the people of the hills. The hillboys would run to meet the one train a day and yell to Huey, "Hello, Huey, what's the news today?" Then, invariably one would say, "God how I would love to be Huey and set up there in that engine and ride—never have to look at a book all day or go home, get in the wood. . . ."

Through the years, when the train carried men away to "cross the waters" for fighting in the war, Huey provided the link with the outside world, bringing the hill region news of the progress of the war and later being the instrument for bringing some of the boys back to their homes with the old E-K engine puffing down the line.

[9] James E. Beard, *Huey, The Engineer* (St. Helena, California: James E. Beard, 1960), 7-8.

Huey maintained his own leisurely pace as local autocrat of the short-line for which he was the engineer. When the boys would go out to a pond to catch frogs, Huey would stop the train and put them off at the right place, or, when carrying a crowd of hunters, he would stop when someone saw a covey of birds, and wait, good-naturedly, while the hunters untied their dogs and brought down the birds, then would take them on again. When one end of the railroad line, Greenupsburg, would play a baseball match against the other end of the line, Grayson, Huey's engine pulled seven coaches, and sometimes box cars, to hold all the people, and the engineer would be an eager spectator, but a diplomat, who maintained "Boys I can't be for neither side. I haul all of you. I live among all of you. I'll just watch the game."

Hangings were holiday occasions, too, and Huey's train was loaded with spectators for these events. Huey's hair eventually became "white as cotton," and his eyes became dimmed. Then, one day, the veteran engineer fell asleep at the throttle, and it was the end of the line for him. The whole mountain community attended Huey's funeral. ". . . We stand and shed our tears unashamed—tears for our engineer that once pulled the train where no track now is—nothing but the wind and dents in the earth and cinders ground down and old bridges—but we remember—we'll always remember—and Huey—our engineer—we wonder on what silent train and to what silent land our engineer has gone" (p. 50).

Accentuating the historical value of this small book is the page attached to the back cover, a reproduction of a page from *The Official Railway Equipment Register* for January 1925, entitled "Eastern Kentucky Railway Company," and detailing the equipment for the short-line railroad, the old "E-K," which had its general offices at Riverton, near Stuart's home.

The stories of Tim and of Huey reflect Jesse Stuart's lifelong interest in the railroad industry, with which his father was associated as a section hand in Jesse's youth. Here, the railroad is a symbol of escapism and of benevolence in the lives of the protagonists, and not the monster sucking the life blood of the workers as it was pictured to be for Uncle Jeff and for Stuart's father on the section. Glamour of life at the throttle and better pay are the lot of the engineer—a true hero to the men and boys of the hills, as Jesse recalls in his tales of Huey and of Tim.

It will be pointed out in the next chapter of this work that Jesse Stuart has achieved distinction in the field of the novel. But the novel, with its relentless requirements of length and of detailed structure, could not hold Jesse Stuart's affection as the short story does. Stuart's innate love of life and action, as evidenced by his writing, makes him admirably suited to the short story, the medium in which he can get his incidents and characters from life down on paper while he is in the grip of mood. For Stuart, it is a natural thing, a joy, to follow Edgar Allan Poe's rule that a short story, in order to have totality, must create a single effect from beginning to end, that it must aim at truth, and that it must be short. This Kentuckian has but to consider the events of any day of the life in his region. There is always something, he says, that will yield a story, and his chronicling of the material seems to fall naturally into the short story pattern decreed by Poe.[1]

[1] Stuart's distinction in the field of the short story is re-emphasized by the recent publishing by Charles Scribner's Sons of *Short Stories for Discussion* (1965), edited by Jesse Stuart and Albert K. Ridout. Stuart's "Rain On Tanyard Hollow" is included and a section by him, "How I Write My Short Stories."

4

···

The Novel

Jesse Stuart's novels have two classifications—the autobiographical and the fictional—although, in the fictional works, with their protagonists based upon actual characters from Stuart's hill region, there is inevitably, with this intensely subjective writer, much of Stuart himself.

In the autobiographical division, *The Thread That Runs So True* has slight fictionalization. Greenup High School becomes "Landsburgh High" and Greenup County is "Greenwood County." The school at Warnock is "Winston High" in the book, and McKell High School is "Maxwell High." The "Dartmouth, Ohio," school described in the book is, in actuality, the Portsmouth, Ohio, school. The people who are given characterization in *The Thread That Runs So True* have fictitious names with the exception of members of Stuart's family and a few others who are mentioned. "Ottis Baylor," in whose home Stuart boarded while teaching at the Warnock, Kentucky, school, is

Otis Taylor. "Budge Waters" was a fictitious name, but "Budge" was a real person whom Stuart brought directly from life to a featured role in his book.[1] Such overlapping of slight fictionalization with fact makes classification of Stuart's work difficult. In this study *The Thread That Runs So True* will be considered as an autobiographical novel.

For an approach to the study of Jesse Stuart in the fictional field, it is apropos to accept Cornelius Weygandt's appraisal of the novel as a form which includes within itself the qualities of many literary forms:

> The novel's inclusion within itself of the qualities of many literary forms both helps and hinders our criticism of it. . . . We have so much more to compare the novel with if it have something of poetry or essay or drama in it . . . the inclusiveness, then, helps us to test the value of any particular novel as literature. . . . The trouble is that there have never been any fixed standards as to what the novel should be.
>
> If this novel have achieved beauty of any kind; if it have insight and understanding and knowledge of humanity; if it have the exaltation that is the very breath of poetry; if it be quick with a personality that reveals life freshly as an essay must be; if it have those moments of tense life breaking into action that we call drama: then there is something to be said for that novel, even if its story be clumsily told or its character drawing labored or uncertain. It belongs to literature, then, even if it fall short of what a novel should be. It is considerations like these that have led critics to say that George Meredith is a great writer but a novelist less than great, that Conrad is a great writer but a poor story-teller. . . . There is, however an approximate consensus of opinion that a novel is a long story in prose that depends for its value on portrayal of character as well as upon succession of incidents.[2]

Carl Van Doren said of Thomas Wolfe, "His whole work was a history of his gigantic desire and desperate frustrations,"

---

[1] The real name of "Budge Waters" is not given because his life ended tragically a few years ago. Details will be noted in Chapter VII.

[2] Cornelius Weygandt, *A Century of the English Novel* (New York: The Century Company, 1925), 30.

that "Wolfe, like Hemingway—or like Byron or Whitman—was a writer with a single principal hero: himself in one form or another," that in reproducing or creating his characters in the "family chronicle, *Look Homeward, Angel*," he had not once looked at them "with cold, disinterested eyes, but with the clannish loyalty in which particular or temporary hatreds could not bar out a general love."[3]

These pronouncements upon Thomas Wolfe might well be made of Jesse Stuart, with the additional one that Stuart has never looked upon the people of his region "with disinterested eyes," except in *Foretaste of Glory*—his one objective novel. And Stuart, like Wolfe, must be considered as poet, dramatist,[4] and essayist in connection with the novel, rather than as straight narrative writer.

Deep rooted in poetry, a great compulsive flow of words was unloosed in Stuart in the writing of his first autobiographical novel *Beyond Dark Hills*. This work thus has the significant dimension in the study of Jesse Stuart as that of *Look Homeward, Angel* in the study of Thomas Wolfe. It is a work filled with a gusto for life and experience, the recording of youth's odyssey of the spirit, the struggle toward finding a solution for inner doubts and fears, and the breakthrough to an affirmation or acceptance of destiny.

In Jesse Stuart's case, acceptance meant a return to his native hills after the finding of emptiness in the life beyond. As critic Richard Sheridan Ames said of Thomas Wolfe and his first novel, one could well say of Stuart and his first long autobiographical work, "He projects no new formula and invents no dewy patois. He seems content to portray character, a love of earth and sky, and the troubled souls of men, all built into an impressive edifice of a poet's integration."[5]

[3] Carl Van Doren, *The American Novel* (New York: The Macmillan Company, 1940), 344, 345, 347.

[4] Stuart's style is so strongly dramatic that many of his short stories have been adapted for radio and television; *The Thread That Runs So True* has been dramatized for amateur production; and, in the summer of 1959, Stuart sent the writer a copy of his first play. It is one-act and unpublished.

There is this sharp difference, however, between the first long prose works of the two. Wolfe, under an editor's meticulous supervision and pruning of his episodes, was forced to attempt to judge objectively his writing as a conscientious artist before it could be published. Jesse Stuart presented his work just as he wrote it, a great kaleidoscopic outpouring of episodes set down as they had crowded into the Stuart mind, and it was published in just that way, with no editing. Where Wolfe is polished and observant of literary dicta, Stuart in *Beyond Dark Hills* is often crude in language in faithfulness to realism, and careless in construction. Yet, there is in both the natural, cyclical construction of an epic, written in close touch with life, showing the great ebb and flow of time as passionate, rebellious youth makes the journey from dissociation to a sense of identification with humanity.

So personal and uninhibited is *Beyond Dark Hills* that no one will ever know Jesse Stuart intimately except by reading this autobiographical novel, which begins with his earliest years and extends through what he calls "the early spring of Life."

Jesse's family history is set forth in this book, with descriptions given members of 'both sides," the Hiltons and the Stuarts. The people of the hill region and the countryside itself are described in graphic detail, also. Stuart's saga, his bitter struggle to gain an education, to participate in the life beyond the rim of his hills, constitutes one of the most powerful and original compositions in contemporary literature in the opinion of numerous critics. It has a freshness of regional language that is unmatched in Stuart's later works, except in his first fictional novel, *Trees of Heaven*, and in his early short-story collections.

Robert Penn Warren, then a Vanderbilt professor, was the first critic to recognize the worth of *Beyond Dark Hills;* he was, in fact, the first critic to read it. This book was written as a term theme for Doctor Edwin Mims by Stuart during his year of graduate study at Vanderbilt University. "Nearly every morn-

[5] Richard Sheridan Ames, *Saturday Review of Literature*, XI (June 1938), 21.

ing I would take my work to Robert Warren," he said, "and he would say it was good, and for me to keep it up if I had to throw everything else aside."

When Stuart finished his work, which was to have been an eighteen-page original theme based upon his own life, he had written three hundred and twenty-two pages. Dr. Mims accepted the manuscript grumblingly, but, after reading it, he said to his pupil, 'Stuart, I have been teaching school for forty years, and I have never read anything so crudely written and yet beautiful, tremendous, and powerful as that term paper you have written."

Beyond Dark Hills was published in its original crude state with small attention to errors of grammar and spelling. Because of this unedited, uninhibited style, the great force of the writer's personality seems to be impressed upon the reader of Stuart's autobiography in an unusually enduring way. Robert Stephens wrote in *The Chicago Tribune*, June 30, 1938: "*Beyond Dark Hills* is incorrigibly unsophisticated, but in desperate earnest. It has alternately quiet and violent moods. It is gay, wistful and immodest, naive and profound, but it has rugged honesty. It has Elizabethan speech, and a persistent Puritanism. No one will ever know Jesse Stuart intimately except by reading this journal of his earlier life. It lacks polish, but it has crude power."[6]

Ralph Thompson of *The New York Times*, was not so enamored of the subjective passages of *Beyond Dark Hills*. He wrote: "Mr. Stuart is naive and utterly winning when he writes about his region and his people. When he starts to unravel his own motives and to explain his own philosophy, he tends to be simply naive."[7]

This naivete, or simplicity, was looked upon as strength, however, by other critics. Among these critics was Harry Hansen, of *The New York World Telegram*, who wrote, "The best quality of *Beyond Dark Hills* is its sincerity, its utter simplicity, its warmth and gusto. It is part of the life of a man, and it shares his faults and his virtues."[8]

[6] Robert Stephens, *The Chicago Tribune*, June 30, 1938, 21.

[7] Ralph Thompson, *The New York Times*, Book Review Section, June 23, 1938, p. 3.

Paul Jordan-Smith wrote, in *The Los Angeles Times*, "This *Beyond Dark Hills* is a book which tells of poverty and beauty . . . how poetry bubbled up out of Stuart and mastered his life. The book has blood in it. It inspires."[9] Writing in *The Philadelphia Inquirer*, Douglas Bement said, "The writing in *Beyond Dark Hills* is often crude and emotionally overladen, but the reader usually finds himself absorbed in the mood created, because of the artlessness, the overwhelming sincerity of the author."[1]

Perhaps the most interesting and thorough assessment of Jesse Stuart's first autobiographical novel was given by Lewis Gannett, in *The New York Herald Tribune:*

Beyond Dark Hills is a novel of stalwart beauty. The curious thing about it is that its naked beauty is accomplished by the author's strength of sincerity, rather than by use of grammatical craftmanship. Mr. Stuart uses the same dynamic language that his pioneering stock of people speak. He wields his pen, like an axe, vigorously and quickly, never failing to strike his mark. This is a sturdy and rugged work. The novel is whipped together with a straightforward, objective pace, with powerful glances from right to left. The writer, using the first person, projects himself into the intensity of life, and with an exultant passion for the people around him. The first chapter is dull, chronological, but interesting in its brutal use of words and phrases, a use for which Stuart has been criticized. . . . He writes, not as one from perspective, but as one still in touch with the life he is portraying. He has stopped beyond the horizon of his native hills only long enough to quicken enthusiasm, and has returned with the same capacity for living intimately with the people, and as happily as he had when he went away.[1a]

Beyond Dark Hills might be called one of the richest sources

---

[8] Harry Hansen, *The New York World Telegram*, June 22, 1938, p. 12.

[9] Paul Jordan-Smith, *The Los Angeles Times*, July 6, 1938, p. 8.

[1] Douglas Bement, *The Philadelphia Inquirer*, July 6, 1938, 16.

[1a] Lewis Gannett, *The New York Herald-Tribune*, June 23, 1938, 2.

of information ever provided by an author upon the subject of himself. In contrast to Thomas Wolfe's oblique approach to his personal recollections and impressions through the character of Eugene Gant, Jesse Stuart's treatment of his life story is frankly given in the first person. He is Jesse Stuart throughout his prodigious chronicle of his personal experiences.

Stuart's autobiographical work opens with an account of the "tall figures of earth" who were his ancestors. These sturdy mountaineers from whom Jesse Stuart is descended on both sides have been described in the opening chapter of this book. In *Beyond Dark Hills* Jesse speaks of his maternal great-grandfather, Preston Hilton, as "a lover of books, a school teacher, a farmer, a warrior and preacher laid to rest." From his great-grandfather Hilton, then, comes Stuart's love of both books and the land. "And now the old generations are sleeping upon the high Kentucky hills amid the primitive lands they cleared and close to the log houses they made. And the stars that I walk under there at night as I worship the drowsy summer landscape, wet with dew, illuminated by the moon and stars, are the same stars that swarmed over my people in their day—maybe creating the same impulse in them to do something worthwhile in life. That was the day when tall figures of the earth were needed."[2]

Like Thomas Wolfe, Jesse Stuart is both realistic and lyric in his approach to the American scene as given through his reminiscences. Along with the poverty and discomfort of life in the eastern Kentucky mountains, where "tobacco is the farmer's money crop," there are the beauties of nature and the excitement of hunting and othr outdoor activities, as remembered by Stuart in this story of his early years. His keen awareness of nature and his love of hunting enabled Stuart to find bright spots in an existence which was characterized by hard work. The whole Stuart family worked hard, because existence in the hills compelled every member to contribute to the work. Jesse was introduced to the use of the axe and the sprouting hoe at the age of six, to the plow at eleven.

---

[2] *Beyond Dark Hills* (New York: E. P. Dutton & Co., 1938), 25.

"There are no vacations for children on the wooded hillside Kentucky farms," Jesse writes in *Beyond Dark Hills.*

He remembers, though, "those fine evenings by the winter fireside—popcorn, roasted potatoes, chestnuts, hickory nuts and walnuts. Mom would be knitting socks and sweaters and the lazy cat would be playing with the yarn. And she pieced many quilts on winter evenings" (p. 31).

School terms lasted only five months of the year in Kentucky in Jesse Stuart's boyhood. School was a fine place to be, young Jesse thought, even though he was usually "kept in" for fighting or playing pranks. He was never "teacher's pet." The two-and-a-half-mile walk from his W-Hollow home to the old log schoolhouse at Plum Grove was, as Jesse recalls, an experience that brought out the poetic side of his nature. On his walk to school with his sister, it was not strange for him to meet a fox in the road, or to see pheasants and quails in a sandhole in the path. Squirrels would ramble through the thick-leaved branches overhead.

This closeness to the things of nature and its relation to his early attempts at writing is well defined in Stuart's third chapter of *Beyond Dark Hills,* which he entitled "Opossums and Poetry." There is a vivid description of Jesse's combining of hunting and studying at night, after he and his sister had started to attend high school at Greenup, four miles from his home.

On a night's hunt, I would take a lantern, a coffee sack, a mattock and a couple of books. I would go off in a silent dark hollow and tie the lantern to a tree. I would sit at the base of the tree and study plane geometry and read English—especially the poetry of Robert Burns. I would get interested and Black-Boy would tree. If he barked fast, I knew I must hurry. If he barked slowly, I took my time. . . . There was loneliness in the dark hill when the wind stirred and withered leaves on the trees. It was music to me. It was poetry. . . . Black-Boy's bark grew to be beautiful to my ear. [p. 55]

That first year of his high school attendance was the year

that he began to try writing poetry. "It was because of the wind

I heard in the dead leaves and the loneliness of sounds at night, not to mention the influence Robrt Burns had on me," he said.

There is a flavor of Mark Twain's *Huckleberry Finn* and *Tom Sawyer* in the account of an episode which occurred one summer in Stuart's high school years.

> This summer I took a supply of Tennyson's poetry and and the songs of Robert Burns and went to live at Carter Caves. I went with Tillman Cartwell. We took a small tent and lived in a place called Horseshoe Bottom. That was a drowsy place there.
>
> We would fish all day long. We made a raft to sit on and fish. But the turtles were vicious and would take our bait. We could not swim in the clear waters of Tygart for turtles. I would sit upon the banks and knock them off logs and rocks down in the river with a twenty-two. [p. 53]

Aside from hunting and fishing, the pastimes of the hills which constituted Jesse Stuart's life away from school and the "laying by" of crops, were those of attending revival meetings and funerals. At these revivals, where everybody came to see everybody else, sinners, "wrestled with the Devil," were saved, then went away, to "backslide." When the next revival season came along, the same people came back to the "mourner's bench" and were strenuously saved again.

Jesse's acquaintance with death, which was to color his writing from his very first attempts,[3] came early in his life when his young brother Herbert died of "pneumonia fever," and Jesse saw Herbert carried away in a pine box roped to the bed of a spring wagon for transportation to Grandfather Hilton's farm, where he was to be buried. Shortly afterward, another of his brothers died of the same ailment, and Jesse was overwhelmed by the tragedy of living in such an isolated area that the doctors had not been able to get to the two boys in time to save their lives. He vowed bitterly that the hills would not hold him, that he would go beyond them some day.

[3] His first short story was "Battle Keaton Dies," and his first published poem, "Elegy for Mitch Stuart."

Death as viewed more characteristically by the hill people is entertainingly described by Stuart in his account of his Grandpa Mitch Stuart's desires regarding his "laying away" and his life after death. Grandpa did not wish to go where he would encounter a Houndshell, the Houndshells being the family with which he had been feuding. Jesse says: "If they meet in the same place, there will be war in either Heaven or Hell, I fear. It is strange how democratic the Kentucky hill-people are in life and then at death they become aristocratic in their own small world. They make requests to be buried by So-and-So. It was the request of my grandfather to be buried beside Jimmie Howe, an old man who could always drink more whisky than Grandpa. He never mentioned about being buried by either of his wives" (p. 23).

Grandpa had missed his old friend Jimmie Howe so much that he had gone once to a place in West Virginia where they "talked to the dead." "In the dark room among the spirits and the people who come to talk with them, didn't Grandpa stand up and say: "Come out, all you dead babies and have a drink on old Mitch Stuart! Come on and have some fun on earth again, for you ain't had none in your damn graves for so long" (p. 21).

Jesse Stuart's keen powers of observation are manifested in the most powerful way throughout his autobiographical novel, but never more impressively than in the part concerning his breaking away from his hill home, after he had finished high school. For a long time, his restlessness had been growing. After attending a carnival in Greenup one night with a girl he went home, took all of his books from his room, and burned them outside, so that his brother, James, "would grow up and be happy and live without the knowledge of my old books." His mother's good-bye speech, as he has set it down, brings a strong picture of the mountain woman, who had been ambitious for her children. When Jesse said he was leaving, she said: "Well, be a good boy and when you come back the key will be above the door where we always keep it. The door might be unlocked when you come back. I trust that you will take care of yourself. I think you will. You know I would not hold you here. But, remember, chickens come home to roost. I have told you often that I would like to get out and go and go and go." (p. 112).

Young Stuart went to the carnival grounds and got a job for himself there, as operator of the "Merry Mix-up," a wheel that turned over and over in the air, like a waterwheel. Envying the young couples their fun of riding in the "Merry Mix-up," Jesse soon was giving free rides to pretty young girls so that he could go up and have some fun, too. Soon he had lost his job. But the small carnival world had served to give Jesse Stuart his first taste of life beyond the hills.

Jesse was fascinated by the outside world, and, although he had experienced periods of homesickness in his few weeks with the show, he was not ready to return home. He dreamed of going to Harvard instead of returning home. He was filled with the desire to go to an old college—"Harvard—a school with a heritage to follow." This venerable institution seemed the most remote, the most unattainable goal which he could imagine for a boy from the Kentucky hills, particularly as that boy had no funds. There was no course to follow except to return home, however, when his carnival salary had been exhausted. He went to Greenup. When he reached Greenup, Jesse found the young men of the town making plans excitedly to go to Camp Knox for a period of military training. He decided to join them.

His days at Camp Knox were among the darkest of Jesse's life. Stuart hated discipline and regimentation. He objected to learning how to kill a man, "knowing he had the same right to live that I had." The Stuarts had always loved to fight in wars, he remembered. None of them had ever been drafted. They had all enlisted. But Jesse decided that he would be in favor of war only in the event of the invasion of his country:

> . . . No country could invade my country and slaughter my people unless they'd do it over my dead body. If a country is not worth fighting for it is not worth living in. Just to think, my home and my people among the hills that I have known . . . these timber-covered hills, are they not worth fighting for? Isn't the rugged earth that holds my dead

and feeds me with bread worth fighting for, and these hundreds of acres of elbow-room. . . . The golden Autumn hills and the full bins of ripe harvest from the slopes, I would fight for these. [p. 133]

This philosophy seems to stem back to that of Jess Stuart's early Scottish ancestors whose lives centered about their small landlocked domains, a philosophy that was expressed in the insular spirit of the descendants in the Kentucky hill country of these quiet, hardy men, in the determination of these mountaineers to protect their own homes and families.

An interesting result of Stuart's reflections during his Camp Knox period is a ballad, entitled "Jim," which he wrote about a cousin who had been killed in World War I. Jim's story is told in the words of his mother. The refrain of "Jim" is:

My Grandma used to say:
"Not men, but women have
The price of war to pay." [p. 128]

Whatever Jesse Stuart's thoughts concerning war may have been later, when he served for two years in the Navy in World War II, his thoughts during his training period at Camp Knox were rebellious and unhappy. Only his easy attainment of the rating of sharpshooter and his leisure hours spent in the reading of Edgar Allan Poe and Robert Burns provided bright spots for him in his Army training days.

There followed for Stuart an even more difficult time after he left Camp Knox. This time was the period which he describes as "eleven months pure hell, forging steel." In a town not far from his home, Jesse obtained a job in a steel mill in order to save money so that he could go to school. Stuart describes his experiences in the steel mill in Chapter VI of *Beyond Dark Hills*. This chapter, entitled "Cool Memories of Steel" contains some of the most realistic passages in contemporary literature. In rugged language that vies with the writing of Hemingway and

Steinbeck, Jesse Stuart takes the reader through his tortured days at the mill, where he worked in the hottest part of the plant. His job was to stand by a track and, with a long steel hook, to keep the white hot slabs of steel from running off the track. One of the poets Stuart admired most was Carl Sandburg. But, at the steel mill, Stuart wrote:

> Get Carl Sandburg to tell you about it. He knows. He's the singer of steel. And I am almost positive that Carl Sandburg has never worked a day in the steel mills in his life. . . . Yet he gives you the beauty of blood and sweat and cinders. . . . Carl Sandburg, you don't know anything about steel. You got your ideas from walking around the mills at night or talking to the Mayor of Gary, Indiana. Go on and write your excellent poems about the wheat fields and the sunflowers in the wind and the great open spaces of the sundown west, but, Carl Sandburg, lay off writing about steel . . . quit singing about the beauty of steel. [p. 141]

Stuart gives an unforgettable description of the "Radnor Home," the cheap, dirty hotel near the mill, the only place he could find in which to live that was close to his work. The inmates of the "Home" were forty-five steel workers of various nationalities; five married women; and a single woman, Mattie, a prostitute; with Henry, a Dutchman, as proprietor of the place. Stuart's description of life in this conglomerate group is as detailed and relentless as that of Steinbeck's picture of the community of *Tortilla Flat*, or that of the ill-fated party in *The Wayward Bus*. As did Henry James, Jesse Stuart stands on the rim of the scene he is portraying and sums up his characters, unerringly, with the vigor, as the aforementioned critic Lewis Gennett put it, of the wielder of an axe, "never failing to strike his mark." Unlike James and unlike Steinbeck, Stuart does not attempt to enter the minds of his characters and probe for the motives for their actions. He presents them as they are from life. He does not dissect them; instead of adopting a dispassionate or psychological probing approach to the people of whom he writes, Stuart assumes the sympathetic attitude of putting himself in their places.

Thus, he is able to say of the men at Radnor Home, whose three escapes in life are "whisky, women and gambling":

> Their lives were cramped. All the poor devils knew was steel, furnaces, the deadly rumble of machinery all day long. Steel, sweat, blood and steel! Life was monotonous. Why not drink whisky and shoot out the windowpanes? Why not do something for a change? Tear up the place—fight each other, fight the Law! Life was ugly and dirty and dwarfted as the little ragweeds growing at the edge of the metal sheds. They were covered with soot and grew weakly where the rain could hardly fall. These men's lives were just dwarfed like the ragweeds. Their faces wore the blank expression of the Armco plant's shotgun dwellinghouses. It was a terrible mess. [p. 156]

Jesse Stuart's escape from this seamy existence was books. At this period in his life, he discovered Rupert Brooke, Alan Seeger, Amy Lowell, Robert Frost, Sara Teasdale, Edna Millay, and Edwin Markham. With his deep interest in the subject of death, he was inevitably drawn to Sara Teasdale's poem concerning the finding of peace after death, "I Shall Not Care." This poem he read over and over again, in the isolation of his room at Radnor Home. He began to write poetry again. *Beyond Dark Hills* contains many poems interspersed among its prose passages, and a wealth of prose that is poetic, along with prose which represents realism in its crudest, most bruising form.

Stuart never lost sight of his goal, which was to become a college graduate. He sent for catalogues from Harvard University, Vanderbilt, and the University of Virginia. These schools were all too expensive for him. He inquired about the smaller schools, and decided upon Berea College as the school which he would attend.

One day, Jesse walked out of the steel mill for the last time. He shipped his trunk to Berea, Kentucky, and with only thirty dollars in his pockt and a pasteboard suitcase in his hand, he set out on the highway to "thumb" his way to college. Upon reaching Berea, Jesse experienced a great disappointment. The student quota had been filled. There was a long waiting list of applicants, and the Dean could offer Stuart no encouragement. The Dean, however, turned out to be a focal figure in Jesse Stuart's life. He sent Jesse to Lincoln Memorial University at Harrogate, Tennessee, with a message to his "very dear friend," Chitwood Langley, the president of the university, which urged Langley to accept Stuart as a student there. This message brought results. Stuart was accepted at Lincoln Memorial. At last, he was a college student.

By sheer force of will and power of purpose, Jesse Stuart fought his way to graduation at Lincoln Memorial University. He worked half a day and went to school half a day. His work—in a hay field and in a rock quarry—was physically exhausting, even for a strong mountain boy. In his second year there which he termed his "golden year in college," Stuart was given work in the dining room. This work assignment was much easier on him than the other work, and he fared better with his grades in his school subjects. He had been writing poetry consistently, and during that year he enjoyed the heady experience of having his poems accepted by many small poetry magazines. He became the editor of the college paper, and for his good work in that post was awarded three honorary hours in English with the grade of "A" at the end of his third, and final, year. The honorary hours were given to replace three hours which were deducted from his record, because, by a mistake made in the college office, he had carried more than the rules of the school allowed. Stuart had carried this heavy schedule in his third year, in addition to performing a new job of carrying the mail from the post office and working in the dining room as well as editing the college paper.

Stuart's greatest encouragement in writing while at Lincoln Memorial University came from Professor Harry Kroll, of the English Department, who was himself a successful writer. "Harry Kroll was the first flesh-and-blood writer I had ever seen. I had borrowed money from him many a time in a pinch. And didn't he give me the job to wash his car every week? Didn't he tell me I could write and for me to keep it up? Didn't I get him out of bed and show him poems and he didn't bawl me out? I worshipped the ground he walked on because he was a writer" (p. 218).

Jesse Stuart was graduated from Lincoln Memorial University in 1929, after attending school only three years. He had made "something like a B average" in his work. He had a sense of great pride in the fact that he was the first of his father's people to earn a college degree. But he was weary of school and of books. The chapter that discusses this period in his life is entitled "Beware: Books Hurt the Flesh."

Long before he had finished his college work, Stuart had felt a great nostalgia for his Kentucky Hills and his people. Soon after graduation, he was at home again, "drinking the lonesome waters." The legend among the hill folks that once one drank of the native waters, "the lonesome waters," he would always return for more, held true for Jesse Stuart. In his heart he knew that his destiny was in the hills. "I had gone beyond the dark hills to taste of life. I found it sour when I went beyond where the blue rim of hills touches the sky. I had wanted to go beyond and find out all that was there. I wanted to taste of life. I tasted of it from books and steel and the merry-go-round. It was not sweet like the life in the hills" (p. 226).

Beyond Dark Hills takes the story of Stuart's life not only through his boyhood and his college days, but also through his years of graduate work at Vanderbilt University and through his years spent as a county school superintendent and as a high school teacher, as well. Stuart's schoolteaching career was made the subject for a separate book, *The Thread That Runs So True*, his second autobiographical work, which will be discussed later.

The period which Jesse Stuart spent as a graduate student at Vanderbilt University was one of the most difficult and one of the most significant periods of his life. In *Beyond Dark Hills*, Stuart entitles the chapter describing his experiences at Vanderbilt "A Stranger Was Afraid."

Once again, Jesse Stuart was to know the persistent pains of hunger, the exhaustion of long hours of physical labor which it was necessary for him to endure in his struggle for an education, as he endeavored to obtain a Master of Arts degree at Vanderbilt University. Once again, he found himself working more than half his waking hours to pay his school expenses, and thus having only half his energies left for attending class and keeping up with his studies. He and some of the other poverty-stricken students would sometimes go all day without food. They would drink warm water in the morning, then go to their classes.

> It is somewhere between eleven and twelve. About twenty of us are listening to Robert Warren talk about Elizabeth Madox Roberts. He goes on lecturing. I don't get it all. My stomach keeps on bothering me. It is empty. I forgot to drink water before I came to the class. Drink plenty of water, for water is good to drink. The head is dizzy and the whole body feels sick. Drink good clear water and drink plenty of it, for it makes the sickness leave the body. (p. 311)

When Jesse received his first grades at Vanderbilt, his "legs weakened," under the blow. He knew the bad grades were coming, he said, but he wanted to make himself believe that they would be passing. His report showed three C's. He wrote a sonnet "To Three Low Grades.[4] The sequel to his experience with the low grades was that, in the final quarter of the year, Stuart made the highest grade, by two points, in the literature class where he had been the trailing member. He received A's in two other courses to replace his three C's. His term papers had not fared so well. He had not made an A on any paper throughout the year. The greatest disappointment for him was the fact that he would not graduate. He had not turned in a thesis. The dormitory where Jesse had been living had burned, and in the fire he had lost not only all of his clothes, but his thesis, the term paper he had rewritten for the fifth time, fifty sonnets, part of a novel, and a number of poems. This setback, which was enough to discourage completely the ordinary person, had not deterred Jesse Stuart from finishing the year. But he had not had the time, nor the energy, to tackle his thesis again. To receive his degree was a dream which he would have to discard.

Jesse's great dream had been to get a degree from the university which had the distinction of being the spawning place of

---

[4] *Beyond Dark Hills.*

the famed literary group, the Fugitives. "I went to Vanderbilt University because I had heard of the Fugitives. I had read poems in magazines and books written by members of this group. I wanted to take graduate courses under these men, whose poems, stories, articles, and non-fiction books, I had read. I believed that I could combine farming and writing" (p. 141).

The young mountain man, with his direct, unaffected ways and his long hours of physical labor at the university, was destined to be outside the magic circle of the Fugitives, always on the rim of their scintillating intellectual life, listening to their doctrines in class and drinking in their conversations when there were opportunities. But he was apart.

He knew that he had to be himself, to write in his own way, his words singing with verbal harmonies and communicating with Anglo-Saxon clarity and strength. His keynote in life and in writing was simplicity. He could not be, nor did he wish to attempt to be, the sophisticate, either in life, or in the affecting of an obscurantism in writing which would have been artificiality for him. Two professors who were noted Fugitives—Donald Davidson and Robert Penn Warren—befriended him, but he was never of the Fugitive group. No cult or school of writing could have held him.

Stuart's year at Vanderbilt was, however, deeply prophetic of his future as a writer. He had never ceased to write poetry, and it was there, at Vanderbilt, that he received the most constructive criticism of his writing efforts, and the greatest encouragement for continuing them. The man who was responsible for directing Stuart's talents into the right channel was the poet and critic Donald Davidson. Jesse was a member of Davidson's graduate class in The English Lyric, a class which Davidson says was "*a very* brilliant class, and certainly I had to work and think very hard, as a young teacher, to keep ahead of them, or even to stay abreast of them."[5]

Donald Davidson's class was the one which stirred the heart

[5] Donald Davidson, letter to the writer, April 19, 1954. Quoted with permission.

and the imagination of Jesse Stuart. Jesse had long felt the desire
to talk with Davidson about his writing before he finally achieved
the courage to do so. As do most students who have questing,
ambitious minds, Jesse had longed to establish an intellectual rapport with his professors, to find that inspiration which supple-
ments the knowledge acquired from books, and which, often, is
the motivating force for outstanding accomplishment by the pupil in his later life.

Davidson did not disappoint Jesse. He listened, sympathetic-
ally and with interest, to his story. He read the poems which
Jesse had brought along. The poems were of two kinds, Davidson recalls. There were in the group the "free verse" sort of
lyric that was featured by the lesser-type magazines. "The other
poems were completely different," Davidson says. "They were
'real poems,' about his Kentucky folks, his Kentucky experiences, his true hopes, his deep affections . . . all were good;
at least they were true poetry. I urged Jesse to throw the 'free
verse' poems away and forget about the little poetry magazines—
to send the Kentucky poems to the best magazines in the country. I suggested two magazines as a starter—*The American Mercury*, then edited by Mencken, and *The Virginia Quarterly Review*."[6]

Acting on Davidson's suggestion, Stuart put aside imitative
lyrics and turned to Kentucky poems. The results started him
on his steady way to fame. As related earlier, the *American Mercury* accepted the poem "Elegy for Mitch Stuart," and Jesse received his first cash payment for poetry. There followed inquiries
from a publishing company which led eventually to the publication of *Man With a Bull-Tongue Plow*.

Today, Jesse Stuart continues to express deep appreciation to
Donald Davidson, just as he did in *Beyond Dark Hills*. "I was inspired to go on with writing through the interest of my professor, Donald Davidson. Davidson is not only one of the greatest
writers in the South, but one of the greatest writers in the nation;

[6] Donald Davidson, letter to the writer, April 19, 1954. Quoted by permission.

and I don't know of a greater teacher teaching than Donald Davidson right now. He was kind to me. He was fine. It was he who
told me to look around me at the things about me and write of
them—not to write of something far away—and I followed his
philosophy."[7]

In reply to a request for information from this writer, Donald
Davidson graciously took the time from his work to answer immediately and in highly interesting detail with his recollections
of young Stuart at Vanderbilt. He gave, as well, his own impression of Stuart as a writer. He wrote, in part:

> As to "form," I never told Jesse anything about it, so far
> as I can remember, other than what may have been said, off
> and on, in that English lyric course. I asked myself, when I
> first saw his poems, whether I should undertake to "criticize"
> them, and decided that it would be most unwise for me to try
> to do more, at that time, than distinguish between good and
> bad in the poems he put into my hands. *How do you criticize
> or teach a flowing river?* It was perfectly clear that Jesse Stu-
> art was a river of poetry—and heaven knew what more. It
> would have been silly for me to try to persuade Jesse to write
> like T. S. Eliot or like my friends of the Fugitive group. Of
> course, Jesse is too profuse and easy, as a poet, and doesn't
> put into his poems the artistic care that goes into his prose
> narratives——or so it would seem. The poems burst out of him.
> I wonder if he *could* be as critical towards his poetry as he
> undoubtedly is toward his prose. All the same, there is much
> fine poetry in Jesse's total accomplishment. He has grown out
> of his early habit of overdoing things—as he did, with the too-
> repetitive sonnets of *Man With a Bull-Tongue Plow,* and has
> steadily become more solid and selective. The more studied
> poems in *Kentucky Is My Land* show the mature Stuart, as
> compared with the hungry, burning, fighting, zealous boy who
> wrote the Bull-Tongue Plow poems. . . . As Allen Tate him-
> self says, in a recent essay, one good poem does *not* compete
> with another good poem, of any time. And the poems of Jesse
> Stuart—the best ones—are not to be thought of as competing
> with the "good" poems produced under the standards of the

[7] Stuart, interview with the writer, March 27, 1953.

"New Criticism," or any other "good" poems.

I would find it very difficult to express *any* critical ideas whatsoever about Jesse Stuart. I have so much admiration and affection for him that I could not be non-partisan. I would always be his champion because of the qualities that he so obviously has in large measure, and because he has touched my heart, and keeps on doing so. I think he is on "my" side in what he writes; and that's what his readers think, I do believe— "He is on *my* side," they must all be saying. "Here is *one* writer who is not on that 'other' side—who is not away from us." Isn't that enough? The larger part of it, though, the gift of art, is there, too, in potent quantity.[8]

Jesse Stuart's year at Vanderbilt brought for him, besides the recognition and help from Donald Davidson, an enlarged vista of life, gained from his classroom competition with students from Harvard, Princeton, Yale, and other leading schools of the country. By the end of his year of study, Jesse had come to realize the worth of his struggle to remain in the university: "Wasn't Vanderbilt University a great school after all! Wasn't it strange to be in school where teachers and students were writing books! If one wrote a book there, what of it? One was just in company with the rest. It wasn't anything to get excited about, as we got excited at Lincoln Memorial University, when Mr. Kroll wrote his first novel" (p. 324).

The impersonal spirit of Vanderbilt, which aroused the spirit of competition in the young Stuart, and the encouragement of Professor Davidson produced a limitless flow of creative efforts from Jesse when he returned to his W-Hollow home. Back at his plowing, Jesse would stop his mule, lean on the plow beam, and write poetry when the thought for a sonnet came to him. Usually he did not have a pencil with him, so he would take a stick and scribble his verse on a poplar leaf. The sonnets for *Man With a Bull-Tongue Plow* grew on piles of poplar leaves. Jesse would take the leaves to his room after his work, and before they shriveled, would copy the sonnets from them in longhand on rough paper.

[8] Donald Davidson, letter to writer, April 19, 1954, Nashville, Tenn. Quoted by permission.

He was "the happiest man in the world," he said, plowing in the sun and writing poetry.

"This was the life, the only life," he recalls. "It was the only life for me. I just could not escape it. I was not cut out to study books. I was patterned for the farm."

Beyond Dark Hills leaves the story of the author's life as he begins to taste the first fruits of success. He has published his first volume of poetry, and has received substantial checks for poems and short stories published in leading literary magazines. He has become a successful school teacher. He has the money now to fulfill a dream for his father and for himself. He buys the fertile bottom land below his family's farm, which has the only possible road into his home. With this dream realized, he begins to look back with nostalgia on his early youth. Could it be that "the early spring of life is passing," he wonders? He entreats spring to "stay a while longer," and dreams that he may allay the "fleeting silver minutes of Time!" [p. 334].

Jesse Stuart's second autobiographical work, *The Tread That Runs So True* is discussed in the chapter entitled, "The Poet As Teacher."

The Year of My Rebirth (1956) is Jesse Stuart's autobiographical work which tells of the shockingly swift heart attack which cut Stuart down in the fall of 1954, when he was at the very peak of his most productive period.

Stuart had turned out in 1953 and 1954 two very poignant and successful works, the full-length novel *The Good Spirit of Laurel Ridge*, and the junior book, *The Beatinest Boy*. As one of America's most-in-demand lecturers, with his humorous and stimulating platform manner and the deep sincerity of his interest in promoting the school teaching profession, he had been keeping killing schedule of speechmaking and public appearances. Vital, and always interested in people, Jesse Stuart had loved this activity, and had paid scant heed to his wife's pleas and to those of his family and friends to "slow down."[9]

Reluctantly consenting to see a doctor after he had suffered chest pains one day, he passed off lightly the physician's advice to go to a heart specialist. "Can't be my ticker, Doc," was his protest. He assured the doctor that for five generations on both sides in his family there had never been a heart attack. When admonished that he was living "in a different age," he was still not convinced. But he was sent to a hospital, just the same, and given a thorough check-up by specialists. It was decided that his trouble was "muscular chest muscles," and he was released.

Consequently, in less than two weeks, he was again in a plane, this time flying across Kentucky, to keep a full lecture schedule. With him on the plane, he had three books to read, four stories and a dozen poems to revise. The following day, he was to give two major talks, one in Kentucky and one in Illinois in the afternoon. It was following completion of his talk at Murray State College, Kentucky, when he was rushing down the aisle of the auditorium to keep his plane schedule, that he suddenly dropped to the floor, as one dead.

He says, in this gripping, personal book, that his last conscious thought was, "I will not die! I will not die!" His tenacious grip on life that held through deeply painful, grueling days spent in the hospital afterward, with his wife's constant encouragement and attention to every detail of his recovery, is portrayed in *The Year of My Rebirth*.

But the real importance of this journal is the strong spiritual growth reflected in Jesse Stuart's daily writing, the very limited periods of writing that were allowed him after a long period of convalescence at his "W-Hollow" home, during which he slowly learned the way back to life again and to hope.

In this year of rebirth, he learned again the rich values of the quiet life bound by his mountains and centered about the two persons closest to him in the world, his wife and daughter. In this year, too, while Jesse was still critically ill, his father died— his father, who had been the subject of so many of his most unforgettable stories—and he could not attend the funeral.

But Jesse Stuart's mountains and the devotion of his family

9 *The Year of My Rebirth* (New York: McGraw-Hill Book Co., Inc. 1956), 5.

worked their spell. He spent long hours in looking out over the low-rolling green hills of his county, the hills broken by deep valleys and sharp ridges, and dotted in brilliant colors, with Kentucky's sweet-smelling trees and flowers, the white plum blossom, blue trillium, foxglove. Jesse Stuart set down in his journal his deep happiness over his reunion with the natural world, the beauty of the daily scene, over which the sky threw a wide, enchanting canopy, or rolled up heavy white mists held up by "props of wind."

An example of Stuart's reflective, essay-type writing in this work, as contrasted with the dramatic dialogue, naturalism, and underlying satire of some of his other writings, is this poetic passage on grass, with its transcendental overtones:

> Green, growing, tender grass in early spring is one of the most fascinating things in the world. I think of the power of the legions of the grass. Hannibal's, Caesar's, Hitler's legions have been covered by the grass. All future dictators and military leaders, leading their legions, will not survive their inevitable battle with the legions of the grass.
>
> Troy, Thebes and Carthage did not. These little, fragile, tender, beautiful stems, one inch high, so soft to touch, so soothing to the eye, are the ultimate conquerors of every living thing. This grass is over all.
>
> I cannot look at these thousands of stems without thinking of them as warriors. I have often referred to the grass this way in poems. Yet I would, if not forbidden for health's sake, lie down on this grass and roll. I would lie face down on it and touch and fondle these soft stems, feel their morning coolness against my cheek.
>
> Grass is one of God's greatest creations. Grass is a food to animals and to man, grass is a beautiful carpet to hide the scars of earth. Think of the living things that would perish without the sustenance of grass. Grass is a lovely flower. All of it blooms in one way or another. All of it seeds in one way or another. Even a few days before the official beginning of spring the grass had made my yard so beautiful that the cattle have already broken through fences to get in.
>
> This grass is a poem. Each blade is a letter, a clump is a strong, selective, poetic word. This yard, an oasis of tender

green, is a small spring lyric. Let the grass grow! Yet this grass will get me in the end, as it has the millions of people who have gone before. It covers them, and then their stones, with a soft green carpet. The grass will cover me someday [p. 65].

There is in Stuart's writing the recurrent theme of the ephemeral quality of the life of man as contrasted with the eternity of Nature. This theme is a human protest against the inequality of things, yet a recognition of God as "the Master" in creating the world with this particular inequality between Man and Nature.

In *Year Of My Rebirth*, after his closeness to death, Jesse Stuart reaches a depth of spirit and thought which might be called his affirmation of faith in the traditional religion of his people. With a renewed awareness of the beauty of nature, he has a stronger awareness of God as over all. "So I shifted my way of living. Once my world had been the American skies, the long train trails that span the continent, the ribbons of highway across this vast and beautiful America. My world had been a thousand friends in a hundred cities, ten cups of coffee and loud talk until three in the morning. Now my world was reduced to my home, my farm, my hills. I lived more closely with my wife, my daughter, my animal friends. I thought more deeply of my God. My heart went back to these. . . . Tomorrow I shall put away this journal, as a child puts away an old toy when he gets a new one. Mine is an old toy that has been given me again, life" (p. 342).

God's Oddling (1960) is Stuart's latest autobiographical work. Subtitled "The Story of Mick Stuart, My Father," this book is "the harvest of all my writing seasons," in Stuart's words in the preface. Recurring again and again in Jesse Stuart's short stories and articles, Mick Stuart here emerges in full stature as the "earth poet" and "stalwart figure of earth" who exerted an even greater influence upon the poet than did his mother.

Though the deep influence of both parents is seen throughout Stuart's writing, there is in this tribute to his father the poet's awareness of the stronger pull which his father had upon him because of the basic antagonism between the two men. For antagonism may be said to be at the roots of the deepest love and desire for approval. Proud of his son's success, but with no real idea of its scope or meaning, Mick Stuart gave first importance always to the land. He went to his death calling his literary son an "oddling," a quaint term which was a seventeenth-century holdover in the region, because Jesse valued his writing above his farm.

God's Oddling is a biography, but not in the traditional objective form. It is highly subjective, humane, and warmly sentimental. For the light which this retrospective work brings to bear on the study of influences affecting the life of Jesse Stuart, for its deep probing of motives and selectivity of events coloring the narrative, this book is examined in the autobiographical section of Stuart's longer prose works.

For it is by reaching back through the years to anecdote and incident that Jesse Stuart builds his montage of memories into the sharp portarit of his father, and reveals his father's significance in his life. This book, then, has a special importance to the student and the general reader of Stuart's works. In includes incidents from *Beyond Dark Hills* (now out of print), and it is written in the same strong, poetic vein as is the earlier work. It includes, also, the celebrated short story, "Nest Egg," the story of the fabulous fighting rooster whose exploits caused Mick Stuart to be accused of chicken-stealing. Here the story does not have a separate entity but falls into place harmoniously in the narrative of the elder Stuart's life.

"Clearing in the Sky," a poignant story of the elder Stuart's secret field at the top of a hill, maintained in spite of his heart condition, is another of the Stuart classics to reappear here. In the story "God's Oddling," from which the book derives its title, there is a character sketch of his father which appeared in the prize-winning short-story collection, *Men of the Mountains*, a work awarded the Academy of Arts and Sciences prize for Literature in 1941, and now out of print.

Here these short stories and sketches of actual persons are less dramatically presented than in their original form. They assume, rather, an inherent place in the wealth of anecdotal material with which Jesse Stuart constructs the picture of his father. As a consequence, they find their proper niche of influence in Stuart's own life story.

In *Taps for Private Tussie*, Jesse Stuart created a prototype of the lazy man of his region, a satire on the relief system and government paternalism for people who would not work. In the story of his father, Stuart presents a man who was just the opposite—a man whose religion was work. With devotion and insight, but occasionally with a harsh objectivity which might be the view of one from outside the region, the son recreates from life the rugged little man who was a coal miner, a railroader, but most of all, a farmer—and a tenant farmer, at that—one who loved the earth as passionately as a miser loves money or a scholar his books. Here is the unlettered dirt farmer, but a man rich in undersanding of Nature, who taught his son to observe Nature's special beauties, to cherish animals, to love and respect the land, to work hard, and "amount to somethin'!"

A book written in the oral tradition of *Beyond Dark Hills*, *God's Oddling* is ballad-like in design, its poetic descriptions of the cycle of changing seasons recurring throughout as in the refrain of a ballad. The tone of the composition varies from felicity as the poet recalls the close union of boy and father plowing the hills or working in the fields under a sunlit sky; to the somber or muted, as he writes of death and of the near-loss of the family farm; to the lively and rugged, as he recounts incidents of fights and of primitive amusements in the hills and describes the superstitions and customs of the hill religion; to the quiet and reflective as he relives in his imagination the last days of his father, and the feeling which he experiences of his father's spiritual presence there in W-Hollow and its periphery of hills.

There is, as always in Stuart's prose works, the occasional rhythmic construction within the sentence which denotes the hand of the poet.

This is seen particularly in *God's Oddling* in the lines describing the world as the embryo poet saw it in following his father about the farm in their work—such lines as "Then I followed him through the woods where the golden, rust-colored, silver, brown, and scarlet drops of leaf-rain slithered from the tall tree-tops through the bright autumn wind to the ground."

The book has the realism, pathos, and beauty of the poem from the collection *Man With a Bull-Tongue Plow*, with which Jesse Stuart introduces this work. The poem, as follows, is reprinted in the preface to *God's Oddling:*

For Mitchell Stuart

I've seen him go among his corn at night
After his day was done—by lantern light
He went, unless it was light of the moon,
And a bright moon was up. He's broken soon;
Lines are groved on his face at fifty-two.
The work he does would get the best of you.
And now his love is wind among the corn;
His love is whispering, talking, green corn blades.
His love is cornfiields when the summer fades,
Oak leaves to red and fodder blades to brown.
His love is raining dead leaves down
And going out on autumn morns to salt the stock.
He loves his mules and whispering corn at night—
Buff-colored corn in full autumn moonlight.[1]

In 1960, shortly after Jesse Stuart completed this book written in tribute to his father and to his father's way of life, he left his Kentucky hill home and went abroad with his family for a year of teaching overseas, which will be discussed in the chapter, "The Poet As Teacher."

With *God's Oddling* Stuart had memorialized the past. Burying deep his nostalgia, he looked ahead to the future, and to the world outside his hills, and plunged into the maelstrom of present-day life with the energy which is as characteristic of him as is the daydreaming of the poet.

[1] *God's Oddling* (New York: McGraw-Hill, 1960).

FICTIONAL

Six long fictional works, novels, by Jesse Stuart have been published. These works are, in the order of publication: *Trees of Heaven* (E. P. Dutton and Company, 1940), *Taps for Private Tussie* (E. P. Dutton and Company, 1943), *Mongrel Mettle* (E. P. Dutton and Company, 1944), *Foretaste of Glory* (E. P. Dutton and Company, 1946), *Hie to the Hunters* (McGraw-Hill–Whittlesey House, 1950), and *The Good Spirit of Laurel Ridge* (McGraw-Hill Book Company, Inc., 1953).

Trees of Heaven, aroused much enthusiasm in many of the nation's leading critics and writers. Henry Seidel Canby was one of the critics who was favorably impressed. He wrote: "In *Trees of Heaven*, Jesse Stuart maks a strong bid as a novelist. Of all the stories of primitive hill life in the American Appalachians, this is one of the best-conceived, most truly written, and most authoritatively human. And it is written, also, in that prose of simple beauty and subtle rhythm which a poet turned prose writer best commands. It has great strength and nurture of the soul. I cannot praise too highly the sincerity and tenderness of this unusual book. Jesse Stuart has contributed something to American literature."[2]

J. Donald Adams, of *The New York Times*, in reviewing *Trees of Heaven*, said, "Jesse Stuart's first novel has that quality which comes out of inner compulsion, a native quality, solid to the core, that is completely without self-consciousness. This is not a labored book; what is written here wells up freely as a hill-country spring."[3]

Trees of Heaven is the story of Tarvin, the young son of a man who owns his own small plot of land, and of Subrinea, a squatter's daughter. The class distinction in the hills between the "landowner" and the "squatter" is so sharp that Anse Bushman, Tarvin's father, is determined that his son shall forget the squatter girl. The successful hurdling of the barriers to the marriage of

[2] Henry Seidel Canby, *New York Herald-Tribune*, Book Review Section, April 14, 1940, 1.

[3] J. Donald Adams, *The New York Times Book Review*, April 14, 1940, 3.

Tarvin and Subrinea makes up the plot of the story. Around the plot are woven some of Jesse Stuart's most colorful incidents of hill life and customs, such as the custom of sorghum-making at a night frolic, where "courtin" is the principal object, square dancing, and the attending of land auctions.

Stuart's description of a Commonwealth of Kentucky land auction, as given in *Trees of Heaven*, becomes "a permanent part of the imagination," in the words of Clifton Fadiman. Everybody rushes to the courthouse square to see the fun when there's a land auction. The women cast "sheep's eyes" at Sebastian Litteral, the Master Commissioner, who is "a sight to see," with his long, flowing white locks under a soft felt grey hat, and a paunch in front that denotes his "easy livin'."

Men whose land is being sold for debts or taxes protest that they are trying to "pay off," and that they want to hold on to their land. They insist that "Pap" or "Grandpa" lived on that land all his life, and they threaten to fight "fists or gun" before they will let it be sold. The Master Commissioner calls in Oscar, the sheriff, for help, from time to time, and the vociferous landowners are carried away, handcuffed.

At one of these sales, Anse Bushman realizes an ambition to own more land. He acquires five hundred acres of land adjoining his own farm. Eventually, he finds that he must have a "renter" to help him till his new land. He decides to hire Boliver Tussie, the shiftless squatter who is Subrinea's father. Before Anse will hire Boliver, he intends to "bind 'im with a good ar-tickle."

This "ar-tickle" of agreement between Anse Bushman, the hardworking farm owner, and Boliver Tussie, renter, constitutes one of the high points of humor in Jesse Stuart's writing. Mr. Stuart says that it is authentic in nature, similar, in every respect, to the copy of a rental contract which he has in his possession.

The Bushman-Tussie contract, after providing the renter with a portion of the new farm, a three-room house, a "tater-patch," a span of mules, a plow and tools, and an account at Grubb's General Store, and making provision for the rules of work and the division of tobacco crops, has a "hard part"—"a few extra things" that Anse has "thrown in." The "extra things" stipulated by the contract are, in part:

> Said Boliver Tussie will not be allowed to have any dances, any sort of frolicking in Anse Bushman's house until the crops are laid by and until the crops are harvested. Tussie will not be allowed to fish from the beginning of crop season until the end of the season—is not to be allowed to make moonshine whisky on the property at any time. If caught operating directly or indirectly a moonshine still, his entire crop and all the work he has done is to fall into the hands of Bushman without any cost, and he is to vacate Bushman's premises within ten days—Will not be permitted to attend church revivals more than two nights out of each week. Tussie will not be allowed to bring a baby into his home each year. "That," says Boliver, "is something a body can't help." "If you have a baby at your house," says Anse, I know who'll haf to foot the Doctor's bill. It will be old Anse Bushman, party of the first part." [p. 182]

These rules laid down by Bushman for the personal living of his renter, Boliver Tussie, illustrate the difference in attitudes toward life between the two men. Anse's wife Fronnie, and his son, Tarvin, are on the side of "the squatters." Fronnie says:

> The people here that makes a little more than the rest air old long before their time to git old and they die before their time to die. The squatters and the rest of the no-count people don't work so hard, and they enjoy life. They can't live as long as they should live, for they don't have enough to live on. It's about the same either way you look at it, starve to death or die workin yourself to death. We have these two kinds of people among these hills. [p. 50]

Tarvin would rather get some fun out of life by "goin' sparkin'" or hunting than to spend all his time working, as his father does. Tarvin and Subrinea have a secret meeting place, the little graveyard of the squatters, a neglected plot of ground that is made a small oasis by a clump of ailanthus trees, or "trees of heaven." Tarvin comes back to the graveyard one day to do some thinking after the Tussie family had been driven away from his father's land for "moonshinin" and breaking most of the agreements of the "ar-tickle." Subrinea is to have a child by Tarvin, but Anse Bushman has determined that his son should not marry a squatter girl. Now Anse has a change of heart. Anse was hit by a falling tree and knocked unconscious for three days. When he regained consciousness, he had a "token," a vision of a lake of fire, where all the land in the world would do him "no good," because he had lost his soul. Now, Anse is "converted." He tells Tarvin to bring Boliver Tussie and his family back to the Bushman farm, and he gives Tarvin his blessing for a marriage with Subrinea. Tarvin reflects about the squatters as he visits their graveyard. He determines that he will be buried by Subrinea in a squatter's grave. He realizes that the squatters' way of life is the way of life that he loves. The squatters had a "good time" while they lived. They hadn't "worked themselves to death." They hadn't "hogged" all the land. They had been a happy lot of people, those people lying in this little neglected graveyard.

The simple moral which Jesse Stuart expresses in *Trees of Heaven* is the moral that life should not be restricted to the sphere of endless work, for the purpose of accumulating material possession, but that life should have some enjoyment. This moral is not stated didactically but is given to the reader in the lively descriptions of the hill pastimes which, the author seems to say, people should take time to enjoy. The moral is contained in Stuart's passages concerning the natural beauty of the hills, which he intimates will go unheeded if people will not take time to appreciate it.

Some of Stuart's most lyrical prose is to be found in *Trees of Heaven*. The following excerpt illustrates his use of repetition and alliteration to produce a poetic effect:

> Dog days pass, and the songs of the beetle, the katydids, cicadas and whippoorwills grow weaker with the passing of summer days. The great white thunder clouds roll across the sky and occasional showers splinter down their soft splashes on the thirsting grass. August showers feed the thirsting throats

of the white corn roots and the budding ears are filled with large full grains.

Days pass in single file; days keep earth replenished with the sun's hot rays and crops grow into maturity. There is the lazy passing of the days and the music of the wind in the corn—music of the flutes among the dying love-vines on the paling fences; music of the cymbals among the coloring sycamore leaves when they beat together, and there are the shrill weird notes of the viols in the dead grasses on the slopes. There is the music of the harp strings plucking among the oak limbs and the pine boughs. Summer is passing and Anse and Tarvin are working in the sprout fields to get the sprouting finished.

Farewell-to-summer is blooming on the cliffs in purple and white masses. Blackbirds gather and fly over the pasture lands and above the fields of buff-coloring corn, flying to the South. Life is changing in the processing of passing days. The multi-colored butterflies flit slowly on fragile wings above the blooming elders beside the creeks and above the rooster-combed pods of shoe-make berries. [p. 49]

Trees of Heaven might be said to be closer to the soil and the life which Stuart knows than are his subsequent novels. This first novel has, for instance, such colloquialisms throughout as the use of "air" for "are," "git" for "get," "norate the news," for "tell the news." While these expressions appear from time to time in other works of Stuart's, they are used consistently only in *Trees of Heaven.*

The test of reality which Henry James says in his *Art of Fiction* must be met by a novel to be successful is more than met in *Trees of Heaven.* One might not expect to be able to put oneself in the place of a sharecropper, but the reader of *Trees of Heaven* finds himself caring about Jesse Stuart's young Tarvin, as he cares for the furze-cutter of Thomas Hardy in *The Return of the Native.*

This sense of identification experienced by readers who have become *aficionados* of Stuart's works is the result of the deep, bardic attachment to his people which Stuart projects into his writing.

Never could *Trees of Heaven* be placed in the genre of the

novel of social criticism, as are Erskine Caldwell's novels and Steinbeck's *Grapes of Wrath.* Throughout, there is evidenced the warm feeling of the author for his subject. He does not write clinically or objectively. Even in his incisive characterization of Anse Bushman, the landowner who is the *bête noire* of the story, there is humor and tolerance—for, was not Anse a hill man, too?

Harry Hansen, *New York World-Telegram* literary critic, strongly supported this view of *Trees of Heaven:*

> Few authors say a kind word for the improvident white farmers of the South. In most cases they treat them as poor white trash, lazy, ornery and dead to change. Jeeter Lester has become the type by which the public judges all. But in Jesse Stuart's first novel, *Trees of Heaven,* the white squatters of the Kentucky hills, who seem to be as fond of laziness and raw liquor as any of their fellows in other states, get a square deal. They love their land; they love the soil where their people are buried, and there is no reason why some of them can't snap out of their bad habits. . . . We get light on the squatter's philosophy, born to some extent of lack of ambition, that there's no benefit in piling up possessions, but the two young people are committed to the belief that work is an expression of energy and health and security belongs to those who fight to win it.[4]

Stuart's philosophy, then, is that an amalgam of hard work and of time off for enjoyment of cameraderie, of human association, and the maintaining always of an awareness of Nature's infinite beauty, is the ideal. This paradoxical view of life, embracing the Calvinistic doctrine of hard work and the deeply ingrained traditionally pious, God-fearing attitude, along with the direct approach to God of the transcendentalist—the conception of God, Man, and Nature as one companionable, all-embracing whole—brings Jesse Stuart, "the American Robert Burns," into line with Burns' philosophy just as, in critical appraisal, he is often compared in his poetic writng with Robert Burns.

Jesse Stuart's second novel, *Taps for Private Tussie,* was pub-

---

[4] Harry Hansen, "The First Reader," *The New York World-Telegram,* May 14, 1940, 6.

lished in 1943. This book, although retaining the atmospheric flavor of *Trees of Heaven,* is completely different in character from
that work. *Taps for Private Tussie,* which is amusingly illustrated
by Thomas Benton, is a hilarious narrative which established Jesse
Stuart immediately as one of the top contemporary humorists in
America.

The outlandish characters and improbable plot are presented
with a broad humor which reflects Stuart's deep regard for his
hill people, even when their foibles and failings are his theme.
And the *joie de vivre* tone symbolizing the bright outdoor world
of the young boy from whose lips we get the story pervades the
narrative in the manner that is typical of Jesse Stuart and his
rapport with Nature. With its frontier flavor, as well, this Stuart
work is highly reminiscent of Mark Twain.

Taps for Private Tussie, a bestseller, is the work by which a
large portion of the reading public both here and abroad
have come to know Jesse Stuart. This book was a Book-of-the
Month Club selection for December 1943. The Metro-Goldwyn-
Mayer Company bought the movie rights for this story. *Taps for
Private Tussie* was published in England, Australia, New Zealand,
Denmark, Argentina, Brazil, Portugal, and Sweden. An edition
was published for the American Armed Services in 1944. A con-
densation of this story appeared in *Ladies Home Journal,* and a
pocket book edition of it was published in 1946.

Stuart's second novel, which brought him fame and financial
success, brought him, also, the Thomas Jefferson Southern Award
in Literature for 1943. This novel continues to bring honors for
Stuart. *Taps for Private Tussie* is included in *Masterpieces of
World Literature in Digest Form,* which was published in 1952
by Harper and Brothers Publishing Company.

Appearing as it did in the midst of World War II, *Taps for
Private Tussie* provided pure escapist reading for a disheartened
public. This story, which is characterized by uproarious humor
throughout, is told by Sid, a young adolescent of the hills. Sid
might be called a present day "Huckleberry Finn." Sid's world
in the Kentucky hills is brought graphically to the reader, as he

relates the story of how the body of his Uncle Kim, who was killed in the war, was brought home for burial, and as he describes the fantastic series of events which follow.

"Press" Tussie, the head of the Tussie family, is Sid's grandfather. Grandpa has shown the natural suspicion of the hill people as he insists that Sid's Uncle Mott open Kim's coffin before they hold the funeral. Kim is identified by the presence of a gold tooth and a missing finger on the body in the coffin.

> I just wanted to be sure it was my boy. I didn't want to bury some other mother's son and think he was my own. When I lay a bunch of wild roses on his grave, I want it to be on Kim's grave. God only knows what makes a body feel that way. But that's the way I feel. I want the bones to be Kim's bones that I put flowers on and keep the briars and sprouts cleaned away! [p. 14]

Uncle Kim is buried on a mountaintop, after the members of the funeral procession have struggled up the steep incline, singing "Beulah Land." "And," says Sid, "if you don't think it's hard to climb a mountain and sing, you try it one of these days."

Uncle Kim is scarcely in his grave before the Tussies are cashing the ten-thousand-dollar insurance policy which he has left for his wife, Sid's "Aunt Vittie." Grandpa supervises the business.

Press Tussie has no trouble in getting Kim's insurance policy cashed. Everyone is helpful. Every one wants the Tussie vote. Press is the head of the "Relief Branch" of the Tussie family.

> It was the Tussie vote was the biggest vote in our county. Every man that ran for office came to see Grandpa since he was the oldest living Tussie and what he said among the majority of Tussies was law. If a Tussie wanted relief, Grandpa got it for him. If he didn't get it, that Tussie was mad at Grandpa. That's the reason a lot of Tussies came to Uncle Kim's funeral that I didn't expect to see and many came that I'd never seen before. They wanted to get in good with Grandpa. They, too, wanted to get relief. [p. 47]

With nine thousand dollars placed in a checking account at

the bank, and one hundred dollars in Aunt Vittie's pocket, the Tussie family begin a new life. Sheriff Whiteapple has put them out of the vacant schoolhouse in which they have been living. For their new home, the Tussies rent a "mansion," the sixteen-room house of George Rayburn, which is situated about three miles from town. Aunt Vittie and Grandma spend money recklessly, buying furnishings for the first real house they have ever occupied. As the house is rented in the name of Vittie, Grandpa can continue to draw his relief check, and pick up his big relief bag of victuals each week. The Tussies are deliriously excited over their good fortune.

There is a rift in the bright outlook for the Tussies, however. They have been established in their new quarters only a short time when the rest of the relief branch Tussies arrive on the scene to share Press Tussie's good fortune. Besides the relief branch members of the family, there is Grandpa's brother George, who is head of the other branch of the Tussies. Uncle George has been living out West, but now he has come home to the mountains to die, he says, after hearing of Press's "fine success."

Uncle George is a "playboy" member of the Tussie Clan. He has had five wives. He is also the musician of the family. Uncle Mott plays the "banjer" but Uncle George is an artist with his fiddle. Sid says that Uncle George can make his fiddle "cry and laugh, and almost talk." Sid wonders if Uncle George has ever had a son by any of his wives that he has called as many pet names as he calls his fiddle.

When all of the shiftless Tussies who can get into the Rayburn house have managed to join Press Tussie, there are "forty-six mouths to feed." One day, a relief investigator calls upon the family. He informs Grandpa that, since he can live in a house like that, he is being dropped from the relief rolls. Without receiving their weekly relief bag of groceries, the Tussies are forced to spend more and more of Vittie's insurance money. They do not worry about it.

There are square dances in the Rayburn house every night. The Tussies provide their own music. They dance wildly, their hob-nailed shoes ruining Mr. Rayburn's dance floor. They drink "moonshine" whisky, fight, make love, argue, and "make up."

George Rayburn calls to inspect his house, and rushes out, horrified. He returns, with Sheriff Whiteapple and an attachment for the Tussie's furniture, which he will hold until they have paid for the damages to his property. Mr. Rayburn sounds like a man "a-trying to cry," Sid says. The Tussies have scraped all the varnish from the hardwood floors of the house. They have ruined the wallpaper with tobacco juice, marked up the bathroom walls, and used fenceposts and the door from the coalhouse on the place for building fires. Sheriff Whiteapple orders the family to leave.

Except for Uncle George, the "sponging" relatives disappear. Grandpa, Grandma, Aunt Vittie, Uncle George, Uncle Mott and Sid carry their belongings and set up a new home in a small shack in a clearing in the woods nearby. Grandma and Aunt Vittie bemoan the loss of their fine furniture. The men are philosophical. Grandpa says that he feels "more at home" in the shack.

Sid has never been to school. Eventually, however, "the law" catches up with Grandpa for not attending to Sid's schooling, and Grandpa is forced to send the boy to school. Attending class at the old schoolhouse where the family has lived before, Sid is embarrassed as he towers ovr the other first-graders. He enjoys school, however, and makes good grades. His spare time is spent trapping wild animals and selling their skins, to make money for the family. With their relief funds cut off, the Tussies have only Grandpa's old age pension to pay for their support.

Aunt Vittie and Uncle George get married. Uncle Mott, a disappointed suitor of Aunt Vittie, hates Uncle George. One night they fight, and Uncle George kills Uncle Mott. Soon afterward, Sid looks through the window of the shack and in the bright moonlight, sees Aunt Vittie walking from the village, with a man in a soldier's uniform. The soldier walks like Uncle Kim— it *is* Uncle Kim! Uncle George jumps through the window, breaking the glass as he does so, and disappears up a hillside. The family is filled with consternation and joy to see Kim. Grandpa says he wishes that he had looked in Kim's coffin, instead of having Uncle Mott do so. Uncle Kim says that Uncle Mott knew the body wasn't Kim's—"Mott had somethin in the back of his head. He had other plans." Now, Mott is dead. Kim says Uncle George will get "what's a-comin to 'im."

Uncle Kim says that he thinks it's time Sid knows who his mother is. Aunt Vittie isn't Sid's aunt, she's his mother. Kim had been paid to marry Vittie by a man who had got her "in trouble." Sid is Vittie's son. Kim says that he is not Sid's father, but he "would love to be." Sid is happy.

> I've always wanted to be your son. . . . I've thought about you more than anybody since they brought you back and buried you. Never a night I didn't think about you. When we lived at the big house and had the dances. I thought about you. I went to bed thinkin about you. I thought about everything we had, even to the clothes I wore, had come from money that we got for your dust! [p. 297]

Thus, this book ends on a reproving note. But the satire on the "relief" program and its abuse, which is the principal theme of *Taps for Private Tussie*, is not stated forthrightly. Instead it is developed by means of the plot, and by such bits of characterization as the allusion to Grandpa's "gittin' down in the back," whenever he is offered work. The style of the humor in this work is broad, and the plot and the characters so outlandish that they vie with the "hill-billy" exaggerations of screen and radio. As previously noted, Mr. Stuart insists that his characters and stories are not exaggerated, but that in his region, truth is, indeed, "stranger than fiction." The characters in *Taps for Private Tussie* are true to life, he insists, and the plot not at all improbable. In this work, the subject matter is treated objectively. *Trees of Heaven*, on the other hand, is strongly subjective in treatment. One learns about the thoughts and dreams of Jesse Stuart, in reading about Tarvin. In Sid's story, there is no analyzation of motives. This book is pure entertainment.

Dorothy Canfield said of *Taps for Private Tussie,* "Jesse Stuart shows himself a master, working in this enchanting story, which may well be one of our American classics."[5]

Mongrel Mettle, the autobiography of a dog, which was published in 1944, is, as Mr. Stuart says, a "complete departure" from his previously published works. He wrote it in five and a half days. Stuart says that he thought he was writing a juvenile book. Instead, *Mongrel Mettle* was published as an adult book, and was hailed both as a social satire and as a special book for dog lovers. This story is reminiscent of those children's classics *Black Beauty* and *Beautiful Joe.* It recalls, too, the animal fables of Chaucer's day.

Jerry-B Boneyard, the lovable Kentucky mongrel who is the hero of *Mongrel Mettle,* is a dog of many masters and mistresses. He is befriended first by Glenna Powderjay. He loves her dearly, but when she goes away to college and leaves him, he feels that he is not wanted. Jerry-B runs away from Glenna's home to make a name for himself out in the world. The little dog falls into many adventures, but the most exciting is the period when he runs wild with a family of foxes. He enjoys a romance with Fair Fox, running the ridges, and catching rabbits with her. But he cannot forget the Powderjay Farm, his old mistress Glenna, and Trusty-Red-Rusty, a dog there on the farm, with whom Jerry-B had had many discussions about the Democracy of Dogs. Jerry-B had said that he was glad he was a mongrel and free to choose his own wife. He was not a pedigreed dog who must be bred with one of his own kind.

During one period of his wanderings, after he has fallen into disgrace for being a drunkard while he is supposed to be a watchdog at a still, Jerry-B vows that he will find the Powderjays again. At last, he arrives at his old home. His mistress is overjoyed to have him again. The mongrel renews his friendship with Trusty-Red-Rusty, but finds that this pedigreed gentlemen, who talks of a Democracy of Dogs, is not really dem-

[5] Dorothy Canfield, *News of Books and Authors* (New York: E. P. Dutton & Co., May-June, 1944), 1.

ocratic when it comes to sharing things. Jerry-B falls in love
with Dossie, a pedigreed dog, who says she will be his wife.

> I was fulfilling one thing; I was a mongrel marrying a
> pedigreed lady. I was helping to mix the dogs of America
> and make them a Democratic Race of Dogs, one that would
> become powerful as a race of dogs in our future that was
> to be. I thought of this as I trotted beside my true-love
> Dossie toward the sunrise of an August morning that prom-
> ised to be a fair day for love, security and a more Democratic
> World of Dogs. [p. 201]

Foretaste of Glory illustrates Jesse Stuart's versatility in subject matter and in manner of approach in the field of fiction.
The novel is treated objectively, in contrast to the subjective
treatment in *Mongrel Mettle*. *Foretaste of Glory* is a *tour de
force*.

Blakesburg, "a town beneath the Southern sun, fenced in by
two rivers, a mountain, and the wind," is obviously Greenup, in
this story. At sundown, one evening, there appears over Blakesburg a mysterious arc of light, "more brilliant than the light of a
thousand moons." We find Jesse Stuart at his poetic best in the
strong, dramatic Prologue to his Narrative: "Great splinters of
light darted across the heavens from the east to the west and from
the north to the south. They criss-crossed each other on falling seas
of liquid fire, as God had promised for the last day. The people
of Blakesburg gazed upon this awesome beauty of ten thousand
rainbows as a heavenly portent" (p. 11).

The terrifying effects of this phenomenon cause many of the
Blakesburg citizens who witness it to make frantic confessions of
their sins and to attempt to make last-minute amends for them,
as they are certain that Doomsday is upon them.

Each chapter in *Foretaste of Glory* treats of an individual or
group of individuals in the town and the circumstances in which
they are found at the time of the appearance of the arc of light.
The effect of this work is that of a number of short stories bound
together by a common, or unifying, theme. Thus, the construction of this story could be said to parallel that of *The Bridge of*

San Luis Rey, in which a group of widely dissimilar characters are caught in the same spot at an awesome moment in time. Again, it might be said that *Foretaste of Glory*, in its panorama of characters, is a *Spoon River Anthology* in prose.

When the great lights flash over Blakesburg, Liam Winston, Aunt Effie's old bachelor son, dashes out of the house, in terror, searching for his brother, Booten, to "make everything right" with him for the brutal knifing he had given him. Booten will not forgive him, even though he knows the "end of time" has come. Liam's teeth rattle with fear.

Attorney Joe Oliver, a "clean, decent and upright gentleman of great moral integrity," in the opinion of the town, a lawyer who makes a specialty of sending guilty people to the penitentiary questions his wife as to her loyalty to him, when the light appears over the town. Arabella is frightened at his attitude. She says, truthfully, that she has been loyal. She cannot understand Joe's mumbling and his agonized contortions that resemble the actions of one of his witnesses whom he has prosecuted on the stand. Because he has put the question of loyalty to her, it occurs to Arabella to question Joe as to his own loyalty. She questions him, and is horrified at his answer. Joe confesses painfully that, for fifteen years, he has been having an affair with their housemaid, Mattie Pratt. Arabella is stunned. Mattie is the girl who has been cleaning her house, who has been cooking for her and her children. She cannot bear the thought. She screams and rushes out into the "approaching doom."

Bruce Livingstone, a leading citizen, who is always busy trying to "improve" his city, and who has been accused of being a Communist, has never taken the time to read about the beginning and the ending of the world. He has no time or thought for church. But when the strange light appears, he begins to tremble and to feel his terrible aloneness. He begins to run toward the center of town, and begs everyone to gather at the courthouse. "Let us not forsake one another at the ending of the world!" is his plea.

Foretaste of Glory has thirty-six chapters, with each featuring a different protagonist in the drama of the Doomsday light. The next morning, as the end of the world has not come, the people go on with their old ways. Life goes on for them and their city "like the slow turning of a paddle wheel pushing a steamboat up the broad river." This work is a clinical study of hypocrisy. It lacks the depth of Stuart's other novels, as the characters are not developed, or given any real determination. It is a "surface," not a probing, novel.

Hie to the Hunters (1950) is a novel based directly upon incidents from Jesse Stuart's boyhood in Kentucky. Stuart says that the idea for this book—the people, the background, the episodes—were stored in his memory for years and that he was eager to put it down on paper "in order to preserve a part of American life that has now gone into oblivion."

With a strong nostalgia for his childhood, Stuart wrote *Hie to the Hunters* as a juvenile book. It was published as an adult book, but, soon after publication, Harcourt, Brace and Company brought it out as a high school textbook. In the introduction to the textbook edition, Jesse Stuart said: "Soon after *Hie to the Hunters* was published as a novel for grown-ups, something happened that pleased me more than anything that could have happened to one of my books. *Hie to the Hunters* was accepted as a textbook for high school English courses. . . . I regard this book being published as a high compliment, for now it will be placed where I intended it originally to be, that is, in the hands of high school students."[6]

This novel of Stuart's is one which expresses most deeply his affinity with the soil and his love of the life in the hills, particularly of his love for hunting. "Hie to the Hunters" is the hill expression for saying "Good luck to the hunters."

The story begins with the meeting of Jud Sparks, "Sparkie," sixteen-year-old mountain boy, and Didway Hargis, "Did," a slender town boy of fourteen. As Sparkie is making his way down the street, Did is being "jumped upon" by the "twin bullies" of Greenwood. The twins are much larger than Did. Sparkie comes

6 Stuart, *Hie to the Hunters* (New York: Harcourt-Brace & Co., 1951),

to Did's rescue, and the smaller boy is pathetically grateful to his champion. The two boys exchange introductions. Sparkie learns that Did is the son of the owner of the largest store in town, the Hargis General Merchandise Store. Did learns that Sparkie is from the Plum Grove Hills, "where there's a war going on between the fox hunters and the tobacco growers. . . . That's where they're burning tobacco barns and poisoning hound-dogs."

Sparkie suggests that, as Did has no one to protect him from the Greenwood bullies, he should come home with him to the hills. Did is afraid of what his father will do, but he agrees to go with Sparkie when the mountain boy promises to teach him how to hunt and shoot.

The story of Did's life and education in the hills is a sequence from the boyhood of Jesse Stuart. Stuart based the characters of Did and Sparkie upon two of his real-life companions, and the incidents were taken from life.

In the story, Did comes to love the tang of the fresh air and the feel of the sun in the hills. From his very first meal cooked by Sparkie's mother, Did develop a strong appetite for the food of the region: "When Did pulled up his bark-bottomed chair at the end of the table, he was surprised at the food before him. There was a dish of steaming hot soup beans, a dish of fried potatoes, pork ribs, kraut, pumpkin, a dish of apples, two small dishes of jelly, and coffee and milk. There was a flat plate of cornpone with steam oozing from the places where the brown crust was broken. This steam smelled sweet to Did's nostrils, giving him an appetite he had never had before" (p. 24).

The poverty of Sparkie's people did not preclude their enjoyment of good food and the exciting pastimes of the hills, Did learns. The hill people are moneyless, but they live rich, full lives in their circumscribed world. Did learns the thrills of the 'possum-hunts at night, which he and Sparkie enjoy with "Shootin' Star," Sparkie's dog. The small-town boy is taught how to trap foxes and other animals to help Sparkie collect skins for selling. He learns the nature lore of the hills. Sparkie takes him to square dances, and he is fascinated by a pretty young mountain girl. Did's father learns of Did's hidingplace, and he comes to take him home. Sparkie's mother and father prevent Mr. Hargis from seizing his son, when Did says he wants to stay with them and Sparkie. Hargis returns to Greenwood and organizes a posse of men to "rescue" his son. They surprise Did, Sparkie's family, and their friends at a corn-shucking party. There is a fantastic fight between the Greenwood faction and the Plum Grove crowd in a cornfield, where the city people are put to flight when they are pommeled with pumpkins and wet cornstalks. Did fights on the side of the hill group. The fight has been the most exciting adventure of his life.

Did stays in the hills with Sparkie for Christmas, and he is sure he has never seen a Christmas card as beautiful as the winter nights in the Plum Grove hills. Did has the pleasure of giving Sparkie's family gifts which he has secured from his father's store. Sparkie gives Did a brandnew holster and a .38 Special pistol, so Did will be "properly dressed at the square dances." Did has promised his father that he will decide whether he is to come home and finish Greenwood High School or stay in the hills. He decides to go home and finish school, then return to Sparkie's family for the summer. He urges Sparkie to go with him to school. Sparkie refuses. School isn't in his nature. He belongs in the hills.

Before Did goes away, he gives Sparkie a blue-speckled "hound-pup." When Sparkie discovers the new dog in the kennels, he throws his arms around the pup, and tears glisten on his tanned cheeks. His mother says, "That boy couldn't be such a bad boy. . . . Shucks, bad boys can't cry."

Hie to the Hunters has the elements of humor, simplicity, and the combined study of adolescence and outdoor life which invite comparison between Jesse Stuart and Mark Twain.

The novel *The Good Spirit of Laurel Ridge* (1953) is, perhaps, Stuart's best fiction work.[7] Certainly the critics do not seem divided in their estimates of this novel, which manages to convey, around a slender plot, the full, rich store of balladry and folklore

---

[7] Jesse Stuart stated in a letter to the writer (April 20, 1953) that he believed this to be his best novel. On January 13, 1954, Stuart sent clippings

of the Kentucky hills, as well as to expound the deep-seated philosophy of Jesse Stuart concerning the rewards to be gained by
living close to the soil.

A cross section of criticisms taken from representative papers
throughout the country shows a concerted opinion that the stature achieved by Stuart as a novelist in this latest work was one
of increased distinction. John D. Paulus, of *The New York Times*
Book Review, says: "Jesse Stuart has written here a heart-warming folktale that is a real delight. He telescopes time to bring the
world of today and the world of a hundred years ago in amazing
(and revealing) juxtaposition. And in Old Op Akers, he has fashioned a giant of noble stature, a self-sufficient man who fears

George H. Favre, of the *Christian Science Monitor*, had this
neither the 'adam bumb' nor the 'evil sperets' that I am sure all
of us know exist."[8]
to say: "Jesse Stuart has done it again. In a simply conceived and
artlessly executed work, the author of *Taps for Private Tussie* has
revealed a character reflecting his own boundless love for the
beauties of the Kentucky hills. Beyond developing a warm and
completely lovable character, Jesse Stuart brings us, through Op,
a rich textural study of the folklore that weaves itself into the
rough homespun philosophy, strongly reinforced by simple faith,
of the hill people. *The Good Spirit of Laurel Ridge* is not just
good fiction. It is authentic Americana. It is history with a heart."[9]

The Good Spirit of Laurel Ridge has some of the outlandish
characterizations of *Taps for Private Tussie*, but the humor of the
book is more restrained than in the earlier work. This latest novel
is strongly subjective, containing much in it of Jesse Stuart's
feelings and beliefs.

Stuart's philosophies are projected through the central character of this story, Theopolis (Old Op) Akers. Old Op is a weath-
er-beaten squatter who loves passionately his cabin home on

---

of reviews of *The Good Spirit of Laurel Ridge* which confirmed his judgment.

[8] John D. Paulus, *The New York Times* Book Review, November 1,
[9] George H. Favre, *Christian Science Monitor*, November 1, 1953, 15.

Laurel Ridge. He finds peace and contentment in hoeing his small patch of corn, and in gathering nuts for food, roots and herbs for his few physical ailments. Everything a man could ever need is on Laurel Ridge, he believes, and what happens in the outside world could only be disturbing.

Op is a folk poet of legendary dimensions. The old mountain man is a naturalist, a wise philosopher—and a staunch believer in "sperets," friendly "sperets," who knock on his walls at night, sit at the table with him, and commune with him. Op sits on his porch in the moonlight, and listens to the weird music of his horsehair harp, as the wind blows across it. He listens, too, to the musical belling of the hounds as they chase the foxes at night. Old Op kills giant fish with bow and arrow, catches forty-pound turtles with his bare hands. He gathers huge strawberries from patches that only he knows about.

Op's world is a true dream world. One day, however, there comes into his primitive paradise a disturbing element. An intruder from the "Outside World" invades his peace. The invader is Op's daughter, Lucretia Akers, who has been living with relatives for many years. Op is skeptical of Lutie, but he responds to her care, as she has come at a time when he has been blinded by cataracts. Lutie takes him to a doctor and stays with him during his operation for removing the cataracts. The operation is a success. Op and Lutie go back to Op's cabin, and Lutie is sympathetic with Op in his belief in the "sperets." One spirit is especially interesting to Lutie. This spirit courts her by singing to her in the glen below the cabin and by bringing her flowers. Op insists that Lutie's ghostly suitor is Ted Newsome, a young man who has long since gone to his "long home" in the graveyard. Ted is strangely suspected, however, of being another invader of the hills, a wild man who is said to roam the ridge, living on roots and berries and killing foxes for eating. The killing of the foxes incenses Op's fox-hunting neighbors. They set out to find the killer and to hang him. Hootbird Hammertight, an unwelcome suitor of Lutie's, is on the trail of the 'speret" too. Hootbird is one of Stuart's most outlandish hill characters. In appearance and action, Hootbird belongs to the oafish hillbilly type of motion pictures and radio. But Hootbird is also in the tradition of the *Taps for Private Tussie* characters who, Jesse Stuart insists, are not exaggerations.

Into this situation of the "speret" hunt come Alf and Julie Pruitt, Lutie's cousins from Dayton, Ohio. These cousins are "thorns in the flesh" to old Op. Op has never heard of the "adam bumb" which Alf and Julie say is an imminent threat to the world, and from which they seek protection in the hills. For Op, the threat to the world, his world, is the intrusion of these "city folks." Op is friendly with the cousins, but, from the moment of their appearance, he schemes to get them out of the hills. He wants his private world again.

Op resorts to slyness to accomplish his purpose of driving Alf and Julie out of the hills. He houses them in his dirty old smokehouse. He chuckles to himself over their many discomforts, and frightens them with spine-tingling stories of the spirits roaming about on Laurel Ridge. While putting the cousins through the worst tests he can devise, Op never ceases to proclaim the good life of his hills. In this philosophizing of Op's, as well as in the old man's storytelling, Jesse Stuart gives expression to his own belief of living close to the land, and he relates some of the most interesting legends of folklore of his region.

Op explains to Alf about snakes and their habits, about ground hogs making coffee, "the clouds a-hanging over the valleys" being the "steam from their coffee boilers." He tells Alf about "young spiders a-throwin' out ropes of silk and a-raisin' up on the warm winds and ridin' away to other places beyond Laurel Ridge."

> The whippoorwill is a strange bird that makes its nest on a leaf on the ground. . . . I've seen their red eyes shin'in in the moonlight like wind-fanned embers. I've walked right up on their nests. They set on the eggs, hatch the young on the ground. . . . They can sing as purty as any bird I've ever heard but they're too lazy to build a nest. They take life easier than any bird I know. Sorta like me, I guess. [p. 112]

Strange birds, snakes, spiders, and knocking "sperets" make wonderful friends, Op tells Alf, but Alf does not agree. In the story's exciting and hilarious denouement, Alf and Julie make their exit out of the hills as abruptly as they have come into them. The killer of the foxes is caught. Lutie and her phantom lover are united in "real life," and they plan a happy future for themselves as husband and wife. Op is left to his peaceful world, his ridge. The owner of Laurel Ridge "has got the deed on paper," Op says, "but I've got the deed for it in my heart. I own this land more'n anybody else."

Jesse Stuart's storytelling is at its best in this book. *The Good Spirit of Laurel Ridge* has natural, rollicking humor instead of the more uproarious humor of *Taps for Private Tussie*.

This story is rich in colloquialisms. The sentences which follow are illustrative of the use of the colloquial. "The snake didn't get outten my way. It quiled, ready to strike." "Dadwrought it, Little Op," he said, "ye'll go out in a world a weaklin'. Can't ye take a water-mocassin bite?" "I-gollies, I've never heard a thing about all these bomb saucers and pizen dust," Op said. "You've already said he was bushwhacked over the Dortch girl. . . ." "Hootbird's smile showed two rows of "dead-phlox-colored" teeth." Showing the influence of Old English is this brief passage, "Ye wait and see! I won't be cuckolded in love. . . ."

Balladry, which is prominent in Stuart's novel *Trees of Heaven*, adds a particularly colorful note to the regional picture presented in *The Good Spirit of Laurel Ridge*. In this book are such Kentucky favorite ballads as "On Top of Old Smoky," "The Little Rosewood Casket," "Goin' Back to Lickin'," "The Hoot Owl Song."

Stuart's poetic prose is notable in this work. One remembers such passages as: "The sun had gone down on Laurel Ridge. The calico clouds were spread like thin sheets above the Sandy Valley. They were held up in space with props of bright evening wind" (p. 58). Another poetic passage is: "There was one wild-rose blossom, a beautiful thing, pale pink in color, soft as satin, with one layer of petals. Op wondered how a flower so beautiful as this could come from such worthless earth" (p. 64).

The Good Spirit of Laurel Ridge has brought Stuart some of his most enthusiastic reviews. George Matthew Adams, syndicated columnist, wrote of this book: "This new book matches his [Stuart's] most famous one, Taps for Private Tussie, though I have yet to read a Jesse Stuart book that doesn't put you in a spell of excitement and amusement, even in his extraordinary book, The Thread That Runs So True, a book about teaching and teachers that should be in the library of every school in the land. Stuart is a born writer of fiction and poetry, a combination most rare. His home and particular region are located in the hills of Kentucky. Many have aptly called this writer the 'American Robert Burns.' "[1]

Chad Walsh, of the Chicago Tribune, in reviewing Stuart's latest novel, said: "There is something refreshing about Jesse Stuart, and I do not think it is entirely the appeal of remote and primitive settings. He is one of that minority of contemporary writers who instinctively believe that homo sapiens is interesting, lovable, and worth continuing in his own right. A sense of natural dignity which has almost been stripped from the human animal is still strong in this chronicler of the Kentucky hills. . . . Old Op and the other mountaineers who roam through the present novel are real humans, worthy of respect on their own terms, though also good for friendly laughs. . . . the plot is gloriously rollicking. . . ."[2]

Josef Dignan, of the Louisville Courier-Journal, wrote: "Jesse Stuart has a way with a story, an inimitable way that can, at its best, charm and delight the most exacting reader. Although it is, in a few minor ways, akin to Taps for Private Tussie, The Good Spirit is, in my opinion, a distinct artistic advance over the earlier book. Its humor is mellower, less boisterous, and its poetic beauties are more integrated and moving. And—this above all—few writers, aside from the mystics, have expressed so well as Mr.

---

[1] George Matthew Adams, "Today's Talk, "Dallas News, November 8, 1953, 12.

[2] Chad Walsh, "Magazine of Books," Chicago Tribune, November 15, 1953, 19.

Stuart the freedom, the joy and serenity of the true individualist. Old Op is a fine character, one that any author might be
proud of creating."[3]

An occasional disparaging note has appeared in the criticism
of Jesse Stuart's latest novel. Josef Dignan tempered his endorse-
ment of *The Good Spirit of Laurel Ridge* with the observation
that "If one applies the strictest standards of judgment, this book
is a little too slow in 'getting going,' a little too contrived, and
unsubtle. . . ."

If the plot is "a little too contrived," the empathic Stuart
reader does not mind, and even the literary critics dismiss this
weakness in favor of Stuart's "way with a story." Stuart's method
is obliquely narrative, in the oral tradition, his story told usually
without expurgation, though *The Good Spirit of Laurel Ridge*
is considerably toned down from the more rugged vernacular of
Beyond Dark Hills and the earlier short stories. Here, as usually,
the story is told without conscious didacticism, but achieves moral
significance through choice of episodes and selection of descriptive material and dialogue. With power and illumination, Stuart
pictures the strongly beautiful elemental life of the "figures of
earth," of those who live close to the soil.

In *The Good Spirit of Laurel Ridge*, which was translated
and published in Germany in 1957, there is a rich tapestry of local
color. And there is this to be emphasized: In Stuart's local color
there is nostalgia, a technique of inclusion, the welding of the
past of his region with the present, which shows the ways of civilization moving in upon a circumscribed world where the inhabitants had followed, almost undisturbed, for at least a century,
the ways of their pioneer ancestors from Scotland and England.
In Stuart's writing, there are themes but not the rawness of the
writing such as that of Erskine Caldwell which makes of the
mountaineers hillbilly caricatures. From the beginning of the
novel, with its description of Laurel Ridge in its legendary days
of the retreat of General Morgan and his men from the determined fighting of the mountaineers, to the Ridge's present status

---

[3] Josef Dignan in *Louisville Courier-Journal*, November 1, 1953, 6.

as the domain of Snake Blue, rightful owner, and "Old Op," natural owner, Stuart is master of his technique of inclusion.

Carl Carmer, of the *New York Herald Tribune*, wrote "it would take a word magician to rescue a novel from so flimsy and trite a plot, and readers are indeed fortunate that Jesse Stuart is able able to stretch over this unsubstantial structure a shimmering fabric of such exquisite poetic prose that few will complain. . . ."[4]

Of *The Good Spirit of Laurel Ridge*, Joseph Henry Jackson wrote, in *The Los Angeles Times:* "His [Stuart's] readers will find in it everything they want to find when they read Stuart—the homely setting (rough in its way, yet beautiful); the people who are a part of it, tight, simple, but also wise in their generation; the straight story line that is invariably there, even when you forget it for the moment—because Mr. Stuart, behind the facade of his apparently rambling, folksy manner, always knows exactly what he is doing."[5]

Josef Dignan, of the *Louisville Courier-Journal*, observed that "Not many writers have the energy and the range of Jesse Stuart. He has written stories, novels, autobiography and, not only poetry, but poetry that sells! What is even more astonishing, he writes well in all these forms."[6]

One feels, after reading *The Good Spirit of Laurel Ridge*, that it is in the field of the novel that Jesse Stuart has found his metier for the maturer, more deeply reflective years of his life.[7] It is in the novel that he has found his ultimate literary expression. It is this form which allows him the full play of his many-faceted genius. He can be, at one and the same time, the spontaneous poet, the writer of sharp, dramatic scenes and description char-

---

[4] Carl Carmer in the *New York Herald Tribune*, November 8, 1953, 3.

[5] Joseph Henry Jackson in "Bookman's Notebook," *The Los Angeles Times*, December 3, 1953, 5.

[6] November 1, 1953.

[7] In 1960, while breakfasting in the Stuart home in the Kentucky hills, the writer listened to a recording of Beethoven's *Pastorale*, which Stuart loves, and heard the poet describe a long symphonic poem he plans to write with thematic structure based upon this musical work.

acteristic of the short story, the narrative artist, and the social philosopher who makes incisive commentary upon modern life through opposing its ills with a cultural primitivism, finding in Nature the cure, in individual purpose and integrity the answer.

5

....

Lectures and Additional Writings

The many-faceted Jesse Stuart may not be seen in totality through study of his books alone, prodigious as the number has been, and as revealing as the books have been in autobiographical detail. To know Stuart through his works, one must consider his remarkable output of writings that are published each year, in addition to the usual contribution of a novel or a short story or a poetry collection.

These additional writings include commencement addresses and lectures, which Stuart delivers at universities and schools in many parts of America and which are usually published later. Such works and the innumerable articles for periodicals and news-papers which he contributes annually show the multiplicity of Jesse Stuart's interests.

Before his heart attack in 1954, Stuart was one of America's busiest lecturers. He thought nothing of delivering three lectures in as many separate states within twenty-four hours, utilizing a

[1] Stuart, *The Year of My Rebirth*, 7.

private plane and pilot to keep his rigorous schedule.[1] The disastrous result of this routine was a near-fatal collapse, following a public address, but an amazing recovery after years of rest and of careful return to normal activities has brought Stuart once more into the lecture field. There has been, of necessity, a great reduction in the number of lectures which he gives, for in his lecturing, as in his writing, Stuart throws himself into his work with such emotional intensity that there is danger of physical exhaustion if the schedule is too heavy.

Stuart's lectures, except for commencement addresses and those written for specific occasions, such as that of the first annual Burns lecture delivered at Centre College, Kentucky, in 1959, are extemporaneous orations, built usually around two themes—the inspirational story of Jesse Stuart's life, with its pioneer ideals of hard work and of simple piety, and the cause of schoolteachers and of education in America. In the lectures, as in the autobiographical works, there is throughout a fervent, forceful note of sincerity, offset by a running thread of humor, a combination which is usually productive of a profound effect upon the listeners.

The emotional character of his speaking causes Stuart to lapse into the rich, flavorful language of the mountains. While startling to the grammarians, this use of the regional dialect gives to Stuart's lectures a heightened fascination, a unique quality, which makes them linger long in the memory. Entertainment value and inspirational value are well balanced in the speeches, and the dynamic manner of Stuart's delivery is as stimulating as it is in his writing. Donald Davidson says: "To those who have never before heard Jesse Stuart speak, the experience is stunning: The modern audience is not used to hearing 'winged words' come at them with Homeric force. That is particularly true of *college* audiences—most of all, of the faculty members in those audiences. I saw it happen at Bread Loaf a few summers ago when Jesse spoke there."[2]

The writer has seen it happen on several occasions, the three sium, held at Vanderbilt University in April 1959, when Stuart

---

[2] Donald Davidson, letter to the writer, May 11, 1959.

most memorable being those of the Vanderbilt Literary Sympo-
and Robert Penn Warren were the featured speakers; and of the
"Jesse Stuart Day" observed by the University of South Carolina
in March 1960, and again, by the University, in 1963.

Although Jesse Stuart was not completely at ease when he
spoke at Vanderbilt, the result was the same—a strong feeling of
communication established between speaker and audience and a
tremendous ovation given at the close of the speech. The quality
of sincerity which characterizes his speaking, as it does his writing, brought for Stuart on this occasion, as it brings usually on
lecture occasions for him, the deep sympathy of the audience for
the speaker. In the relating of his struggles to gain an education
and to win recognition as a writer, Stuart entertains with stories
and anecdotes of broad, frontier type humor, in the natural style
of his writing.

At Vanderbilt, he was laboring under heavy emotion, as it
was his first return since finding fame as a writer to the university
where he had worked with such difficulty as a graduate student,
but with such devotion to the ideals of the university. Not only
was he immensely stirred, but he was self-conscious before such
of his former professors in the audience as Robert Penn Warren
and Randall Stewart. The man who could have put him at ease
was not there—Donald Davidson, the professor to whose direction,
sympathy, and understanding Jesse Stuart always gives credit
for the success of his career, was too ill to attend the symposium.
Stuart felt his absence keenly, and from his heart spoke words of
eulogy for Davidson, "one of the greatest teachers and poets in
America today—one who has not received his proper recognition."

Stuart's speech was impassioned, eloquent. But he spoke so
rapidly and so vehemently that many in the audience said afterward they had been fearful of the consequences. They had feared
that he might be seized by a heart attack such as the one which
he had suffered following a speech at Murray State College, Kentucky, in 1954—the attack which had been near fatal. The reception of the Vanderbilt speech, however, was in the usual pattern.
Townspeople and university students and professors gave such

prolonged, enthusiastic applause that it amounted to an unreserved ovation for the man from the Kentucky hills.

When Jesse Stuart spoke at the University of South Carolina in the spring of 1960, the atmosphere of the events leading up to the lecture, the feeling of warm hospitality and enthusiasm which surrounded him, had engendered a feeling of ease which put him in top form for the occasion. The university's Russell House was packed, and the audience was eager, responsive. Stuart reacted with deep pleasure. A speech which was to have been limited to a few minutes' remarks, after a long day, was stretched by the speaker easily and happily into a talk lasting more than an hour. This was Stuart at his extemporaneous best, and the response by the Carolina audience was tremendous, as is the usual response when Jesse Stuart speaks at ease in his forceful, ebullient style.

JESSE STUART CHARMS AUDIENCE AT USC the headline stated over writer David Abeel's story of the lecture in the Columbia newspaper *The State* the following day (March 24, 1960). When Representative Edmund G. Grant, who had attended the lecture, presented Jesse Stuart to the South Carolina Legislature, he said:

> Mr. Speaker, ladies and gentlemen of the General Assembly: Today we have as our guest a great American—a truly great American. Yesterday, I was asked to make this introduction. I found some fine-sounding adjectives. It was to be a kind of "Pink-laced" introduction!
>
> Last night, I had the pleasure of hearing Mr. Jesse Stuart, after which I threw the introduction into a waste basket. It just didn't apply to our guest.
>
> He is a combination of Will Rogers, Frank Howard, Billy Graham, and Henry Mills![3] Jesse Stuart has been called "An American Robert Burns." I wish that many of us could leave these Halls and follow this man for a few days. I am sure that much of his goodness would rub off on us. (I have an idea that many taxpayers wish we would do just that!) Our guest has published 21 books, and his books have been translated into

[3] Mr. Grant added to the copy of this speech the following notation: "Frank Howard is the coach of Clemson College; Henry Mills a big, round jovial man, is the Sergeant-at-Arms in the Legislature."

many foreign languages.

It has been said that "One has not really lived until he has dipped with a gourd and drunk water from a cool, clear, bubbling spring, and has eaten pinebark catfish stew cooked in Florence County." Now. after having heard Jesse Stuart I must add—"One has not really lived until he has heard, and known, Jesse Stuart."

His is a rugged character, unaffected by fame, unpretentious in manner, moved by a love of his fellow-man and by a compulsion to lead people to a greater understanding of one another.

William Saroyan says of Jesse Stuart: "A 'natural' is somebody who has genius, and is therefore great, but who has in his greatness no strain, and is therefore a 'natural.' Jesse Stuart has greatness and simplicity. He is a 'natural.' "

Ladies and gentlemen, the Poet Laureate of Kentucky— Mr. Jesse Stuart!

When Jesse Stuart visited the University of South Carolina in 1960, he was a guest in the hospitable campus home of Dr. Robert L. Sumwalt, president, and Mrs. Sumwalt. In 1963, again he enjoyed the special hospitality of the president as a guest in his home. Upon this occasion, Mrs. Stuart was with him, and they stayed at the beautifully re-decorated home of the new president, Dr. Thomas F. Jones, and Mrs. Jones. Mrs. Jones arranged a dinner party in honor of the Stuarts, and, with her deep interest in literature and the arts, persuaded Mr. Stuart to read from his poetry, as a highlight of the evening. This was a rare event, as Jesse Stuart seldom reads his poems in public, or even in private gatherings, though, on this occasion in Columbia, he said that he thought more poetry readings should be held. He read a number of the same selections which he had read at the Award celebration staged for him in New York in 1961 by the Academy of American Poets.

On that memorable evening in Columbia, Dr. Chapman Milling, popular South Carolina writer and folklorist, interspersed Stuart's readings with folk songs, playing his own accompaniments on the guitar, again through Mrs. Jones' persuasion. It was indeed, a rare event, enjoyed by the large group of leading South Carolinians from numerous areas of the state.

Memories are evoked of a distinguished guest who took a special pleasure in the success of that evening—the late Dr. Havilah Babcock, head of the university's English department and sponsor of Jesse Stuart's USC visits. Professor, writer, and sportsman, Dr. Babcock was a lover of outdoor life, as is his friend Stuart, and he usually shunned social gatherings. At this notable party, however, he was a delighted guest.[4]

During his 1963 visit to the University of South Carolina, Jesse Stuart delivered a major address at Russell House, the University's student union building, as he had done in 1960, again to an enthusiastic "full-house" audience. This lecture was different, however, from that given in 1960. In the interim, Stuart had made his extended lecture tour in Europe, the Middle East, and the Far East under the auspices of the U. S. State Department. Into his rollicking accounts of his experiences as a youth in the Kentucky Mountains and of early schoolteaching days, he interjected a sobering note. He described educational conditions in foreign lands as he had observed them, attitudes toward the United States, both favorable and unfavorable, his personal encounters with Communists and "fellow travelers," the sense of urgency which he had felt everywhere for the need of international understanding. He urged the students in the audience to make the most of their educational opportunities, so superior to those which he had found to be prevalent abroad, and urged both students and others present to reflect seriously upon international responsibilities and to take an individual part, however inconsiderable, in the fight against Communism. As usual, he stressed the power of the individual. No individual effort made in this fight is "unimportant," he emphasized. On this visit, Stuart was honored at a luncheon given at Russell House by Dr. Babcock's class. A highlight, too, was a special WIS-TV interview program on Jesse Stuart, written and presided over by Don Upton and featuring a discussion of the humanities by Stuart, President Jones and Dr. Babcock. He was featured, also, over Lois Quattlebaum's WNOK program.

An interesting sidelight of Jesse Stuart's USC visit in 1960

[4] This writer and her husband were among the guests that evening.

was his meeting with the late Julia Peterkin, South Carolina's famed Pulitzer Prize winner, author of *Scarlet Sister Mary* and other distinguished books, at Lang Syne, her plantation home not far from Columbia. Although Dr. Babcock, a longtime friend of Mrs. Peterkin, was responsible for the meeting of those two strong personalities, so highly dissimilar in background, he was unable to be present. With Mr. Stuart, he sent along a group from the English department, including this writer, at that time a graduate student, who was also a friend of Mrs. Peterkin.

Julia Peterkin greeted the group in her typically gracious and welcoming manner at the door of antebellum Lang Syne, served them refreshments in the dining room, assisted in the hostess duties by her daughter-in-law and her grand-daughter-in-law, then, in the drawingroom, seated upon a sofa beside Stuart, with the group in chairs close by, engaged the Kentucky poet in a wide-ranging conversation. She expressed admiration for *Taps for Private Tussie*, which, she said, she had read after its first publication, and Stuart told of his enjoyment of the realism of her works, her direct, particularized style in portraying her characters and her region, her humor and understanding, qualities which he had always tried to show in his works. In reminiscing about their careers, the two writers found that, though differing so greatly in background and in personal experiences, they had much in common in their love of the land and in their purpose of presenting the life of their regions as authentic contributions to Americana. Julia Peterkin told this writer later that she had found Jesse Stuart "very dynamic and stimulating—very much like my good friend, Carl Sandburg, who has visited me at 'Lang Syne'—he's a *young* Carl Sandburg!"

Two other such high emotional moments in Jesse Stuart's life as his return to Vanderbilt have called forth his deepest eloquence, the words cascading in strong, subjective, unrestrained flow, as they do for him on the typewritten page. One such event was the Jesse Stuart Day proclaimed in Kentucky by the governor, in October of 1955, and organized by Stuart's former pupils and his fellow members in the Lions Club of Greenup. This day celebrated Jesse's recovery from the heart attack which had almost claimed his life in 1954.

To the thousands of Kentuckians who had streamed into the small hill town by Chesapeake and Ohio trains, by automobile and by springboard wagon to honor him with the unveiling of a marker on Greenup's courthouse lawn—a bust of the youthful visionary Stuart of the early poetry days—Jesse Stuart spoke in an emotion-filled voice. His thanks for the rare honor, which had come to him, a writer, in his lifetime, were expressed from a prepared speech. His doctor, who was present, had insisted upon this precaution, as he knew his patient's proclivity for speaking dynamically and at great length when speaking extemporaneously. Even so, the words were deeply moving and forceful. In concluding, he charged his listeners to "have courage in the face of these troubled times . . . have the will to live forever. We have to live now, the present, rejoice, dream and lay plans for those tomorrows that never come."[5]

The second event was the celebration staged in New York City in November 1961, by the Academy of American Poets, in honor of Jesse Stuart's winning of the Academy's 1960 $5,000 Fellowship Award "for distinguished poetic achievement." In a simple extemporaneous speech Stuart spoke movingly of his overwhelming joy upon receiving the news of the award by cablegram in Cairo, Egypt, where he was teaching at the time, and of what the award meant to him after a long hiatus in his poetic career.

Jesse Stuart wrote two articles for *The Peabody Reflector* in 1953, which are of special interest to the student of Stuart and his life. For the February issue of this publication, the magazine of the Alumni Association of George Peabody College for Teachers, Nashville, Tennessee, Stuart wrote, "Is the Short Story at a Dead End?" In this article, he describes his method of developing short stories from incidents of his daily life in the hills. He predicts that the combined media of radio, newspapers, magazines, motion pic-

[5] Elinor Richey's report of the event in *The Herald-Advertiser*, Hunt-

tures, and television will prove to be stimulants for the short story which will make that form of writing "again the most popular of all literary media of creative expression."[6]

Jesse Stuart's creed concerning his deep love of his region and the determination to remain there for his literary inspiration is embodied in an article called "Background and Results of Regional Writing," which appeared in *The Peabody Reflector* for January 1953. The final paragraph of this article set forth Stuart's philosophy, under the heading of "The Values of Regional Writing":

> I believe that through regionalism we can get stories, poems, and novels that have universal extension. It all depends upon the writer. And this is one of the ticklish problems this writer has had to face. I have debated it over and over and have often thought of leaving my own locale for other books. If I didn't think one could get universal extension through regionalism as Robert Burns, Sinclair Lewis, Robert Frost, Edgar Lee Masters, William Faulkner (to mention only a few) have done, then I would leave regionalism immediately. I wouldn't pick up the stories on my farm, my own backyard, my hometown, and my county.
>
> There is something greater than monetary value in writing. There is the bigness of the dream. And that bigness of the dream can be in many forms. I feel I have a region to depict, to make nationally known in my life and time. I put this dream above all monetary reward. If I make just enough to live, I might make a greater writer, for all of that.
>
> I've not been ambitious to be a prolific writer. I have recently decided not to mention the number of my published stories and poems again. But I have the feeling that if I write in my lifetime three hundred stories, and if one hundred of these stories are considered good, from these one hundred I might have from one to five live when I am gone. That if I do a thousand poems, a dozen might live after I am gone. If I write twenty-five books, one might live after I am gone. I put this possibility above all monetary value. *There is a simple headstone* of immortality in a book, a poem, or a short story.[7]

Since his heart attack in 1954, Stuart has had to cut down on

---

ington, W. Va., October 16, 1955, 1.

[6] *The Peabody Reflector*, XXVI (February 1953), 28.

the continuous flow of articles and short stories, as well as upon the lectures. From his typewriter, however, have come several highly significant results of his long reflections made during the period of convalescence. The most important writing, of course, was the autobiography covering the illness and slow progress toward recovery, *The Year of My Rebirth,* published in 1956.

An article appeared in 1955, however, in the August 13 edition of *The Saturday Evening Post.* It was entitled, "My Heart Attack and I." Dramatic, straight-from-the-shoulder, this account of Jesse Stuart's near-brush with death was not only an eloquent description of his own experience, but it was a sobering warning to the millions of Americans courting heart attacks by overwork, as Stuart had done. The article received wide attention, foreshadowing the interest with which *Year of My Rebirth* would be received in the following year. It showed Stuart in a new light, commentator in the field of medical research relating to the heart and to the heart patient. What he had to say about disease of the heart was coined from personal experience and from long hours of study of writing about methods of treatment and of new methods discovered. In a subsequent article, "Comeback From a Heart Attack," in *Today's Health,* published by The American Medical Association—an issue which featured his picture on the cover— Jesse Stuart wrote:

> I have kept separate scrapbooks on all the new medicines and discoveries by doctors and scientists regarding the heart, cancer, polio and tuberculosis. I am chairman of the Greenup County Heart Fund Drive, which has almost doubled its quota the last two years. I know the dollars given these worthy causes are the most valuable dollars ever contributed by man. I am a member of the State Board of the Kentucky Heart Association. I went to the West Coast and appeared on the program of the American Heart Association. And I recommend to young teen-age girls they go into the profession of nursing to help save human lives. I know now nursing is one of the greatest professions. And, too, I am so thankful I had the second

---

[7] *The Peabody Reflector,* XXVI, (January 1953), 5.

chance, that I am above the ground and not under it. I cannot get too chummy with God. It is such a glorious feeling to return from the fingers of death and to live again.[8]

A strong didactic note has crept into his lectures and articles since Stuart's close escape from death. Although he had always proclaimed the doctrine of hard work as a means of securing what one wants from life and had urged the bettering of schools and deplored the situation of underpaid schoolteachers, in all of his lectures he had avoided the consciously evangelical strain. As his fiction had usually pointed a moral by implication only, so had his speeches and articles taught their lessons in moderate manner. But the near-fatal illness brought an added religious fervor to his life, a fervor which tends to make both his writing and his public speaking evangelical in tone.

At the Vanderbilt Literary Symposium, he told the writer, "I have to watch it since my illness, not to get too preachy with people."

The intensity of the quality of sincerity pervading Stuart's written and oral narrations of his experiences carries its own didacticism, according to many critics, and "sermonizing" would spoil the effect. Only in a few short stories, which have been noted in the chapter on the short story, does Stuart overtly moralize.

A most graphic description of Jesse Stuart's speech style, both on the lecture platform and in conversation, was written by Cyril Erick Bryant, who interviewed Stuart in 1954 for *The Christian Herald*, before his heart attack: "Words and ideas explode from him in a torrential rush. As he speaks, his husky body twists with the restlessness of a man who cannot wait to expound his hopes and convictions. Yet beneath his volcanic vitality, one senses the delicate soul of a poet. Warm, sensitive, and friendly, Jesse is genuinely interested in everyone he meets."[9]

This intensity which characterizes both Stuart's speaking and his writing and which is sparked by his love of people and life,

[8] *Today's Health*, XXXVIII (February 1960), 69.
[9] "Kentucky Is His Land," *The Christian Herald*, LXXVII (November 1954), 74.

results in his constant stream of articles for magazines and other publications. Articles for such widely dissimilar publications as *Reader's Digest, Saturday Evening Post, NEA Journal* (published by the National Education Association) *Nature Magazine, American Forest, The Georgia Review, The Arizona Quarterly, Wildflower,* and *Together* (published by the Methodist Church, of which he is a member), denotes some of his many and varied interests.

"Love That Land," a piece which appeared in the magazine *The Land and Land News* (January 1953), a quarterly publication issued by Friends of the Land, Bel Air, Maryland, was reprinted in *Reader's Digest* of May 1953. "Love That Land" tells of the elder Stuart's methods of soil conservation, which he calls "pertectin' the land." Jesse's father would not drag a plow up or down hill and leave a mark that would start a ditch. When he had to cross a slope to get to the tobacco field, "he would drive his team ahead and carry his plow. He was that careful with the land." All of his life, Mitch Stuart followed the contour of the hills with his plow, Jesse says, and the hills did not erode for him.

"My Father Was a Railroad Man" was published in April 1953, in *Tracks,* which is a monthly publication of the Chesapeake and Ohio Railway Company. This article tells of Jesse's father's love for the railroad. The senior Stuart had worked for twenty-three years on "Section 201" of the Chesapeake and Ohio, which was at Riverton, Kentucky, four miles from the Stuart home in W-Hollow. It had been necessary for his father to get up at four o'clock each morning in order to make the walk to his work, Jesse said. In the evenings, after leaving the section, Mr. Stuart would come home and farm his few acres, and attend to his livestock, chickens, hogs, and his plow team.

On his small paycheck from the railroad company, the father helped as much as possible to send his five children through school, paid for his little farm, built a house, and managed to take care of his family. Three of the children finished college, and four of the family became schoolteachers. Mitch Stuart had held the profession of schoolteaching above all others as a goal for his children.

In "My Father Was a Railroad Man" Jesse Stuart describes an automobile trip which he and his father made one day in 1952. The father and son had started for the stock market at Catlettsburg, Kentucky, to buy more cattle. On the way, the father observed two of his old friends of the "C & O" Railway, working on the tracks beside the road. He ordered Jesse to stop, and he got out of the car, excitedly, to greet his old friends, Press Moore and Choppie Thomas. Press and Choppie, like Mick Stuart, had been small farmers in W-Hollow and were now working for the railroad. They told Mick about new methods, new tools. Mick spotted a "low joint" far up the track and pointed it out to the workers. Trains and tracks were in the old man's blood. Jesse had a difficult time getting his father to leave. Mick was not interested in buying cattle. He said, regretfully, as he finally left his former fellow workers, that he was not sure that he had as much "the matter" with him as they had told him at the hospital. Jesse knew better. His father, at seventy-two, could look back on many years of hard work that were lived after a doctor had told him, when Mick was thirty, that he should go home and "put his affairs in order," because of a bad heart. That advice had been ignored. All of Mick's railroad work had come after his visit to the doctor.

"The Man Who Painted Schoolhouses"[1] is another of Jesse Stuart's many nostalgic stories of his schoolteaching days. The theme of this story is the painting of the small, dilapidated schoolhouse where Jesse was teaching at the time, by "Screech" Sutherland, who did the painting "for nothing." "Screech" did his painting job free because he had a strong belief that "pretty schoolhouses, clean attractive schoolyards and birdboxes around a school" would make the children love school. "Screech" believed that "we'll have a new crop of fine citizens in this county in the next generation" if the children were happy in their pretty, newly painted schoolhouse. This simple sketch is an interesting study in character, as are the two articles on Jesse Stuart's father. As in the sketches of his father, this short piece by Stuart is rich in the language

[1] *Country Gentleman*, CXXIII (July 1953), 30.

and color of the Kentucky hill region.

Stuart writes countless stories and sketches of the kind just described. He donates many of them to small publications or schools that are trying to build up a department of regional literature. In addition he often contributes articles to publications of the schoolteaching profession.

Jesse Stuart wrote an article entitled "What America Means To Me," which was published in the May 10, 1951, issue of *American Magazine*. This article won for Stuart the American Freedom Award for 1951, given by the American Freedom Foundation at Valley Forge, Pennsylvania. The *American Magazine* editors had requested Stuart to write on the subject "What America Means To Me." In an explanatory note preceding Stuart's article, the editors say:

> When a book of poems called *Man With a Bull-Tongue Plow* was published in 1935, critics hailed the author, Jesse Stuart, as an unknown genius—"an American Robert Burns." We asked this distinguished American writer to tell his own story, as an inspiration to other young people, competing for the education and the opportunities offered to all under our democratic system. It is a simple and powerful story of faith and fulfillment, and a decisive answer to those who criticize the American way of life. Where else but in the United States could a poor mountain boy find such opportunity and achieve so much?[2]

Stuart tells, in this article, of speaking before an audience of fifteen thousand educators in Milwaukee and of autographing copies of his books afterwards for many of the people who attended the lecture. He says that it is difficult for him to realize that he has reached this point of success in attaining his goal in life of becoming a writer and teacher. He reviews his boyhood in the Kentucky hills, where his home was a poor mountain cabin, but where he had the inspiration of his parents' love and dreams for his future.

Stuart recalls his days of hard work to obtain a college educa-

---

[2] *American Magazine*, May 1951.

tion. He describes his winning of the Guggenheim Fellowship for creative writing in 1937, which made possible his European travels.

> After fourteen months spent among the different nationalities of Europe, people whose antecedents had made America, I returned to America with this feeling: I never knew America until I went to Europe. The Europeans were fine and hospitable people. But their opportunities were so limited as compared to ours in America. I wondered what would happen if the young men and women in Europe had the chances America offered. I had the feeling that the majority of these young people would not wait for the opportunities which might never come to them. They would be able to go out and find them.
>
> I returned to America on the Countess Savoy. When we passed the Statue of Liberty, if my arms had been long enough to reach from my ship, I would have hugged her neck. America is the dream. America is the place. America is it.[3]

Jesse Stuart's integrity as a fighter for individualism is most recently affirmed in his hard-hitting article, "Are We a Nation of Digits?" in the July 28–August 4, 1962, number of *The Saturday Evening Post*. In the *Post's* regular feature, "Speaking Out," Stuart sets himself squarely against the sweeping tide of objectivity which is engulfing our lives in the form of digital designations that replace personal names. Characteristically, he relates his antagonism to such submersion of the individual to early experiences suffered in his native Kentucky hills, and highlights his article with autobiographical data and incidents that strike a universal note. "I have never wanted to be called a number in my life. Not from the time when I was a small boy at Plum Grove Rural School, when the teacher called our numbers in the order we had been chosen to come up front and spell. I resented being called a number then as much as I do now."

Thus he pinpoints his numbers phobia at its very beginning, and traces it through his days of playing football with a number on his back and his days of active duty in the United States Naval

[3] Ibid.

Reserves in World War II, when he was "a numerical abstraction" on a dog tag. Bringing his irritation up to date, he deplores the loss of the name in his telephone number, and the loss of his friendly operators to a seven-digit impersonal system. Nell, Sue, and Tillie are gone.

"Gone is Jesse Stuart, for he is now 473-4813," is his succinct observation.

The most poignant reflection on the impersonality governing the citizen in today's national scene centers about the author's treatment of the subject of Social Security, though he has expressed impatience about the many numbers identifying himself with which he must keep in touch in his daily living—gasoline credit cards, bank numbers and the like. His name, Jesse Stuart, has been an individual force among neighbors and friends, and on stories, poems, and articles which he has written and which have been published in this country and numerous other lands. But this, he sadly concludes, will carry little weight in the engulfing wave of nonentity which the present digital craze in America typifies.

> Owing to changes in America, this, my real name, was mere window dressing. My name, the one that had real meaning in Social Security and death, had been recorded for all eternity in groups of figures with dashes separating them. We are becoming, if we haven't already made it, a country where number substitutes have become names, and names have been reduced to substitutes. I wonder whether in years to come numbers will be more appropriate for tombstones than names. I suppose that for the sake of our descendants we had better have numbers marking our graves, so they can identify us without mistake.

The article has an easy, colloquial style combined with the swift pinpointing of fact characteristic of the debater—a style Stuart uses on the lecture platform and in his nonfictional writing. A loose, seemingly undesigned handling of his subject is discovered at the end of the article to be Jesse Stuart's camouflage for the pointing of a moral, an uncompromising truism, without resort to didacticism. Thus in selectivity of subject matter and in the underlying moral seriousness to be found beneath the often humorous conversational manner of treatment in his articles, as well as in his other forms of writing, Stuart makes his critical comment and follows a guiding principle of being himself, a stubborn individualist. He maintains integrity of purpose, however apart he may be in his beliefs from the accepted, or popular, attitudes.

This Is the South, published in 1959, a symposium of articles written by natives of the South, contains "Up the Branch," by Jesse Stuart. This work, which might be called an extended essay, describes some of the speech characteristics and customs of Stuart's Kentucky region. He writes:

> In spite of mass communications, mountain people still use an Appalachian Mountain dialect that reflects its old Anglo-Saxon origin. In it may be found obsolete forms used by Chaucer and Shakespeare, and in the original King James Bible. It is most difficult for one who is a native of the mountains, and who writes from the inside looking out, not to have his work searched for folklore and obsolete forms of Old English, even when he is under the impression he uses the modern words and definitions of his American tongue.
>
> I found epitaphs on gravestones at Chester, England, in both old and new cemeteries at Stoke Poges and Linlithgow, Scotland, that are almost word for word the same as those carved on stones in our own mountain village, town, and city cemeteries. We held rural folk dances similar to England's—and as fast and furious as Scotland's Dashing White Sergeant—for a hundred and fifty years before the advent of TV.[4]

In discussing the humor of mountaineers and their fighting qualities, he says:

> Our humor is often grotesque, vigorous, with dry remarks, sky-high anecdotes, and roaring, whooping exaggerations. . . . We have been, and are still, too much like the phlegmatic Spartans of ancient Greece, and not enough like our Celtic ancestors to produce a great humor. We inherited and held onto

[4] *This Is The South* (Chicago: Rand McNally, 1959) 227. Reprinted with the permission of Jesse Stuart.

the mournful ballads; when we have not been engaged in one
of our country's wars, we have been fighting private wars of
our own. . . . I was born after the beginning of the twentieth
century. In my day and time, the governor of this state has
had to call out the National Guard many times to quell fights
between families. At Pearl Harbor, they went off together to
fight a common foe.[5]

Striking a nostalgic note, while at the same time anticipating
progress for his region, Stuart concludes:

> Our forebears had to work harder than the "outlanders" for
> everything they got. Today America is a land of promises
> for all, there is no difference here and elsewhere. Many
> types are united to make the whole. . . . Maybe we will not
> lose all of the tenacious fight, the dream, the usefulness and
> skill of our hands, and the physical stamina of our rugged
> forebears. Maybe we will retain some of our heritage,
> and our Appalachian Mountain culture of music, ballad, song
> and dance, and our skills at craft. Maybe with more enlight-
> ened youth, we'll expand our rich inheritance into drama,
> book, music, and art! Maybe we shall! But we have definite-
> ly become, or we are fast becoming, America's Last Original
> Type.[6]

One of Stuart's most vigorous and poetic tributes to his region
written in recent years is his article entitled "Ascend the High
Mountain," which appeared in the magazine *Country Beautiful*
for February 1962, and is beautifully illustrated in color. This is
an excellent example of Stuart's lean prose of current times, poetry-
filled, but containing an economy of words which differs greatly
from some of the earlier prolixity of style for which he was criticized.

He describes the intrepid pioneers who "ascended the high
mountains," bringing their rifles, tools, Bibles, and musical instru-
ments with them, and holding a firm belief in the fable of the ant
and the grasshopper, with its moral of work. "Resourcefulness
was their stock in trade; to survive, they *had* to have something

[5] Ibid.
[6] Ibid.

above their ears and their elbows. The men were seasoned Indian fighters, experts with rifle and axe. They feared God and hated the Devil, the Indians and the British."

Speaking for the descendants of these pioneers, he says:

> Our small farms that we own and love, farms our fathers and fathers' fathers farmed before us, have made us free men. And one free man, after some of my observations, is worth thirty *yes men* who bow to despotism. In all of America, no segment of the people like private ownership more than the highlanders. We are believers in freedom and will fight for it. We have received much criticism for our acts against what we think is unfairness, but, after just having visited fifteen countries in Africa, the Near East and Europe, I am convinced that we should be proud of our individualism, our fierce love of freedom, our original culture within a country's culture. [p. 13]

There is this lyrical paragraph on springtime in the highlands, a springtime that is "different from that in any other part of the United States":

> Springtime in the highlands will not let anyone stay in the house if he is able to walk. The love songs of birds that are building nests, mating, laying eggs, hatching and feeding their young—the Kentucky Cardinal and the hawk, redbirds in their slow flight over white sails of dogwood blossoms, blackbirds in the blooms of the wild plum groves, gray hawks skimming over the blankets of redbuds on the slopes—are permanent remembrances.
>
> The autumns are as memorable as the springs. . . . During the past year when I was in Egypt where there is really no autumn at all, I missed the poetry of the colored leaves more than anything. And when I received pressed autumn leaves in letters from relatives and friends, I wept. [p. 11]

In Stuart's articles about his region, there is a certain repetitiveness, but always a freshness of description through different word selections and transposition of phrases, and one may usually come across some inconspicuously placed personal item such as the above about the poet. Or, there may be an opinion expressed, which is of literary interest, such as the following, in a paragraph from the aforementioned Country Beautiful article, which discusses the balladry and the vernacular of the mountains: "Our traditions, our way of life, flavors, permeates, and colors what we write, even to a portion of the late Thomas Wolfe's work, for he was one of us, and our greatest writer" (p. 14).

JUVENILE BOOKS

Jesse Stuart, as one of America's most prolific writers, has contributed five books to the field of juvenile literature. These are *The Beatinest Boy, Penny's Worth of Character, Red Mule, Rightful Owner,* and *Andy Finds a Way*.

The Beatinest Boy, Stuart's first juvenile book, published in 1953, is the touching story of a penniless orphan and of how he solves the problem of getting a Christmas present for his beloved "Grandma." The boy, David, caught some opossums, planning to sell their skins, but could not make himself kill them. He sawed down a bee tree, hoping to sell the honey, but Grandma needed the honey to ease her coughing. Just a week before Christmas, a neighbor showed the lad how to make things out of old feed bags. He stayed up late every night, making a fringed table cloth and nine napkins from two sacks printed with an autumn oak-leaf pattern.

On Christmas day in the cabin, Grandma was the happiest woman in the world.

> "David, look," Grandma Beverley said softly, tears coming from her eyes and rolling down her wrinkled face. "I wonder where this nice tablecloth and napkins came from."
> "Made them from feed sacks," David said. "The prettiest things I ever saw in my life," she said.[7]

As usual, Stuart tells his story with effective realism, for he has taken it from life. He actually knew such a boy, and, without stating his moral, in his narration he points up the resourceful-

[7] Stuart, *The Beatinest Boy* (New York: Whittlesey House, 1953), 195.

ness of the boy and his respect for the knowledge and experience of his elders. He illustrates for modern youth the point that the best gifts are not always bought with money.

In *Elementary English*, magazine of the National Council of Teachers of English, Paul C. Burns and Ruth Hines say of Stuart's juvenile stories:

> They might be likened somewhat to an Aesop's Fable or a modern McGuffey story. He tells of children's good un-trained minds, but also of their sterling character. Through his writing of stories for children, he aims to help youth to find a path that will lead through fields of frustration and mod-ern pitfalls of destruction until he finds the best self. . . . He points again and again to the good, the essentially and poten-tionally fine characteristics that are to be found—and de-veloped—in children.[8]

Stuart's other juvenile books have the same poignancy and refreshing quality as that of *The Beatinest Boy*. In *A Penny's Worth of Character*, a young boy, Shan, is given a refreshing les-son in honesty. Sent along to the store to get some things for his mother, he takes with him ten paper sacks to trade for candy. The tenth bag has a hole in it, and Shan's mother has told him to leave it at home, but he takes it along, too, as ten sacks are needed in order for him to get a dime to buy his favorite chocolate bar and lemon soda pop. The storekeeper does not discover the deception, as he trades the sacks for the candy and drink. Shan does not enjoy the fruits of his trade as much as he had thought he would. At home, he discovers that his mother has learned of the deception. She sends Shan back to the store to confess to the storekeeper. Though this is a most unhappy mission for the young boy, he fol-lows his mother's instructions and when the storekeeper forgives him, he returns home, feeling "as light as a June bug in the Au-gust wind." This story has particular meaning today, Burns and Hines points out, when "it is so often considered 'smart' to be dis-honest if one can avoid detection."

[8] "Kentucky Is His Home," *Elementary English*, XXXVIII (March 1961, 138.

Red Mule, the juvenile novel published in 1955, is a story which reveals Jesse Stuart's deep love of animals and his regret for the replacement of animals, as well as the replacement of men, by machines. Red Mule is something of an outcast in his little mountain town. He is a crusty old stable hand, whose faithful team, Dick and Dinah, have been doing through the years the work around town which is being taken over by noisy tractors. Red Mule is joined in his campaign to keep mules in the work picture by the young boy, Scrappie Lykins, who works with him in his spare time.

Scrappie meets the challenge of responsibility in this partnership for a while, with the aid of his father. Then the mules prove their worth when they pull the tractors out of the mud in which they have become stuck during a work project. Finally, a letter which Scrappie has sent to the President of the United States in behalf of mules, produces results. A government agent comes to town to buy mules to be sent overseas for use in underdeveloped countries. The mules are saved, and the business of Scrappie and Red Mule prospers. Stuart's sympathy for rejected draft animals, as reflected in this story, symbolizes his regret for the passing of an ancestral way that he has found good.

The adventure and love between a boy and his dog is a universal theme which Jesse Stuart develops in *The Rightful Owner*.[9] Poignancy is present in much of Stuart's writing, and there is a special poignancy in this work. Mike, the young protagonist, finds a dog, "Speckles," one spring day, but realizes that he will have to give the dog up to his "rightful owner," if he appears. Mike's father has warned him that "A good hound dog never forgets his real master." But Mike and Speckles spend many happy days together through the summer, with the dog accompanying the boy in the fields and in his fishing, as though he had never had another master.

There is a fox hunt, which Speckles wins, and jealous neighbors, the Addingtons, claim that he is a dog of theirs stolen in a chase. Mike's father proposes that the dispute be settled by having

⁹ *The Rightful Owner* (New York: Whittlesey House, 1960), 104.

the Addington boy and his son call to the dog. "A dog will go to his rightful owner," he says. The dog will be given to the boy to whom he runs, after the call. The contest is decided when Speckles races joyfully to Mike.

One night, however, during a chase, Speckles's former owner appears. He is an old man, Tom Adams, who has blown one long lonesome call on his horn, followed by seven short ones. Speckles recognizes the signal. He bounds toward the old man and there is an ecstatic reunion between the long-lost dog and his owner.

The old man says tearfully, "I've been everywhere in Carter County hunting for Rags. I've been over most of your Green-wood County. I have traveled hundreds of miles blowing my horn on the ridges and hilltops. I knew if he ever heard this horn he would come. A good hound never forgets his rightful owner."

Though Mike has been well disciplined by his father for the separation, he is heartbroken. Tom Adams tells him, gratefully, that he is going to bring him a hound puppy, a son of Rags, as a present the next day, in return for his good care of his dog, and this brings the boy some comfort. Tears continue to run down Mike's cheeks, but he tells his father, philosophically, "I will have a Speckles of my own . . . that nobody can take. He'll always come to me because I'll be his rightful owner."

Andy Finds A Way has a theme similar to that of the story of Mike and Speckles. Stuart's latest juvenile novel, published in 1961, is noted in a *New York Times* review as ". . . the tale of a boy and his need for a playmate, to which Jesse Stuart brings all his skill in presenting country people and places. . . . "[1] Life on the backcountry farm in Ragweed Valley was a lonesome one for Andy. When he tried to make pets of wild animals, invariably they returned to their own kind. Soddy, the bull calf, is the an-swer to Andy's prayer for a real pet, but the boy's happiness is threatened because his father needs the money which Soddy will bring as veal. Secretly, Andy embarks on a money-raising project of finding ginseng root for market and Soddy does his part to help.

---

[1] Marjorie Burger, in *The New York Times Book Review*, October 29, 1961), 6.

The author injects suspense into the story, and it is not until the very day when the buyer comes for Soddy that the reader learns whether Andy will get to keep his pet, or whether, as Mike did, he will suffer disappointment. In this case a boy's dream comes true. Soddy stays with Andy.

Burns and Hines conclude: "It is to be hoped that Jesse Stuart will continue for a long time to bring his many talents to the field of literature for young children. The reasons are obvious: Here is indeed a born story-teller. His plots are simple, straightforward. A poetic quality in his use of language, full of word pictures, adds to the charm and appeal of his stories."[2]

Certainly the junior books, along with inspirational autobiographical essays written for textbooks for secondary schools, are a well-established part of Stuart's work. Through his teaching experiences, and through his acute memories of his own early years, Jesse Stuart has shown throughout his writing career a preoccupation for the inspiring of youth. Columnist Meyer Levin, of the *Newark Star-Ledger*, Newark, New Jersey, wrote in 1953: "Jesse Stuart stories have already become part of the literature our children grew up on. They have read them in the schoolbooks along with the tales of Hawthorne and Mark Twain."[3]

Stuart's idealism concerning youth is expressed in his numerous high school and college commencement addresses. Typical of his belief in youth is the concluding paragraph of his speech entitled "The Sensible Six Percent," which he delivered at the commencement exercises of Murray State College, Murray, Kentucky, in the spring of 1960: "Modern Youth is a river of clear shining water that is flowing endlessly out into a vast new world. Some impure drops are bound to get into this river, but in its constant flow and surge, these impure drops will be purified and hidden in the crytal immensity of the whole. Not any part of young humanity's flow that can be purified should ever be lost."

Jesse Stuart traveled through Europe and the Middle East with

[2] Burns and Hines, "*Elementary English* (March 1961), 140.
[3] Meyer Levin, "The Candid Critic," *Newark Star Ledger*, October 22, 1953, p. 6.

his family in 1950 and 1961, and he kept voluminous diaries of his trips. One of these—*Italian Diary*—has been published in serial form in the *Herald-Advertiser*, Huntington, West Virginia, the first installment appearing on Sunday, July 29, 1952, and the others following in consecutive Sunday editions through August.

Italian Diary has importance in the study of Jesse Stuart's works as it is the first major published account of his experiences with a people outside America—indeed, one might say with a people outside his region. An article, "Challenge in Cairo," written for *The NEA Journal* in 1962 after a year spent in Egypt, two separate articles on "Jesse Stuart in Lebanon," which appeared in March 1963, in Huntington's *Herald-Advertiser*, and features written for the small local papers of his region concerning the period which he spent in Europe on his Guggenheim Fellowship in 1938 and 1939 have resulted from his travels. But *Italian Diary* is the first, published book-length work of Stuart's describing his experiences abroad.

In this autobiographical narrative, Jesse Stuart undertakes an extended study of the people of a foreign nation, as he has come to know them, both in America and in their own country. From the moment he embarks, with his wife and daughter, upon the SS Augustus, an Italian ship sailing out of New York, he documents the manners and customs of the Italians and relates them to the ways of his own people. Throughout the voyage, and in his tours through the Italian countryside and through Italy's major cities, Stuart brings the individual into focus.

His viewpoint in this series reflects his own divided interests—those of the poet, who thrills to the sunset at sea, to the Italian gardens and museums, and to the visit to the birthplace of Dante; and those of the practical farmer. Along with the lyricisms of the poet, there is this passage from the farmer: "How could a people be so gifted in music, art and literature and be so far behind in the science of farming, which also is poetry, is art and even life itself! We certainly could have given these people lessons in the

---

[4] Stuart, "Italian Diary," *Herald-Advertiser* (Huntington, W. Va.), August 5, 1962, p. 5.

art of growing tobacco, hay and corn. Smith-Hughes teachers of agriculture in public schools would teach the young Italian farmers, and in a few years they would change the face of Italy."[4]

Italian Diary introduces a new and significant phase of Jesse Stuart's literary career—a phase in which his source material for books, as well as for his lectures and additional writing, assumes global extension.

6

The Poet as Teacher

IF poetry has been the passion of Jesse Stuart's life, schoolteaching has been both cause and passion, and any comprehensive study of Stuart must take ample note of him as a figure of importance in the field of education.

He is important in this field, not only for his autobiographical work *The Thread That Runs So True*, the story of his schoolteaching experiences, which won the award as "The Most Important Book of 1949" from the National Education Association, but also for his representation in numerous college-level and secondary-school-level textbooks.

In addition, his work as a lecturer in colleges and universities and in writers' forums throughout the country has won him wide acclaim. The lectures have contributed immeasurably to his stature as a social commentator, a crusader for equality of opportunity in education. Speaking with "Homeric fire," in the words of his great friend the poet-teacher Donald Davidson, Jesse Stuart has championed on the lecture platform, as he has in *The Thread*

That Runs So True, the cause of educational improvements for children in America's remote areas and the cause of underpaid schoolteachers. Through his speeches and his writing, there has been the constant theme of pride in a profession so vital to mankind as the profession of teaching.

Entering actively again into the teaching field in the summer of 1960, he carried this high sense of dedication abroad for a year of teaching at the American University of Cairo, Egypt, accompanied there by his family. His subjects were education and creative writing.

Jesse Stuart's career in the field of education, paralleling his career in literature, has kept him in constant touch with life. The two careers have intertwined like wistaria and pine, one being the sturdy tree at certain points of the writer's life, the other the vine, and vice versa. Each has complemented the other, lending substances to beauty and beauty to substance. The poet has inspired the schoolmaster, and the schoolmaster has brought to the poet powerful material straight from life. Of the great writers, it is Robert Burns, idol of his childhood years and throughout his life, with whom Stuart has the closest affinity. The Burns' occurpations of writer and farmer, Jesse Stuart adds the vital and busy one of schoolteaching, and through this means has found his closest touch with life.

Jesse Stuart dedicated *The Thread That Runs So True* to the schoolteachers of America. In 1950 this work was selected by the National Education Association as "the most important book of 1949, because it is concerned with the unique institution which gives strength to all other institutions in American life. *The Thread That Runs So True* is truly a great book—the kind that comes but once in a generation, a book that will live to entertain and inspire new readers as Eggleston's *Hoosier School-master* has lived to be read decade after decade. . . . This story of Lonesome Valley and other schools is good literature . . . it is good history . . . it is good pedagogy. It shows what happens when a strong, honest, earnest, and loving personality gives himself to his students. . . . This book is sound Americanism. It exalts the aspirations and ideals by which our people have risen rapidly to national and world greatness."

"When the National Education Association came out and made *The Thread That Runs So True* the best book of 1949, I walked on the wind," Stuart said, in an address at the seventy-seventh annual convention of the American Association of School Administrators, held at Atlantic City, New Jersey, in 1951. "This was the greatest honor I have received—the people of my profession had chosen by book."[2]

Stuart's philosophy on education is embodied in Chapter Seven of *The Thread That Runs So True:*

> I thought if every teacher in every school in America—rural, village, city, township, church, public, or private—could inspire his pupils with all the power he had, if he could teach them as they had never been taught before to live, to work, to play, and to share, if he could put ambition into their brains and hearts, that would be a great way to make a generation of the greatest citizenry America ever had. All of this had to begin with the little unit. Each teacher had to do his share. Each teacher was responsible for the destiny of America, because the pupils came under his influence. The teacher held the destiny of a great country in his hand as no member of any other profession could hold it. All other professions stemmed from the product of his profession. [p. 82]

Jesse Stuart began his schoolteaching career in the smallest of units, the Lonesome Valley School, back in a remote section of the Kentucky hills. Jesse was not quite seventeen, had not finished high school, when he took over the Lonesome Valley School. The school was a one-room, dilapidated structure, which had to be cleaned up and painted by the new teacher and his pupils before it was habitable. Young Stuart had chosen the Lonesome Valley

[1] Joy Elmer Morgan, *Journal of the National Education Association,* XXXIX (January 1950), 7.

[2] Jesse Stuart from an address entitled "Schools to Keep Us Free," delivered before the seventy-seventh annual convention of The American Association of School Administrators, Atlantic City, New Jersey, 1951.

School for his first teaching assignment because he wanted to avenge his sister who had been beaten brutally by Guy Hawkins, one of the students, while she was teaching there. Jesse's first trial as a teacher came when this same overgrown bully attacked him. Stuart won the fight. At the same time he won the respect of the community of Lonesome Valley.

These "beardy-faced figures of the earth" who were the fathers of Jesse's pupils were "men who, when they liked and respected you would die for you, men who, when they hated and despised you would kill you." The new teacher had proved himself in their eyes, and they were willing for their children to attend his school instead of staying home to help strip cane and cut tobacco.

Stuart had fifty-four classes to teach in six hours of work. The classes ranged from the primer to the eighth grade subjects. The teacher was at his wit's end to keep his smaller pupils occupied while he heard the advanced classes. But, one day, while watching the children play their favorite recess-time game, "The Needle's Eye," he received the idea of making play out of the schoolwork, in order to hold the interest of all the pupils. The teacher would be the "needle's eye" and play would be the thread that bound them together.

With crayon, pieces of cardboard, scissors, and paste-pot, he evolved jigsaw puzzles for the beginning pupils. For the older groups, he organized arithmetic matches, spelling bees, ball games. The school became the liveliest place in the community. The pupils were proud of their school. "It was the only place they could go, and many would never go beyond this school. Their education ended when they finished at Lonesome Valley. These were their happy days. Beyond these days, for those that remained in Lonesome Valley, it was eternal work, work, work, and the sameness of life. It was marriage, children, death, and burial in Lonesome Valley" (p. 58).

Some children were forced to come to school barefooted and thinly clad, but they would not stay away. Many times Jesse saw red spots on the frost-covered ground where the bleeding feet of these children had left their imprints. In his own straitened circumstances, the teacher could not buy shoes for these children, though he longed to do so. For one little boy and girl, whose father was serving a sentence in the penitentiary, Jesse did buy shoes, because, as he said, "When I saw blood on the snow from this moonshiner's children who were coming to my school, it did something to me. I wanted to fight for them harder than I had ever fought Guy Hawkins" (p. 59).

Jesse Stuart taught his pupils practical things—how to write letters, measure land, be clean with drinking water. He taught them to use screens for their windows. He instructed them about personal sanitation, "and so many things aside from the dry-as-dust uninteresting textbooks I was forced to teach because they were standard, selected by someone in the state department who didn't teach, perhaps never had, and if he had taught once upon a time was far-removed from it now. When I gave them assignments, I never gave them the topics listed in their books. I told them to write about the things they knew about: people, places, things and adventures in Lonesome Valley" (p. 71).

During the next five years, Jesse Stuart finished his senior year in Landsburgh High School. He worked at the Auckland Steel Mills, for a hard, bitter period, then managed to get into Lincoln Memorial University, and graduated in three years. He was ready for a career.

His next schoolteaching job, however, was that of serving as one-man faculty for the fourteen pupils of Winston High School, an isolated county high school. At this school Jesse met one of the most amazing characters of his life in Budge Waters, one of his pupils.

"If you're not awfully smart, he'll be teaching you," one of the other pupils warned Jesse when he met Budge.

Budge Waters was tall, gangling; pimply faced. He had peculiar "elongated eyes" that squinted at Stuart. When Budge walked, he had an awkward gait, and his hands seemed to "pull against the wind." But this boy more than made up for his appearance with his phenomenal mind. Budge did not read a page by sentence. He read by paragraph. When he and Jesse disagreed on dates, they would look them up in the encyclopedia, and Budge Waters would always be right. He had a photographic memory.

The young teacher worried often about keeping ahead of his brilliant pupil. But, Budge was Stuart's mainstay and pride when a scholastic contest was arranged with the small school of Winston and the great city high school of Landsburgh. Stuart knew that his school would be the victor. When the contest results were in, Budge Waters had won first place in English literature, first in grammar, first in history, and first in civil government: Winston High School had earned the honor of representing the county in the district scholastic contests, an unheard-of situation for Landsburgh High.

For his "future citizens of America," his fourteen ambitious young students, Jesse Stuart once made a seventeen-mile walk through a snowstorm into Landsburgh, to obtain sorely needed books. He lost his way in the storm, spent the night in a cornfield. He saved his life by building a makeshift shelter from fodder shocks, by pulling off his soaked clothing and substituting dry clothes from the suitcase he was carrying. He came very close to freezing. but continued his journey the next morning to Landsburgh. When he returned to Winston, he brought his suitcase filled with novels, books of short stories, books of poems and essays for Budge Water and his other book-starved pupils in the back hills.

As a result of Winston's sensational victory over Landsburgh High School, Stuart was offered the job of principal of Landsburgh High for the following year. When he accepted this job at Landsburgh (which was in reality Greenup High School), Jesse gave his mother and father a great feeling of happiness and pride. Jesse was the first member "on either side" of his family to receive a college degree, as far as his parents could recollect. Most important, he was following in the footsteps of his schoolteaching great-grandfather Preston Hilton.

After an eventful year spent as principal of Landsburgh High School, Jesse Stuart went to Vanderbilt University for his year of graduate work. He still loved schoolteaching, but he had decided to embark upon a career which would combine farming and writing. Before he could get started on this course, however, he was urged by the Greenwood County Board of Education to accept the post of Superintendent. His father took the day off from work, dressed up in his "town clothes," and told his son proudly, "You've amounted to somethin'. You've gone as high as you can ever go. . . ." His "Mom" advised him, "Be honest in all things, Jesse. You're going into the biggest job in this county. The County School Superintendent's Office has been the graveyard for many a man's reputation. I'll pray for you" (p. 146).

Stuart's career as County Superintendent proved that he had, indeed, needed his mother's prayers when going into that job. He was bitter in his denunciation of the school trustee system—a system whereby "each little rural schoolteacher had nine bosses: three trustees, five county board members, and the county school superintendent." All of these people were trying to tell a teacher how to teach. Jesse knew of this by experience, and his sympathy was usually with the schoolteacher. This attitude was one of the things which gave him trouble in his new post.

Jesse Stuart's philosophy of education is well stated in the following quotation from his recollections of those days spent as county school superintendent in a poor Kentucky county, where the school system was in debt very badly:

> I proposed we cut one month from all the schools in Greenwood County. This would reduce all the rural schools to six months, and Maxwell High School from nine months to eight. I could not understand why high schools have nine months when the rural schools only got six and seven. For, according to statistics, only a small percentage of the pupils from the rural schools go to school. It seemed to me that the rural schools and the graded schools were the underpinnings of the whole public school system. So why shouldn't the public school tax money, paid by the people, be used for the greatest good for the greatest number of their children? [p. 154]

Thus in striking out against inequalities in education, and later in fighting for consolidation of schools, he was entreating that pupils in remote, poorly equipped schools in the county, such as Winston High School, be transported at county expense to large, modern, centrally located schools. This crusade caused many of the people in Greenup to rise up and protest against him as "a dangerous critic of cherished instructions."[3]

While the people who had cheered him when he had been a football star at "Landsburgh" High School turned against him for his policies and many of his old friends refused to speak to him, Jesse endured this difficult time, keeping his hurt thoughts to himself. Meanwhile, he continued to carry out his duties. While he served as superintendent, he and the county school system were involved in approximately thirty-two lawsuits. Jesse and the schools won thirty-one and one half of these thirty-two suits.[4]

Stuart was the kind of administrator who went out to see for himself what conditions were in his area of responsibility. With a friend who had a broken-down car, he toured the back hills of the county. Where the one-room schools could not be reached by car, he would get to them by foot. He told teachers to hold up their heads because they were members of "the proudest profession" in the world, though "one of the poorest-paid ones." When he returned to Landsburgh, Jesse reflected upon what he had seen on his tour:

> There were ten thousand things I wanted to say about schools and schoolteaching. I couldn't begin to say all the things I wanted to say: I couldn't begin to do all the things I wanted to do. The need was too great. One had to be with them, see them, be a living part of the whole. For when one was a part of the rock-bottom reality, then he could have vision for vast improvement. The thought must precede the action.[5]

It was as county superintendent that he had evolved in his

---

[3] Joe Creason, "The Author who Writes so True," *The Courier Journal Magazine* (Louisville, Ky.), January 15, 1950, 7.

[4] *The Thread That Runs So True*, 173.

[5] *The Thread That Runs So True* (New York: Charles Scribner's & Sons, 1949), 196.

mind a consummate vision of what should be done for the improvement of his profession of teaching. "Vision: first, good roads until we could have consolidation of schools, then consolidated schools, well-qualified teachers, who would teach pupils how to get along with one another. Teach them elementary principles of health. Help them find a vocation in life and work toward that vocation. Not let the talent of any pupil, born upon this earth with a fair amount of intelligence, be lost to the world of humanity" (p. 196).

Through this vision, there emerges strongly the stature of the poet as teacher, the following through of his problm in careful architectonic pattern, as in the construction of a sonnet, to the goal of the harmonious whole, and accentuating always the theme of the individual. In the schoolteaching vision, the pupil was the individual about whom everything was to be built.

An incident which illustrates strongly his deep feeling of identification with the pupil as an individual occurred during Jesse Stuart's days as a high school principal. Jesse was called upon to witness Lyttle Brier's disgrace and to prescribe his punishment for tearing paper from his science notebook—an act that his teacher had pointed out as "destruction of school property." Says Jesse, "There was a poem written on each page. In some places, Lyttle Brier had selected eight to ten words before he chose the right one." He told the teacher, "This is poetry. When a poetic mood like this strikes a pupil, he should be given a chance to get paper. If he doesn't have it, let him write on his notebook." Then he told Lyttle Brier where to send his poems. They were accepted by a nationally known magazine (p. 253).

"It is this heroic idealism, rising here and there into passionate eloquence, but present always as a kind of interlinear light, that constitutes the greatest charm of the book," says Fred G. Walcott, of the University of Michigan, who prepared in 1949 the *Manual* for accompanying *The Thread That Runs So True.*[6]

Under the general title of "The Poet As Teacher," the *Manual*

[6] Fred G. Walcott, *Manual* (Minneapolis: Professional Books, Inc., November 1949), 3.

terms the work "a grand epic," a sort of poetic "Odyssey" of trials and tribulations which Jesse and his fellow teachers endured among a people where the education emerges "as though from the primitive roots of the culture."

Continuing in this vein, looking at Stuart's contribution to teaching as the manifestation of the fervent, evangelical spirit of the poet who seeks to inflame others with his own idealistic beliefs, the writer of the *Manual* states:

> Considering the background of such conditions, one is compelled to ponder the amazing professional stature of the author. It is as though he had recapitulated the educational experience of the race in one short generation. Examining the simple, cultural needs of his people, he seems to have discovered for himself all the philosophical tenets of the humanistic school. . . . Stuart acts, as it were, from the springs of sympathy and fellow feeling.[7]

The best mark of the master teacher, Walcott emphasizes, is to be found in his liberating of the creative genius in his pupils, and Jesse Stuart, prompted always by his own urge for creation, sought in each of his pupils the signs of incipient self-expression and encouraged it.

"It is a rare thing to find the poet as teacher," the *Manual* points out, "rarer still to have him speak as a teacher, to think as a teacher, to understand as a teacher. But it is only in the professional sense that this is true: in a larger sense, he has always taught and prophesied, and foreshown. The poet is a man of deeper insight into the affairs and conditions of mankind; he is the seer, the revealer, the interpreter—all of which taken together constitute the act of prophecy. The poet is, moreover, a devotee of the free spirit, and abjurer of the formal strictures that bind the aspirations of children and of men. He more than any other knows, deep within his nature, that 'it is the letter that killeth, the spirit that giveth life.' "[8]

[7] Ibid., 4.
[8] Ibid., 6.

In Jesse Stuart, there are combined two antipathetic strains, the visionary and the practical, and, far from producing stalemate, these two strains seem within him to be so balanced as to motivate action both well considered and daring. As soon as he could find the time, Stuart sat down and turned his attention to the outlining of his bold plan for democratic reform of Kentucky's dual school system. In days and nights of arduous writing, he elaborated on his plan, which he called the county-unit plan, a great simplification of the one prevailing.

After his long and grueling hours of writing, Jesse found that no one would print his article. This would have been crushing disappointment to many, but Jesse Stuart plunged on stubbornly with his reform ideas. One article concerned "seniority rights" for teachers, a term which Jesse had borrowed from his father, this expression being in common use among the elder Stuart's railroad laborer associates. Jesse was not familiar with teacher's tenure systems which were in effect in many states, but he was angry about what he had observed in the treatment of teachers, particularly in the rural districts. He had seen "excellent teachers" who had been "pushed around" from school to school, and often completely out of the school system, for no justifiable reason. This pushing had been done by "ignorant school trustees . . . by persons who hadn't the faintest idea what schoolteaching was all about, by school trustees who never had what it takes to make teachers themselves."[9]

This article, too, was rejected, as was another which advocated old-age pensions for teachers, and additional ones which denounced school trustees. Stuart had sent the articles to newspapers and to a local educational magazine. If he had sent them to publications of national circulation, his fight might have had a different outcome, he observed, in retrospect. At the time, the outlook seemed hopeless. Bitterly, Jesse gathered together his numerous reform writings, including a 450-page manuscript *The Cradle of the Copperheads*, a nonfiction satirical denunciation of certain educators "who fought against school reforms for their own personal

[9] *Thread That Runs So True*, 214.

gains" (p. 215). He filled a coffee sack to the top with these manuscripts, and burned them by a big rock in the Stuart pasture, where customarily the sheep were salted. To watch his ill-fated labor go up in flame and smoke was catharsis for Jesse Stuart. His violent feelings were dissipated in this manner as they were at the time of his first leaving home in his early 'teens, when he had gone out to find life beyond his "dark hills."

Books had misled him, he had decided, then, in disillusionment. They were "deceitful things," inspiring him to false dreams of becoming a Robert Burns in the Kentucky hills. "Life can be put into a book, but life cannot be taken from a book," had been his anguished and belligerent thought, as he tossed his books, a small, meager collection, under the kettle beneath a hickory tree where his mother had washed clothes, and set fire to them. He would not leave books behind to mislead his brother James, as he had been misled. He wanted him to stay at home and be happy in nature, without the distraction of books. With the burning, Jesse had felt that his own life was purged of books and of futile dreams.[1] "The man that gets life must get down and put his hands on it. He must hide his face in the wet leaves of the earth. What good had the books done me? I had even acted crazy over them for a little while. Little Sandy River, the River Ayr—Maria Sheen, my Highland Mary? W-Hollow the land of Robert Burns? It was all a joke. It was all a big joke! A Kentucky farm boy put his face against the quilts his mother had made for his bed and cried."[2]

But, just as the books and the dreams returned, and Jesse Stuart became, in the opinion of many critics, the "Robert Burns of America," so did the forward-looking educational ideas return to Stuart's life. They were, through the years, and continue to be, innate with him.

He went on to be principal of McKell High School, which was in the west end of the county, an area where he was well liked. McKell High School was a large, luxurious school plant

[1] *Beyond Dark Hills*, 109.
[2] Ibid.

located on extensive acres donated by an Ohio philanthropist. To be principal of such a high school was satisfaction, indeed, and meant a larger salary though it was a step down from being county superintendent. Jesse had decided not to attempt another term as county superintendent, when he learned that his friends on the school board would be defeated for reelection if they supported him. The reforms he had effected during his incumbency as county superintendent, while not the far-reaching ones proposed in his articles, were still revolutionary enough to have won for him dangerous enemies.

"You've done too much good in too little time," Benton Dangerfield, his best friend on the board had told him. "You're honest. The politicians can't handle you."[3]

So Jesse had bowed out of the situation, but not to take on a more passive life. At McKell High School there were problems along with pleasures. The biggest problem was dealing with the people of the community and their hostile attitude toward the school. Ruffians from the steel mills and shoe factories in Ohio, across Big River from the McKell High School area, crashed the school football games, plays, and other activities to make trouble. In one instance, Jesse decided that since there was no law to protect the school it was time that the school should begin to protect itself. Once again, in his schoolteaching career, he resorted to his fists to gain self-respect. In this fight he was aided by the football coach and two other men and a victory was gained which proved to be the turning point in the community relations. Ignorance and superstition were replaced by a healthy interest in the school and by cooperation with the school program.

One policy which Stuart put into effect at McKell High School is apropos today, with the return of many veterans to both high school and college classrooms. Jesse opened the doors of McKell High School to any person, regardless of age, who was qualified to enter. Many rural teachers were thus enabled to return and work toward high school diplomas. The ages of McKell High School pupils ranged from eleven to sixty-nine. Martha

[3] *Thread*, 216.

Binion was the pupil aged sixty-nine. She returned to high school as a sophomore, after teaching in the rural schools of Greenup County for many years. The pupils called her "Grandma" and held her in high affection. Often she acted as a substitute English teacher and presided over the study halls. She graduated with honors, and went back to rural teaching. Far from being a source of friction in the school, as some members of the faculty had feared, these older pupils proved to be a steadying influence and inspiration to the younger ones, and Jesse's innovation was considered a a great success.

Along with the satisfaction over the working-out locally of new ideas, there was for Stuart the greater triumph of seeing state-wide changes made in educational policies and practices during his second year at McKell High School. These were changes for which he had fought so zealously, and as he had thought, futilely. He had burned his articles, but letters and spoken words had had their effect in the campaign to improve Kentucky's school system. Not only was there legislation abolishing subdistricts, thus doing away with the hated trustee system, but later a Teachers' Tenure Law and a Teachers' Reirement law were passed. The crusading spirit which figures so largely in the make-up of Jesse Stuart was here indelibly repaid.

Literary success also had come to Jesse Stuart by this time. His collection of sonnets *Man With a Bull-Tongue Plow* had been published in 1934 and acclaimed by many of the nation's top critics. In his fourth year of teaching at McKell High, Jesse was in demand at numerous schools and colleges as a speaker, and his teaching was often interspersed with travel. It was at this time, in reward for his creative writing, that he was granted a Guggenheim fellowship. He asked for and received a leave of absence from McKell High School, and spent fourteen months in Europe.

When he returned from overseas, he found that his leave of absence had been disregarded. The son of a new member of the school board was principal of McKell High. In retaliation for this and other injustices in the system, Jesse started a newspaper of his own, the *Greenup County Citizen*, in which he pounded so for reforms that his life was endangered. Members of political gangs and even former friends and neighbors were stirred up against him. They hated and feared change. The newspaper was short-lived. Meantime, Jesse had crossed the Mason-Dixon Line to take a good teaching job at Portsmouth, Ohio, the fictitious "Dartmouth" High School..

This school was a big, modern plant, and rated as one of the best in the United States. The salary was high, the work interesting, but Jesse disapproved of the assembly-line methods used, the "'factory-like coordination and mechanism." Teacher and pupil entered the schoolhouse in the morning, had classes all day with only a thirty-minute break for lunch, didn't come out until the school day was over.

"In a large school, pupils didn't get that friendliness, love and warmth from teachers they could get in a small school,"[4] Jesse said. He felt strongly, as he does today, that each pupil should be given a chance to grow up "individually and originally," as trees in a forest not so crowded, rather than as the trees stiffly patterned in an over-crowded forest.

He came to a momentous decision. He decided to return to the land of his father at "W-Hollow," to raise sheep, and to make a full-time career of writing. Most important, he was determined to marry Naomi Deane Norris, the young schoolteacher of his region, whose books he had carried in high school, and to whom he had long been engaged.

With these plans consummated in 1939, Jesse Stuart began the era of lyrical reunion with the land which has resulted in his prodigious flow of poetry and of poetic prose, sonnets, short stories, novels, and autobiography.

But, his thoughts are ever upon schoolteaching and its problems. Looking back over his years of rich experience in the field, which began at the eager age of seventeen, he set down incidents and ideas for a book about teaching that has become a classic of its kind.

---

[4] *Thread That Runs So True*, 276.

In selecting *The Thread That Runs So True* as "The most important book of 1949," the National Education Association was following its well-established policy to call attention each year to a volume which "if read by the great body of American citizens would help to build the common understanding essential to the successful operation and growth of our democratic society."[5]

In its brief survey of this work, the *NEA Journal* considers it first as "good literature":

> Comes now the adventures of a young teacher told by a born story-teller whose writing has the rugged freshness of his native Kentucky hills. . . . It records life throbbing with energy, aspiration, conflict and love, is full of suspense and vivid imagery—difficult to lay down until one has finished. . . . It appeals to a wide range of readers, young and old, city and rural, teacher and layman, the little and the much-schooled.

The *Journal* points out that Stuart's book is "good history," as well, recording life in our American highlands among people who still retain many of the characteristics of the original pioneers. "It reveals the immense lifting power of our free public schools and tells of an experience that in various forms has been repeated on one frontier after another as our country has swept westward and forward. It should help us to understand that whatever we do in home, church, or business must begin with sound education."

The New York Herald Tribune reviewer wrote: "It is every American's book, as indigenously epic as the Paul Bunyan saga and with a hero possessed of brains as well as brawn."[6]

The Thread That Runs So True does not have the emotional power and drama which characterized Stuart's first autobiographical work, *Beyond Dark Hills*. This work has, instead, a mature, quiet, reflective power. The burning young poet who poured out his feelings about the world and the beauties of nature about him

---

[5] Morgan, "Editor's Note," *National Education Association Journal*.
[6] *New York Herald Tribune* Book Section, June 1949, 6.

has become a more subdued poet and a philosopher in *The Thread That Runs So True.* The consciousness of the beauty of his hills is still there, and there is much poetic prose in this second autobiographical work, as well as humorous descriptions of the hill life. But in the eleven years that elapsed between the publication of Stuart's first autobiography and the publication of his second, the young writer had been brought in touch with the realities of life beyond his hills in even larger measure than before.

As stated, he had been awarded a Guggenheim fellowship for travel to Europe in 1937, as a result of his published works. He had married Naomi Deane Norris in 1939, the dark-haired, blue-eyed sweetheart of his high school days. Naomi Deane had stood by him staunchly throughout his stormy period as County School Superintendent. She had done so, even though Naomi Deane's family, "one of the quietest and most highly respected in Greenup," did not like disturbances, and even though Jesse's enemies were Naomi Deane's friends.[7] Naomi, a schoolteacher, had understood Jesse's vision for the profession. She had encouraged him, too, in his writing of poetry.

His marriage, and the birth of his daughter, Jane, had caused Jesse to reflect a great deal about the future—the future of education and the future of his country. His service in the Navy during World War II had intensified these thoughts of the future.

One may find Jesse Stuart's views upon a great many subjects in *The Thread That Runs So True,* but these views resolve mainly upon the subject of education. In this book, Stuart is preoccupied with the problems of education in Kentucky. There are many intimations of his decision to remain always in his home state:

> Illiteracy in my state was high. My portion of the state—the hill country of eastern Kentucky, settled by the pioneers who had helped to make this country, who had won the Northwest territory, and who had fought for the very life of this country . . . had remained static intellectually while the progress of of a nation had swept around them like a great

[7] Ibid.

cyclone. If there was ever a man who wanted to obliterate il-
literacy from the hill country, I was that man. I thought that
if any pupil I might get into college would graduate and return to the hills to work, his influence would be like the dropping of an acorn into a deep pool of mountain water. The little waves would spread from the acorn the entire breadth and
length of the pool. [p. 256]

The Thread That Runs So True has been one of Jesse Stuart's
most widely read books. In May of 1949 a condensed version of
the work was published in the magazine, *The Ladies' Home Journal. Adventure in Reading,* an impressively illustrated secondary-
level textbook, has a section entitled "Toward Better Living" devoted to biographies and autobiographies of such world-renowned
figures as Winston Churchill. An extract from Jesse Stuart's *The
Thread That Runs So True* leads the list in this section. The introduction to the section says, in part, ". . . the ones who make
the deeper footprints on the sands of time, the ones who challenge our interest and emulation are the brave ,the wise, and the
generous. . . ."

In his new Preface written for the 1958 edition of the work,
Jesse Stuart noted that when he had begun writing *The Thread
That Runs So True,* eleven years before, he had said that teaching
was the greatest profession in the world, and that not too many
people had agreed with him at that time.

> Now, the interest of all America is focused upon Amer-
> ica's schools and their importance to our survival as a nation.
>   No one can ever tell me that education, rightly directed,
> without propaganda, cannot change the individual commun-
> ity, county, state and the world for the better. It can. There
> must be health, science, technology, the arts, and conserva-
> tion of all worthwhile things that aid humanity upon this
> earth. And there must, above all, be character education. [p.
> vii]

This emphasis upon character recurs throughout Stuart's writings and lectures upon education. His oft-stated principle is "I
would rather have a student with a A-character and a C-grade
than a student with C-character and an A grade. Teachers should

take time——more time—to stress honesty above everything else."[8]

In a letter to the editors of the *Ladies' Home Journal* in March 1960, he wrote: "In this second half of the twentieth century, we need to teach that which goes far beyond personal security, a full stomach and a fine automobile. We have boasted too loud and too long about our high standards of living. Shouldn't we aim also, and primarily, for high moral standards, for honesty—in a word, for character? We who are older should set a better example for youth to follow."[9]

In much the same vein, he elaborated on the subject of youth in a WIS-TV interview staged by Alice Wyman, of the University of South Carolina Extension Division, on March 23, 1960. This was the occasion of the special "Jesse Stuart Day," arranged in Stuart's honor by the university's Department of English. "Every youth is important. I think that if you can make a good citizen of a youth, this youth doesn't become an expense on the county, the state and the nation. We make a mistake, I think, when we discard a youth and say, 'He shouldn't be in this school.' We should hang on to that pupil as long as we can—do what we can for that pupil. If we get him to be a normal good citizen, we've accomplished something. I never let one go, that's my point, as long as I can possibly help it."[1]

Stuart reiterates, too, that teachers, with all of their overwork, their large numbers of pupils, should take time for problems of the individual.

"Say something kind to that student," he urges. "Help that student, and believe in an individual. Believe in a group and let them work together, but let each student still be an individual."[2]

Throughout Jesse Stuart's schoolteaching philosophy there is, in the insistence on character and discipline and hard work, the quality that symbolized the schoolmaster of "Little Red School-

---

[8] Stuart, interview with the writer, March 17, 1953.

[9] Stuart, "Do Our Schools Teach Dishonesty?", *Ladies' Home Journal*, (March 1960), 6.

[1] Tape-recorded interview, WIS-TV, March 24, 1960, Jesse Stuart, with Alice Wyman, the late Dr. Havilah Babcock, and the writer, University of South Carolina, Columbia, S. C.

[2] Ibid.

house" days, a nostalgic quality which, in part, belongs to a time and place alien to today's institutionalized program of education. Above all, there is the impassioned sense of dedication to his profession which Chaucer's Clerk of Oxenford epitomized in "And gladly teche." These schoolmaster tenets, however, may be considered forward looking, as well as nostalgic, it seems. For, in an era which has tended to force individuals into strict conformist mold in education, as well as in the arts, is not the pendulum beginning to swing back ever so discernibly to enhancement and development of individual potentials in education, to the recognizable figure in art instead of complete abstraction, to the Voice of the Poet instead of genuflection to the dictators of the obscure and to modern formalism?

The intense individualism portrayed by Stuart in his teaching, as well as in his writing, would seem to be in the vanguard of the movement toward this new sentiment of protest.

The potential of each student, no matter what the rating, should be kept in mind, Stuart believes. Again, speaking on the telecast at the University of South Carolina in 1963, he agreed emphatically with the late Dr. Havilah Babcock, Chairman of the University's English department, who stated that a great many colleges are making the error of encouraging or admitting only the upper ten percent of high school students. The leaders, Babcock pointed out, are frequently not in this group, and the B student or C student is just as entitled to what he can get, or absorb, as an A Student. Stuart labeled this practice of catering only to the top ten per cent as "Un-American." Such great leaders as Benjamin Franklin, Woodrow Wilson, in our country, and Winston Churchill in England, were not in the highest-rating group in their classes, was his vigorous comment. Under today's practices, Woodrow Wilson might not have been admitted to college. He was poorly prepared for college entrance, Ray Stannard Baker points out in his biography of Wilson, but once in, he improved his standing by conscientious study. He came out in the second highest group at graduation, and became a world leader.[3]

Qualities of leadership may emerge in various strata below the level of the top ten percent of intellectuals; therefore let the average as well as the brilliant student have due consideration, Stuart argued.

His high sense of devotion to the individual and to his profession of schoolteaching was expressed most poignantly in a poem which he wrote in 1959. He was being photographed in various scenes at his home in W-Hollow and at other parts of the region for illustrations of a *Saturday Evening Post* article written by John Bird. When Jesse arrived with the photographer at the ruins of Warnock School where he once was a schoolmaster, he was so moved that he sat down on the platform where his desk had once been and wrote this poem, which appeared in the *Post* article:

It is most painful now as I
Schoolmaster once return to this;
Master of learning, all they had
Until they grew and went beyond.
This barn was dear to them and me.
Only the skeleton remains;
Parts of the roof, windows and doors
And master's desk and window panes
Are gone into oblivion.

The birds and bats now carry on,
Where elm trees have reached new heights;
Young winds blow over greened-up fields
That lie in all directions here
Where fields of grass run with the winds.
These friendly winds have not erased
The memories of what has been
From those who caught fire here that spread
The flame of learning to the world.[4]

[3] Ray Stannard Baker, *Woodrow Wilson—Life and Letters* (Garden City, New York: Doubleday, Page & Co., 1927), I, 85-7.

In a most lasting way, and a highly dramatic way, Jesse Stuart's pupils proved to him and to the world that they had, in truth, "caught fire" from him and that his words had motivated their lives. In 1955, following Stuart's slow and painful recovery from the near-fatal heart attack, his pupils began a project which culminated in "Jesse Stuart Day"—on October 15 of that year—in all-out tribute from the State of Kentucky to its poet laureate, who was not only poet, novelist, and short-story writer, but also schoolmaster and philosopher in the field of education.

Greenup, the seat of Jesse's county, was the center for the celebration. Here where the poet-teacher had had some of his bitterest battles over new teaching ideas, and on the courthouse lawn, where he had sat so often, listening to talk, gaining speech and flavor for his famed short stories and novels, here, amid great fanfare, a marker was erected to Jesse Stuart. High school bands played, floats depicted *Taps for Private Tussie, Trees of Heaven, Hie to the hunters, The Thread That Runs So True,* and others of Jesse's most noted works. College presidents and various other dignitaries of Kentucky eulogizd him, but to Jesse the most heart-warming part of it all was the knowledge that his former pupils had initiated the big event.

Carved in bas-relief on the face of the vertical tablet of the granite marker dedicated to Jesse was a bull-tongue plow, symbolic of his first sonnet collection. The life-sized bust atop the tablet showed the youthful, visionary Stuart of the early schoolmaster days. Lines below the bust, from Pakenham Beatty's essay, "Self-Reliance," and chosen by Jesse himself, reflected the creed by which the poet-teacher had pointed the way for his pupils through the years. They were:

By your own soul's law,
   learn to live,
And if men thwart you,
   take no heed,

[4] John Bird, "My Friend, Jesse Stuart," *Saturday Evening Post,* CCXXXII (July 25, 1959), 81.

If men hate you, have no
    care,
Sing your song, dream your
    dream, hope
Your hope and pray your
    prayer.

In studying the schoolteaching facet of Jesse Stuart, into which field he projects his intense ideals of individualism, of developing each individual to his greatest potential in society, it can be said that Stuart is in the tradition of two great Victorians—Carlyle and Ruskin—whom Stuart came to admire in his Victorian literature course under Dr. Mims at Vanderbilt University.

These Victorians, in crying, "Educate or govern—they are one and the same word," in advocating enlightenment and accentuation of culture in a world of industrialization,[5] inspired Jesse Stuart to write as follows, in *The Thread That Runs So True:* "O hypocritical, shortsighted, ignorant politicians, living in the middle of this twentieth century ,allowing schools to remain closed for lack of financial appropriations, perpetuators of continued ignorance and future crime, I, at least, shall go on record to rebuke you! Tax us. Tax us to death to pay our teachers. Let them work upon immortal minds to brighten them to all eternity. We educate our people or we perish . . ." (p. 284).

And, as a creed, in the opening pages of the second edition of *The Thread That Runs So True,* Jesse Stuart chose this quotation from Daniel Webster: "If we work upon marble, it will perish; if we work upon brass, time will efface it; if we rear temples, they will crumble into dust; but if we work upon immortal minds, if we imbue them with principles, with just fear of God and love of our fellowmen, we engrave on those tables something which will brighten to all eternity"

---

[5] William S. Knickerbocker, "Victorian Education and the Idea of Culture," *The Reinterpretation of Victorian Literature,* ed. Joseph E. Baker (Princeton: Princeton University Press, 1950), 97.

ADDENDUM: EGYPT

In July 1960 Jesse Stuart sailed to Egypt with his wife and daughter, for a year of teaching at the American University in Cairo. He had left his region for extended periods only twice before since his year of graduate study at Vanderbilt. Those periods included the year of 1937, when he traveled and wrote in Europe, on a Guggenheim Travel Fellowship, and the period of his service in the Navy during World War II. He had taught creative writing for a summer at the University of Nevada in 1958, but, usually, his periods away from W-Hollow had been of only a few days' duration, for lecture tours or guest appearances for literary events in New York and other major cities. His stay in New York was never prolonged, for, after taking care of the business at hand and visiting with publishers and other friends, he would be restless to get back to his land, to his hills.

It seemed surprisingly out of character that Jesse Stuart should suddenly accept an offer of a year's teaching assignment overseas, especially in the exotic country of Egypt, the greatest contrast one could imagine to his Kentucky region.

When this writer, in a tape-recorded interview at W.Hollow, on July 2, 1960, asked Stuart why he was going to Egypt, the answer shot back, "To meet new challenges!"

Here was the Poet, with his "heroic idealism" in teaching, aflame with the determination to carry his ideas to larger spheres. Stuart said that he was "in deadly fear" for his country, in its battle with Communism. In his characteristically dynamic way, he had felt impelled to do something tangible in the furthering of ideals of Americanism in the Cold War. To meet the ever-intensifying program of Communist propagandizing, Americans whose talents were needed should give of those talents in representing their country abroad, Jesse Stuart felt. His lecturing activities had been restricted because of the massive heart attack of 1954. But his thoughts had often turned to the possibilities for teaching or lecturing overseas, he said.

When the request came, then, from the American University

at Cairo, which had as its president a former head of Transylvania College in Kentucky, Dr. Raymond L. McLain, Stuart did not hesitate to accept it, after receiving permission from his doctor to do so. Not only did he wish his family to have the experience of living overseas, but also he felt a definite "call" to teach there and to help fight the Communists in the idea war.

Jesse Stuart kept a journal of his year in Egypt—a report of events and a study of the people. This journal, entitled *Egyptian Diary*, has not, as yet, been released for publication. When Stuart and his family arrived back in America in July 1961, the writer met them in New York and Stuart showed her a portion of the manuscript of *Egyptian Diary*. From this reading, from conversations with Jesse Stuart, and from the brief, but colorful, letters received from the poet while he was in Egypt, the writer believes that this diary will prove to be an absorbing human document, resulting from the keen powers of observation of the Kentucky hill man and from the perceptive talents of the poet.

Typically, Stuart's letters from Egypt had reflected, even amid the fascinations of a foreign country, his schoolmaster preoccupation with his students: "Here I sit, not thinking of what has been, but of more books—and teaching more students—trying to plant into students' minds a broader basis, and broader concepts of education, in these parts."[6]

"Detached in time" is the phrase used by Stuart to describe his feeling about living in the Middle East. But being "detached in time" did not deter the energetic teacher-poet in his wholehearted carrying out of the ideals of personal ambassadorship which had brought him overseas. The clipping of a story in French from an Alexandria newspaper, which Stuart sent to the writer, tells of his enthusiastic reception as a lecturer at a literary gathering held in that city under the sponsorship of the United States State Department.[7] Clippings from *The Campus Caravan*, newspaper of the American University at Cairo, tell of his par-

---

[6] Letter to the writer, October 24, 1960.

[7] H.T.H., "Un Grand Poete Americain," *Le Progres Egyptien* (Alexandria), March 7, 1961, 2.

ticipation in student activities, of his interest in the students and their interest in him—of particular note being the story and picture showing students clustered about him on the campus, in excitement over his news of receiving the 1960 Fellowship of the Academy of American Poets.[8]

Most indicative of his dedicated interest in the students were his letters written back to America, as the time approached for his return home. They were filled with plans for getting teaching fellowships in America for the top members of his creative writing class.[9] He did succeed in placing his three "most brilliant" members in American universities for the year 1961-62. These three were all of Greek descent—the nationality which, in a class of some twenty-three nationalities, rated highest in scholarship, Stuart wrote.[1]

Nadia Khalaf, an Egyptian who was one of Stuart's students in Cairo, and who came to Duke University as a political science major, said, in answer to a request from the writer for her impressions of Stuart as a teacher:

> The first time I was introduced to Jesse Stuart I realized one thing immediately: Here is a person who talks to you freely and kindly and who shows real interest in the person to whom he is talking, no matter who that person may be. Jesse is a man with a big heart and this is what we love and appreciate in Egypt. Such a man is kind, understanding, helpful, and would give generously. Then I became one of his students and confirming my beliefs I realized that all the students in the class reacted in the same way to Jesse as I did. His simplicity struck everybody. We enjoyed having him in Cairo. His students will always remember him as the man with the "Big Heart."[2]

This simple and natural approach to his students overseas was not achieved by Jesse Stuart without some difficulty. In an article, 'Challenge in Cairo," which appeared in the May 1962 issue of *NEA Journal*, he described the fears which had possessed him

---

[8] February 13, 1961.
[9] Letter to the writer, May 8. 1961.
[1] Ibid.
[2] Nadia Khalaf, letter to the writer, June 1, 1962.

when he arrived upon the scene as visiting professor of English for 1960–61 at the American University. With students of such diversity, both racial and geographic, he would be "abysmally ignorant" of their personal backgrounds and could not follow his usual practices of visiting in their homes and of getting to know their parents. He had grown up "free as the wind in the hills of Kentucky . . . and had taught with the same freedom" he said.

I had lived in a country where my views on any subject (if not obscene or treasonable) could be freely expressed. Given my American political heritage, my Western culture, how could I teach in a country where newspapers, magazines, publishing houses, radio and TV were "nationalized"? . . . . When I first looked into my students' faces, a new fear struck me. Some of the countries from which they came were hostile to the United States. Had national attitudes rubbed off on these young men and women? Would personal hostilities nullify my efforts to teach them?[3]

Stuart's students ranged from Persian, Egyptian, Armenian, Kuwaitian, and other nationalities of the Middle East, to German, Finnish, and Greek. But, he said, to his great relief, he found no hostility or distrust in the faces of any of them.

A sense of the missionary teaching zeal that had prompted me to accept the AUC job in the first place came flooding back. I wanted my students to get something from my courses that they wouldn't find in their textbooks, and I resolved to teach them just as I would have taught at the college level at home. I told them to relax, that I was an easy grader. I knew that grades meant a great deal to them because those with high grades might win that highly coveted prize, a scholarship in America, with all expenses paid. . . . I told them that since there were twelve of them I hoped for twelve schools of writing—each was to be an individual and find his own way. Actually, however, I don't think they needed my green light. If ever I found individualists, I found them at AUC. Here was no mass culture, no set specifications for writing.[4]

Under Jesse Stuart's teaching philosophy of personal encour-

[3] Jesse Stuart, "Challenge in Cairo," *NEA Journal,* LI (May 1962), 46.
[4] Ibid., 47.

agement and of the promotion of individualism, the students were inspired to enthusiastic and prolific writing. When Stuart returned to America in 1961, he showed the writer one of his brief cases which was bulging with special works of his Cairo creative writing class—poems, short stories, articles, a play, and part of a novel—works for which he himself would attempt to find publication.

In his article, "Challenge in Cairo," Stuart described his twelve writing students individually, their backgrounds and ther personal problems, for, contrary to his initial misgivings, he had found that he could get to know his students and their families in Egypt, as he had come to know his students in America. His intense interest in the future of his class members and in the future of their young friends is given summation in the final lines of the article: ". . . theirs is a new generation. Where education is reaching, it is producing a more enlightened age for the youth of the Near East. Professionally, it is enormously satisfying to have played a minute part in the war for intellectual liberation. Personally, I am delighted that I was caught for a while in the middle of the struggle, pushed on all sides by my brilliant, creative students."[5]

The parallel careers of schoolteaching and of writing will, no doubt, provide the motif for Jesse Stuart's life in the future as they have in the past. As his horizon has broadened and his sense of urgency for aiding in his country's fight against Communism internationally, as well as at home, has pressed upon him, Stuart seems destined to leave his native hills, from time to time, for assignments in foreign countries.

"This overseas schoolteaching may turn out to be the thing," he said cryptically, to the writer during her visit to W-Hollow in 1960 a few days before the Stuarts' departure for Egypt.

The Poet as Teacher has now gone beyond the regional to a universal field of operations.

[5] Ibid.

7

Jesse Stuart Today

Jesse Stuart today is living the life which he has advocated from the beginning of his writings, a life close to the land, in his native W-Hollow, near Greenup, Kentucky. This is the land of his ancestors, the land where he was born. Stuart has acquired the farms which his father rented as a tenant farmer, and to those original acres he has added other ones until today he can stand on the porch of his modernized log cabin home and say, as he said in Sonnet 7 in *Man With a Bull-Tongue Plow*, "And far as eyes can see this land is mine." For this land, however, he has a deed.

This is "Jesse Stuart country," and these verdant acres rimmed by the hills prove that the poet is, indeed, "a brother to the tree." As he has realized his ambition of combining farming with writing as a career, he has made the regeneration of his valley a lifetime project, along with his literary projects. Although his thousand-acre estate is a model farm which draws countless visitors in fair weather, many of the acres which he acquires are barren,

eroded slopes that are not rehabilitated for crops. Instead, they
are reset with trees, according to the plan of "The Builder and
the Dream," in Stuart's *Kentucky Is My Land:*

> Ben Tuttle looked to Nature's Book for guidance.
> He reset trees adapted to this soil and seasons,
>
> . . . .
>
> He has the mastpoles for a thousand ships,
> Telephone and electric poles for a thousand
>   miles of wire,
> Fence posts to reach across this State. [pp. 89, 94]

Years of success for Jesse Stuart in the strenuous fields of
schoolteaching, writing, and lecturing have been matched with
his accomplishments in his valley as a leader in soil conservation
and in the resetting of trees. He has been devoted to his ideal, as
expressed in "The Builder and the Dream":

> *To build with the substantial and the good,*
> *To build, to build and never to destroy*
> One hundred thousand people lifted up
> Until their eyes are level with the stars,
> They have found Nature's book of rules
> And they have learned to read her language. [p. 94]

These free-verse lines in *Kentucky Is My Land* comprise an
eloquent statement of the Stuart creed in life. The importance
which he attaches to the mission of "Ben Tuttle" and Tuttle's
scheme of reforestation in the carrying out of this creed is shown
in the final lines of the long stanza:

> He has done as much as the dreamer
> Who sends his message to people in books,
> Much as a composer whose symphonies
> Are greater than the music of wind in the trees.
> He has brought back beauty for the people
> To see and feel and know,

To make them happier than
They would have been had he not dreamed.
He takes his place beside the dreamers
And the builders of our human destiny
Because he has produced a great forest. [p. 95]

This important facet of Jesse Stuart—Stuart, the scientific farmer and leader of his people in the ways of progress, as well as chronicler of their past—is best understood by a firsthand study of the poet in his region. The privilege of making such a study came to the writer in July of 1960 when she, with her husband, was a guest of the Stuarts at W-Hollow.

Seeing the poet in his environment is to see the environment through the poet's eyes, romanticized, heightened, transmuted by the imagination of the poet into a place of highly special meaning. For the follower of the poet, it is natural to envision what the poet sees in his region. For one who does not follow, there may be, of course, no enchantment. Certainly Jesse Stuart has been accused by some critics of "overstatement" or overenthusiasm in the image he has built up in portraying his region, just as Yeats was accused by some of creating a fantasy in his portrayal of Ireland.

"There never was an Ireland like Yeats' Ireland," Robert Penn Warren stated, in debunking tone, at the poetry colloquium held during the Vanderbilt Literary Symposium of 1959, when the conversation of the panel centered upon Yeats. He might as well have said that there never is a land like any poet's land, because the transmutation by the poet makes of it a realm outside reality. Stuart, who was a member of the panel, did not agree with Warren.

"Kentucky," for the empathic reader of Jesse Stuart, is a word of infinite magic and beauty, as is the name "Big Sandy" for the river that Stuart has celebrated in poetry and in prose. In entering the state at Catlettsburg, where the large figure of a Kentucky Colonel atop the bridge spanning Big Sandy welcomes the traveler, one is instantly conscious of coming into a land set apart in the imagination, and the Stuart line, "Kentucky Is My Land," runs through the mind. This land of wind and sun differs sharply from the area just left, neighboring West Virginia, with its deep cuts in the hills, showing sandstone and coal, slag piles, and scattered, abandoned mining settlements. Even in these cheerless areas close by his region, however, there had been evocations of Stuart and of his observant eye for realism, as he had demonstrated in the atmospheric poem, "Deserted Coal-Mine Camp":

> This is a place of
>   desolation here,
> Not any sign of life
>   and all is still,
> Except a blackbird
>   on a berry briar—
> And lizard sunning on a
>   window sill.[1]

Crossing the bridge out of the industrial center of Ashland, the traveler meets the figurative portal of the "Jesse Stuart country" in a large sign which states *Entering Greenup County*. Here, for the first time, flowers may be seen edging the road. On the left trees grow down to the roadside, and on the right, Big Sandy is lined with trees, luxuriant in leaves. On the horizon are Jesse's hills.

"The trees are greener here!" the writer exclaimed, when first viewing "Stuart country," the pastoral scenes which recall Stuart's lyricism. Outside of Ashland, one had passed the steel works which had been the setting for Stuart's nightmarish encounter with that segment of life. Not far from the steel works, one had noted the rows of "shotgun dwelling houses," in one of which Jesse had lived and watched a "life that was ugly and dirty and dwarfed as the little ragweeds growing at the edge of the metal sheds."[2]

[1] *Kentucky Is My Land*, 29.
[2] *Beyond Dark Hills*, 156.

The town of Greenup, small, and with a sleepy nineteenth-century air, faded old brick buildings still standing between occasional new ones, is centered by a typical courthouse and square It could be duplicated by hundreds of towns throughout the South and Southwest, this little town of Greenup. There is a difference, however. The spotlighted place of interest in front of the courthouse is not a military figure of the War Between the States but a bust of the young hometown poet, Jesse Stuart, who went beyond his "dark hills" to achieve fame—a poet honored in his own lifetime by his people. The loiterers on the courthouse square whose colorful stories have supplied material for so much of Stuart's writing do not show any undue curiosity when one stops to take a picture of the Stuart marker, the writer learned. They wave in a friendly way, but do not ask questions. They are accustomed to the interest in Jesse now and take it in their stride, though, when questioned, will answer with pride in the native son.

These lounging farmers from the hills and people of the town who find leisure for talk on the square, the business people who belong to the Greenup Lions Club, of which Jesse is a member, and who are former pupils of his, were the people who provided the Stuart marker. Not all Greenup citizens are Jesse Stuart enthusiasts, however. In spite of the literary honors which have come to the Kentucky writer, and the publishing of his works in many countries of the world, he is still regarded by some old resident families of the town with the age-old prejudice against the mountaineers.[3]

As the writer first glimpsed the Stuart home, the modernized log cabin, brown with white trim and covered with shingles riven personally by Jesse's father from oaks on the place, as a wedding present, this rustic home blended aesthetically against the hills, she was filled with respect for the vision of Deane Stuart, who saw for her young husband—as Donald Davidson had seen

[3] "Some of the old families have never forgiven me for marrying Naomi Deane, a towngirl, and taking her to the hills to live," Jesse Stuart said, with a slight note of bitterness, during the writer's visit.

for his young student at Vanderbilt—a future of highest promise set right in the periphery of his own hill region, among the people whom he had known all of his life.

It was Deane who took the initiative in sentimentality toward working out the plan of their lives upon a firm basis of continuity of the past and the familiar with a dynamic future which would enrich the tradition of the hills so beloved to both of them.

Few writers, it would seem, have had wives so closely identified with their work as has Jesse Stuart. Of his region, she has known instinctively what he has tried to express in his work, and has been able to give him assurance and true guidance when he has turned to her for opinions. As a schoolteacher herself, she has been an invaluable critic of his writings on educational experiences, as well, giving sound editorial advice and assistance, "here in the hills where we have no editors to turn to!"

Still "neatly patterned as a willow tree," as Jesse said of her in one of his early sonnets, tall, slender "Deane," is still the inspiration of many of her husband's poems. A superb cook and housewife, devoted mother to daughter Jane, amanuensis, nurse— she fulfills many roles, but none more conscientiously than that of nurse. It was her devotion, her meticulous, tireless attention which enabled the poet to pull through his long year of isolation and recovery following his major heart attack.

It is natural that Deane Stuart should say, when urged by this writer to give an answer, that *The Year of My Rebirh* is her favorite of Jesse Stuart's works. It is a journal of the poet and his family, the closely knit family of three. The convalescent could have no visitors. Not even the nearest of neighbors could drop by that year and that was difficult both for the people who love to visit the writer, and for the writer, who had always been interested in their activities and had taken his stories from life. Once Naomi Deane and the doctors brought him back to normal living, the strong gregarious side of Jesse's nature took over again and once more he was a vital part of the community, aiding, and often, spearheading, projects for progress.

Stuart is tremendously proud of the work of the hill neighbors who have followed his lead in farm improvements. One such neighbor, the owner of a fine farm, is Ott Taylor, the farmer near Winston High School at Warnock, Kentucky, in whose home the schoolteacher once lived (described in *The Thread That Runs So True*). During her visit to the region, the writer met and talked with Mr. Taylor, who was "Ottis Baylor" in the book. Mr. Taylor told in his own words the story of Jesse Stuart's long walk into town for books for his pupils, and of his nearly perishing when he become lost in a snowstorm.

"I tried my best to talk him out of going into town," Taylor recalled. "The weather was very threatening—but he insisted on going. What he didn't write in his book was that the weather was just as bad on his return trip. His fingers were frostbitten, and I stopped him from rushing up to the fire in our livingroom until I could thaw them out for him."

Taylor's sons, whom Stuart had taught, had been the schoolteacher's roommates in their farm home.

"He used to keep us awake till two o'clock in the morning sometimes, pounding on his typewriter!" one of the sons said, smiling with indulgent pride. "He was always writing."

Jesse returned the pride as he exclaimed, on leaving the Taylors' place, "Look at those rows of tobacco!" The symmetrical rows of green on the hillside were on a plot which had been cultivated by the son who was living still at the family home.

Taylor was among those models of Stuart's book characters who spoke with deep admiration and affection for Jesse.

"We read everything he writes," he said, for his family. "Please let us know when your book comes out. You have a good subject!"

The Warnock school which figured so prominently in *The Thread That Runs So True* was in a sad, dilapidated state, and was no longer a schoolhouse, but a meetingplace for a local club. Members of the old board of trustees would do what they could to preserve the old schoolhouse because of its importance in Jesse Stuart's autobiographical works about his schoolteaching days, Mr. Taylor assured Stuart, who had felt a great nostalgia, he said, upon seeing the place and his former pupils again.

Most of the townspeople and people of the hills echo the sentiments of Ott Taylor, a pride and deep regard for the region's native writer. Jesse Stuart has achieved fame through his writings and lectures, and he spends much of his time in traveling about the country, lately even filling extensive engagements overseas. The people of his region are impressed that this neighbor who paid for a college education by hard, physical labor can now write nine honorary degrees after his name—the Doctor of Laws degree from Baylor University, Waco, Texas; Doctor of Humane Letters, from Lincoln Memorial University, his Alma Mater; Doctor of Letters degrees from the University of Kentucky, Marietta College in Ohio, Morris-Harvey College in Charleston, West Virginia, Marshall University, Huntington, West Virginia, Eastern Kentucky University, and from Berea College, Kentucky; and the Doctor of Literature Degree from ths University of Northern Michigan. He received also, in 1955, the Berea College Centennial Award for Literature.

The people are impressed, and at the local drug store where Jesse's books are stacked for autographing, there is always someone around, waiting for Jesse to put in an appearance when he is at W-Hollow, the owner of the store told the writer during her visit there in 1960. But more important to the people than Jesse Stuart's honors is the measure of the man who continues to join them in community events, continues to be an active member of the Greenup Methodist Church, and of the Greenup Lions Club, heads the Heart Fund drives of the county, and finds time when he is in town to join the group on the courthouse square, keeping up with the news of the family members, many of whom he has taught "through the fourth generation," he says.

Stuart keeps a file at his home on each student with whom he has corresponded through the years, and the correspondence has been voluminous. His file on Budge Waters, the brilliant pupil whom readers of *The Thread That Runs So True* remember and ask about, has been closed away, he said to the writer, with deep regret. Budge Waters, it seems, was a misfit in life. He had tried to teach school, but he had taught "over the heads" of his pupils. He could not come down to their level of thinking. He had tried selling real estate. At first, this had been disastrous, too, but he had persisted and eventually had found success, his keen, "photographic" memory serving him spectacularly in real estate competition. Apparently, he had come to terms with the business world. One day, however, Budge's body had been found in the Detroit River near his home. Had there been inner despair, such strong despair, that Budge had ended his life? Had the drowning been accidental, or had a crime been committed? This matter has never been settled. Whatever the answer, Jesse Stuart grieves for Budge Waters.

But, as the poet celebrates his fifty-eighth birthday this year, 1965—there, in his scenic rural home in W-Hollow, with Naomi Deane, his wife, busily aiding him in his many activities, and his prize student, daughter Jane, a brilliant college graduate and poet in her own right, in Indiana, not far away—he can reflect, with satisfaction, upon the many pupils he has had who have not given up in life, but who have followed, or who seem destined to follow, his dynamic lead to success.[4]

[4] Jane Stuart, now 22, was her father's pupil in his creative writing class at the American University in Cairo. She has had numerous poems published in highly rated literary periodicals. She is married to Julian Juergensmeyer, who is teaching in the Law School at the University of Indiana. She is teaching Latin at the University and is working there on her Doctor of Philosophy degree in Classical Languages.

8

Conclusion

What will be Jesse Stuart's place in literature? As Stuart himself reiterates from the lecture platform, "Time will be the great critic. Only Time can give the answer to the question of what will endure."[1] This writer predicts, however, that scholars and general readers in a future age will be searching for the writers of the movement forming a stubborn countertrend to the critical strictures, depersonalization, and the objective formalism of our time, much as the romanticists symbolized a rebellious force against neoclassicism in the eighteenth century.

In the vanguard of today's dynamic and individualistic writers who protest against the prevailing school of "new criticism," obscurantism, and objectivity is Jesse Stuart, yet he may not be placed with any group or cult. He is an "independent." He is *sui generis*.

[1] Lecture at the University of South Carolina, March 23, 1960, and lecture at Vanderbilt University Literary Symposium, April 22, 1959.

"A marvelous phenomenon," Donald Davidson characterized Stuart, in his essay, "Still Rebels, Still Yankees."[2]

Editor and critic Frederic A. Birmingham, meeting the young author, soon after Stuart's first books had brought him fame, wrote enthusiastically: "Jesse Stuart, a queer sport (as biologists use the term, meaning a deviation from the species, a mutation), a natural-born writer, produced as by a miracle out of the illiterates of backwoods Kentucky, who will make his mark indelibly in the literature of the day—a volcano of energy, pouring out pages and pages of manuscript, as Thomas Wolfe did. . . ."[3]

Jesse Stuart's contribution to contemporary literature, and, if one may predict, his contribution to literature of the ages, is his strong individuality, which has made itself felt in defiance of the prevailing current of his era for aesthetic distance, for objectivity in writing. Stuart opposes these tenets with simplicity and the highly personal.

This determination to write in his own way, to be himself, took possession of Stuart when he first returned to his mountain home, after his adventures in the steel mills and his grueling days of work in obtaining a college education. Revisiting the pastures and woods where he had found time between chores and hunting to read the poetry of Robert Burns and dream of becoming a Burns of his Kentucky hills, he found his nostalgia overlaid with a new confidence in his own powers. As he expressed it in *Beyond Dark Hills:* "I didn't want to write like Burns now. I wanted to write like myself. I wanted to be myself. I didn't want to be a tree like another tree in the forest. I wanted to be a shoe--make with a little different color of leaves, a different kind of bark and different arrangement of limbs, so when the wind whipped through my body, I would sing a different song to my brother shoe-makes. I wanted to be different, not for the sake of being different but being different for something" (p. 229).

[2] Donald Davidson, *Still Rebels, Still Yankees and Other Essays* (Baton Rouge: Louisiana State University Press, 1957), 166.

[3] Frederic A. Birmingham, *The Writer's Craft* (New York) Hawthorne

Poetically, he defined his creed of independence in Sonnet 200 of *Man With a Bull-Tongue Plow:*

I cannot sing tunes that great men have sung.
I cannot follow roads great men have gone,
I am not here to sing the songs they've sung,
I think I'm here to make a road my own.
I shall go forth not knowing where I go.
I shall go forth and I shall go alone.
The road I'll travel on is mud, I know.
But it's a road I can call my own.
The stars and moon and sun will give me light.
The winds will whisper songs I love to hear;
Oak leaves will make for me a bed at night,
And dawn will break to find me lying here.
The winey sunlight of another day
Will find me plodding on my muddy way.

Through twenty-eight books, he has held with integrity to his guiding principle of individualism, and, in both poetry and prose, he has maintained, with equal fidelity, his twin principle of close communion with Nature.

Certainly, in looking back upon Jesse Stuart's full and dramatic life which has been reflected in his works, and upon considering Stuart's prodigious contribution in the fields of poetry, the short story, and the novel, as well as his contribution of an influential book and of innumerable articles in the field of education, it would seem clear that to confine him merely to the category of the regional writer of frontier-type humor is to be not only shortsighted, but dogmatic.

Successful and amusing as was *Taps for Private Tussie,* with which Jesse Stuart gained national and international attention as a humorist in the book's best-selling days in 1943 and 1944, that book represents only one side of the many-faceted Stuart. By my survey of all of his published works, I have hoped to show that

Books, Inc., 1958), 174.

Stuart, the passionate, subjective poet, the writer of poetic prose descriptions of the land, the realistic writer of life in the steel mills, and the writer of works of social significance, must be recognized before a true estimate of Jesse Stuart may be given.

As has been noted, Stuart has received signal honors for his work in each of the literary forms which he has employed, and a number of his books and many individual short stories have been published in foreign countries.

In 1959, terming *Man With a Bull-Tongue Plow* "a landmark in American literature," Dutton, Publishers, reissued the collection in paperback, the original number of 703 sonnets cut down to 622, but the monumental work still, as the publishers said, "crowded with dozens of dramas and scores of characters."

The distinguished awards won by *Man With a Bull-Tongue Plow*, and *Taps for Private Tussie* have been mentioned previously, as well as the extensive foreign publishing of the latter work. In 1952, *Taps for Private Tussie* was included in *Masterpieces of World Literature in Digest Form*, published by Harper and Brothers. The short-story collection, *Men of the Mountains*, brought for Stuart the Academy of Arts and Sciences Prize for Literature in 1941.

In 1962, a special textbook edition of *The Thread That Runs So True* was published by Charles Scribner's Sons. This book was dramatized for amateur production in 1958 by the Dramatic Publishing Company, of Chicago, and has proved to be a very popular play for local groups throughout the country, according to information given to the writer in December 1962, by the agent for the play, Annie Laurie Williams. Miss Williams stated, also, that the play is being adapted for Broadway production as a musical.

A Jesse Stuart Reader, Stories and Poems Selected by Jesse Stuart (and with introductory remarks by Stuart) was published in 1963 by McGraw-Hill Book Company, Inc. The *Reader* includs excerpts from *The Thread That Runs So True*, *The Year of My Rebirth*, and *God's Oddling*, as well as short stories and poems from *Man With a Bull-Tongue Plow*, *Album of Destiny*, and *Hold April*, with Stuart's interesting anecdotal comments about the works.

In 1964, a book was published which attracted little attenion from the critics, but which deserves attention in the study of Jesse Stuart, as does each article or poem, no matter how minor, because it is an extension of the poet's genius. *Save Every Lamb* was the book, a quiet collection of stories of the Jesse Stuart country, many of which had appeared in earlier volumes and had been cited for merit. This collection of tales and short stories, and passages of just pure reminiscing in the Stuart manner, is very special. Its theme is animals. It was written specifically in the cause of preservation of wildlife and it seems destined to acquire a special significance as the problem of wildlife conservation in America becomes more acute.

The title story in the collection is an excerpt from Stuart's first novel, *Trees of Heaven*. It describes the method by which the author and members of his family saved their lambs in winter, whenever food was scarce.

"During World War II, when meat was rationed and sheep and cattle were becoming scarce," Stuart wrote in his Introduction to the book, "this excerpt was taken from my novel and was used in Agricultural Colleges and Universities and by the U. S. Department of Agriculture.[4]

In another part of the Introduction, he writes:

> My world has changed since I was a boy, when everybody in the country lived by digging his livelihood from the ground. No one digs all his livelihood from the soil here any more. Everyone works in industry and drives to and from his work. Men who used to farm and live from the products they grew on their farms now get paid by our Federal government for not farming. This philosophy has changed our country and our people. It has also had a direct bearing on all wildlife. . . . Wildlife is shoved back to its last wild refuge-stands. These wild areas are dwindling year by year. When

---

[4] *Save Every Lamb* (New York: McGraw-Hill Book Company, 1964, 3.

wildlife, rabbits, possums, birds and even foxes, are finally starved into submission and try to find feed around houses, they are killed by ruthless young or would-be hunters who kill for the joy of killing. Not half enough has been said in America about what is happening and what will happen to our wildlife if something isn't done in a hurry to preserve these species we have left. . . . Our wildlife, if not fed and protected, will become extinct, and the youth of tomorrow will not have the kind of wonderful world my boyhood friends and I had in which to grow from boyhood to manhood. [pp. 9–10]

"Or They Perish" is the title of the final chapter in this collection, which is a tangential contribution to Stuart's flowing river" of autobiographical works. "Or They Perish" continues the theme of the Introduction with strong admonitions of what the future will hold for America if wildlife is not guarded, this being a subject highly central in the thinking of Jesse Stuart. It is one upon which he dwells often in conversation, as well as in writing. He is ever the poet, and his concluding line here is that of a poet—"And the saddest and loneliest countries in the world are those without wildlife."

In 1952, *The Thread That Runs So True* was published in Brazil, and in 1963 it appeared in Egypt and in Lebanon, translated into Arabic, as was *Red Mule. Beyond Dark Hills, Hie to the Hunters* and *The Year of My Rebirth* have been published in England. *The Beatinest Boy* was published in India and in Denmark. *A Penny's Worth of Character* has been published in Denmark and in Pakistan. Stuart stated that he was "elated" to receive a copy of *God's Oddling* which had been published in Dacca, East Pakistan, in 1964. It had been translated into Bengali.[5]

The Good Spirit of Laurel Ridge was published in Germany in 1959, and *Hie to the Hunters* was published there in 1960 under the title *Kentuckie Melodie*. Rudolf Roder, Bayreuth, was the translator.

The title *Kentuckie Melodie* emphasizes the lyrical aspect of Stuart's prose, the union with Nature in his works, which, it seems,

[5] Letter to the writer, September 26, 1964.

is particularly recognized by readers in Germany, where, in the eighteenth century, the seeds of romanticism were sown by Kant, with his concepts of reason as transcendental ideas. Jesse Stuart's lyricism, his spirit of cosmic optimism which enables him to view the harmonies of life as transcending the often bitter dissonances noted by his strong realistic pen, these qualities, it seems, make him a writer of interest to Germany and the Scandinavian countries. In existentialist France and Italy, it is the nihilism of Hemingway, the negativism of Faulkner and his preoccupation with degeneracy, which have scored.[6] Stuart's books have not been translated in those countries although his short story "Dawn of Remembered Spring" has been published recently in Italy.

Numerous other short stories by Jesse Stuart have been translated and published in foreign lands. Translations include those of "The Cousins" in *Hiemmet* (Copenhagen, November 7, 1961); and "Walk in the Moon Shadows" from *Ploughshare in Heaven* for special radio reading in Sweden in 1960 by Karin Nellemose, actress of the Royal Danish Theatre. These translations join the growing list of single stories and poems published in European magazines, including magazines in England, Ireland, Germany, Denmark, Norway, and Sweden, and the magazine *Amerika* published for distribution in Russia by the United States State Department.[7]

Jesse Stuart has made his Kentucky world believable, then, not only to his readers in other parts of America, but also to an ever-increasing number of readers in lands around the world. He has portrayed with deep faithfulness the life of his circumscribed region, his microcosm in the mountains, where the people live in close affinity with the land, governed by the cycle of the seasons and clinging to the simple pieties of their pioneer ancestors—superstitious religious faith, love of country, respect for

[6] Harry Modean Campbell and Ruel Foster, *William Faulkner, A Critical Appraisal* (Norman: University of Oklahoma Press, 1951), 179.

[7] Recent data on Stuart translations are taken from the *Jesse Stuart Newsletter*, a pamphlet which is published quarterly by Dr. Hensley Woodbridge, former librarian at Murray State College, Murray, Kentucky, where the personal papers of Jesse Stuart are housed in the Stuart Room.

the past, above all loyalty to family. In portraying his people, he has struck a deep understanding chord in many readers of other countries, and according to critics whose opinions have been cited in this work, has gone far beyond the realm of the regional to attain universality.

Jesse Stuart's conception of his role as a bardic poet, who would speak not only for the people of his region, but also for the common heart of mankind, is well stated in his concluding lines of Sonnet 3 in *Man With a Bull-Tongue Plow:*

I speak of men that live in my lifetime,
And I speak of the men of yesterday.
I do not care to know if this is art—
These common words born in a common heart.

Faults of construction, faults of diction, a tendency at times, in both poetry and prose, to overwork the vernacular, and the impression given by the author at times that, in his eagerness, he is overemphasizing, overstating, are weaknesses of Stuart's craftmanship that have been pointed out by some critics noted in this work. But these critics have, as a rule, recognized the qualities of originality, of elemental strength and simplicity, and of an innate love of humanity, which give to Stuart's works a universal or cosmic meaning, and for which they have been willing to forgive weaknesses of execution.

Other critics noted have disputed the accusation of "carelessness," and have insisted that in Jesse Stuart's "rambling" and "loquacious" characterizations, there is "artful artnessness," a most careful attention to architectonics to portray a subject which will have archetypal meaning for his readers.

The Tussies and the Hammertights are archetypes of the lazy, shiftless people of the world. Jesse Stuart's father and mother are the opposing types, the hard workers, the God-fearing, and the ambitious. Mitch Stuart, Jesse's grandfather, is the archetype of the fighter. Uncle Jeff is the natural man harnessed to a machine, and finally beaten by the machine, the railroad, to which he has been a slave. Old Op, of *The Good Spirit of Laurel Ridge* ,is natural man who refuses to be beaten by the Machine Age, who defies the threat of the atom bomb and clings to his hills and his life of peace. Alec, of "Alec's Cabin," one of Stuart's most poignant short stories, is man engulfed in primordial loneliness, seeking identity and a home in the place where he had once known happiness.

In the summation of Jesse Stuart, the point may be clearly made that he is both realist and romanticist in his depiction of and his interpretation of life, both in his poetry and in his prose. In the midst of his most lyrical descriptions of Nature and her beauties as a backdrop of action for a story, he may create a brutal caricature of a human being or set a scene of ugliness so powerful in its realism that it is shattering to the sensibilities of the readers.

This preoccupation with life as a paradox, with the juxtaposition of the cruel and the beautiful, the evil and the good, places Stuart in the tradition of such a writer as Thomas Wolfe and in the interpretations of the South held by Wolfe. In commenting upon Wolfe's "linguistic combination—the combination of concrete detail, accurate speech, and incantatory rhetorical extravagance," as associated with something in the tradition of Southern culture, critic C. Hugh Holman says: "Wolfe likewise shares the Southerner's willingness to accept and find delight in paradox . . . paradoxes bother Southerners less than they would bother their Northern neighbors, for while they hunger for order and are moved by a rage for tradition, they can at the same time accept instability as a permanent aspect of human existence, and the unresolved contradiction as a part of man's condition."[8]

Though this acceptance of the paradoxical in life may be inherent in Jesse Stuart as a Southern writer, it has a deep source, too, in the opinion of the writer, in the avid study which Stuart has made from his boyhood days of the life and works of his literary idol, Robert Burns. Along with Burns' love lyrics and Scottish

---

[8] C. Hugh Holman, "Thomas Wolfe and the South," *South*, eds. Louis D. Rubin, Jr. and Robert D. Jacobs (Garden City, New York: Doubleday and Co., Inc., 1961), 189.

songs, there were such bitter satirical poems as "Holy Willie's Prayer" and "Address to the Unco Guid," so that for Stuart, in his Kentucky hills, with inheritance from his Scottish ancestors of both *joie de vivre* and a stern Calvinistic conscience, it was natural to follow the example of Burns and mix the lyrical with searing social criticism and a moral doctrine.

The romantic realist, or realistic romanticist, George Crabbe, is another of Jesse Stuart's spiritual forebears, with his "Parish Register" and "The Village," revealing portrayals of the seamy side of life in contrast with the beauty of the pastoral.

Man With a Bull-Tongue Plow is a rivulet of poetry, containing, in the main, sonnets which are a paean to Nature. In the midst of the highest incantational verse, however, there appear such rugged denunciations in the vernacular as No. 380:

To Toodle Wormlake

You are a belly-acher with a rope
Tied round your neck where you can eat the grass;
A belly-acher with a mental scope
Of black-ants and your back is streaked with brass.
Your heart is brass; your tongue is cankered brass.
And round the radius of your pasture rope
Your tongue lolls out—you eat and laze and mope.
Do people fail to watch you when they pass?
Lakewood: You are their politician boar.
The stems of grass are dollars that you flank
Down your intestinal channel with a roar;
You are a liar, hypocrite and crank.
When grass gets short they set and stake your chain;
Gives you the chance to eat high grass again.

Equally striking contrasts in tone and diction may be noted throughout Jesse Stuart's autobiographical writing and his works of fiction. The most realistic passages may be followed by pure poetic prose, as in this passage (after a night service at the Plum Grove Church):

On the outside of the house there would be a yellow moon up in the sky and a cold white glitter of thousands of summer stars. There would be moonlight on the hay fields and the tasseled corn. And there would be darkness in the little patches of oak trees. The air would be filled with the voices of frogs, katydids, whippoorwills and beetles. And there would be the white slabs gleaming in the moonlight where hundreds of dead lie buried on Plum Grove Hill.[9]

Here the prose is rhythmic, and the romanticist's preoccupation with the natural scene is evidenced—a scene which projects an atmosphere of remoteness, of death, in the midst of the animate voices of the poet's hill country churchyard. There is the romanticist's awareness of two time levels, the past and the present, which is found throughout Jesse Stuart's writing. Time past and time present, in dramatic continuity, constitute the theme of No. 484 in *Man With a Bull-Tongue Plow* as Tish Meadows speaks:

I sleep beneath the earth-scarred battle ground;
The English and the Indians were my foe.
Now I have slept here many years below,
Where wind and water and the trees make sound.
America goes on because I sleep
And others sleep—we died to make her go.
Corn will grow over us and ripen brown;
Wheat will grow over us year after year;
Each year a coat of new leaves will drift down;
Farmers will pass, not knowing who sleeps here.
What does it matter who is sleeping here?
For death is death just anyway we die;
And when we died, we were fighting for
The land you keep today—something to have;
America, for you we took the grave!

Contrast these inspirational lines and their evocation of the romance of the past, with the sharp, primitive power of a para-

---

[9] *Beyond Dark Hills*, 87.

graph from an early Stuart short story, "Kentucky Hill Dance":

> Outside in the yard one can hear the licks struck within the
> giant century-old log house. One can hear the cries and the
> curses of the men and the finer cries of the women. One can
> see the tall, strong and brown-skinnd mountain girls (skin
> made brown by working in the corn fields and the tobacco
> fields) come pouring out at the doors. And a voice among
> them is higher than the rest: "They got that old rot-gut
> down to Phil Conley's. I knowed what was going to happen
> all the time. This is the way of all our dances any more. We
> just can't have them for rot-gut whisky. We can't have
> church. We can't have anything."[1]

Rarely are the writings of Jesse Stuart didactic, it must be rec-
terated. His criticisms are implicit. They are expressed most vividly in his selection of material. Once he has selected his area for
criticism, he will present his subjct in relentless documentation
of detail to create reality. But he will not consciously point a
moral, as a rule. He knows his region, and he loves and understands his characters, even the most reprehensible ones. He understands their human failings at the same time that he is exposing
them.

Only in his novel *Foretaste of Glory*, with its dramatic plot
of a false Doomsday alarm, does he lash out at hypocrites much
in the manner of Burns in the "Unco Guid." In this work, he
seems to depart from the subjectiveness that one feels in his other
works, his deep affinity with his characters.

In *The Thread That Runs So True*, which, on the human level
of *The Hoosier Schoolmaster*, has been hailed as a classic of American life, Jesse Stuart has direct and bitter criticism for the enemies of the welfare of schoolteachers and of their pupils, such
enemies as the men in a Kntucky county who allowed four rural
schools to remain closed because of lack of appropriations. "O
hypocritical, shortsighted, ignorant politicians, living in the middle of this twentieth century. . . ." he flayed them.

It is the cause of the schoolteaching profession and the correc-

---

[1] "Kentucky Hill Dance," *The New Republic*, LXXIX (May 16, 1934),
15.

tion of inequities between urban and rural school systems which brings out the unequivocal and fearless crusader in Jesse Stuart. As has been shown in this study, *The Thread That Runs So True* is considered to be one of the most powerful American social documents of our time. Appearing as it does, in excerpts, in high school English textbooks, it may also be considered to be one of the most inspirational and best-known books by a contemporary author for the youth of America.

There is in Jesse Stuart a deep dichotomy, which has been reflected in his works and in his ambivalent view of life, embracing both the stern Calvinistic doctrine of hard work and the traditionally pious God-fearing attitude of his ancestors, along with the direct approach to God of the transcendentalist. God, man, and Nature in one understanding, all-embracing whole permeate the lyrical poetry and the subjective prose of Stuart. In his incantational poetry, Jesse Stuart seems akin to Wordsworth and Whitman, with their pantheistic worship of Nature, and is even akin to Hesiod.[2] Stuart is in sharp contrast to contemporary writers who affect a mystique of the soil. As an actual tiller of the soil, he is especially akin to Hesiod and Robert Burns, whose poetry of unrestrained joy in communion with Nature came from close, daily contact with earth.

"O Gods of Storm, best savage-white and cold!" Stuart intones in *Album of Destiny*, and, in the same sonnet sequence, "Give trees, you ancient Gods, new blood for veins"; "O Sun of gold, ride up with golden light"; "Sing out, you mighty organs of the wind!"

In the poem, "Impressions," in *Hold April*, Jesse Stuart concludes with the line, "Nature. You make; you make; Come often rain!" In the same volume, in "Back Where I Belong," written after recovery from his near-fatal heart attack, the poet writes, in the deep piety of his forefathers,

> I thank God that he granted my stay here
> To count the many songs in winds that blow.

[2] At the Award ceremony held by the Academy of American Poets

The dichotomy which exists in Stuart is recognized by him in what he calls the "dreamer-doer" approach to life. Loving the solitude and communion with nature in his "ivory tower" in the hills, he has, at the same time, an intense love of people, a restless desire to be with them, for he gets material for his stories from life, and he has the profound feeling, too, that the writer has an obligation to society, to make his contribution toward solving the problems of the day. Stuart does not cling to his ivory tower, then, but comes to grips with the hard realities of our times, and, in his works of social criticism, reflects the vital and wholehearted attention he has given to his areas of interest, particularly the field of education.

This moral doctrine of hard work and of social awareness in the life and works of Jesse Stuart was predicted by one of Stuart's favorite professors at Vanderbilt University, Dr. Edwin Mims, in whose class in Victorian literature the young Kentuckian developed a great admiration for Carlyle. Dr. Mims reviewed Stuart's 1958 short-story collection *Ploughshare in Heaven* for the *Nashville Tennessean*, and maintained that the collection showed a "new maturity" in its author, "a broader scope, a new outlook for his powers." He concluded:

> One wonders just what course the writing of Jesse Stuart will take. He will still farm, he will still teach school, but will he, like so many of his predecessors, lose his creative power? Or will he sound the trumpet of a larger faith than he has expressed in his earlier volumes? Not in the mood of the 'Spoon River Anthology' or of 'A Shropshire Lad,' which is so often expressed in his early poetry and prose, but in the mood of Carlyle when he wrote 'The Everlasting Yea,' he may lead us out of the confusion and chaos of the present time. Let the trumpet sound![3]

As Stuart continues to write poetry and prose imbued with

in New York for Jesse Stuart in 1961, Mr. Stephen Xydos, of Columbia University's faculty, a native of Greece and member of the Academy's Advisory Board, remarked to the writer about the affinity between Stuart and the ancient Greek poets.

the fundamental elements of strength and of optimism which were native to the American character of pioneer days, Dr. Mims might well say that Stuart has attained the peace of Carlyle's "Everlasting Yea" though recognizing and recording with realism the brutalities and weaknesses of life and meeting headlong the challenges of today. Dr. Mims' prophecy concerning Jesse Stuart's moral, or social, seriousness would seem to have been fulfilled in Stuart's program of teaching and of lecturing overseas since 1960, the broadening of his horizon from the regional to the global. In his concern for his country and the "free world," in the struggle against Communism, Stuart revealed his deep patriotism in undertaking a seven-months' lecture tour overseas for the United States State Department in 1962, though still a heart patient. On January 30, 1963, nearing completion of his tour, he wrote happily from Taipei, Formosa, of his imminent return home to his Kentucky hills: "This is some trip—it will soon be over! I've crossed the face of the earth—have spoken all the way—have traveled faster than sound! From Taipei to Tokyo, our Mandarin Jet set a record, 800 miles per hour. Yes, deserts, oceans, seas, mountains—barren and snow-capped—Africa, Europe, Near East—Middle East and Far East—the Orient you know and love so well—This has been some tour!"[4]

In a telephone call from Washington to the writer, in response to a letter, the director of Mr. Stuart's tour, Mr. Thomas T. Turqman, Program Officer, Department of State, Bureau of Educational and cultural Affairs, spoke enthusiastically of its success.

"Mr. Stuart has done a wonderful job for us," he said. "He is so patriotic—a deeply patriotic man."

Jesse Stuart was hospitalized briefly, following his return from this strenuous tour for the State Department. Again, early in 1965, he was hospitalized, this time, for a mild heart attack. He spent most of that year quietly at home in the hills, always writing, of course, but, by doctors' orders, avoiding lecturing and teaching.

[3] Sept. 28, 1958.
[4] Stuart, Letter to the writer, January 30, 1963.

This writer's study of Stuart's life and works was officially "completed" in the spring of 1965, yet the collection of material concerning the prolific literary figure continues. Not only through the deep interest of the writer, and through use of endless material on hand, but through Jesse Stuart's generous cooperation in supplying needed information for keeping abreast with his activities, the work will be extended. The establishment in January 1967 of *W-Hollow Harvest*, "A magazine for Jesse Stuart buffs. News and reviews; contributionns by collectors," promises to be an additional aid in the project. Published at 11982 Marwood Lane, Cincinnati, Ohio, 45246, its editors, are David and Phyllis Brandenburg. A monthly, the magazine's January number contains a note concerning the Jesse Stuart High School, a $200,000 complex situated at Valley Station, Kentucky, a suburb of Louisville. When the Jesse Stuart High School was dedicated in November 1966, taking its place with Robert Frost High School and Edgar Allan Poe Elementary, "the Jefferson County Kentucky School System recently became the most 'literary' system in the country," the article states.

After Stuart's comparatively restful years in 1965, the year 1966 proved to be one of the busiest and most significant of his life. He joined the graduate faculty of Eastern Kentucky University as author in residence, plunging full force again into the work which he finds the most inspirational, that of encouraging the nation's youth in creative writing. He has continued as author in residence in 1967. The institution is approximately 150 miles from the Stuart home, and, as usual, Deane Stuart does the driving. The famous author's lectures are recorded, and he talks informally with the students concerning their problems He considers the arrangement ideal, he stated in a letter to this writer in May 1966. Usually he stays at the University for a period of a week, then returns home for a while for relaxation and for work on his own writing. Typically, he fulfills lecture engagements for a schedule as full as his other activities will allow.

His lectures and articles for the past year have reflected his travels in the summer of 1966, when he and Mrs. Stuart lived

in Athens while their daughter, Jane, was enrolled there in the
Anglo-American Cultural Institute for Modern Greek, later
traveling through Europe and the Greek isles in the Mediterran-
ean with Jane and their niece, Vivien Kenney. Always keenly
aware of strong parallels of the past with the present Stuart delivered a most powerful lecture at Commencement at Murray
State University (formerly Murray State College) in Kentucky
on May 29, 1967. This speech was considered to be "a message
so timely and so greatly needed—A Message the World Needs,"
as stated by President R. H. Woods of the University, that it
was published in July by Murray State, in pamphlet form.
Stuart entitled the address "Rebels With A Cause." He urged
his young graduate audience members to take the classic Roman
poet and satirist, Horace, as an example of a "rebel with a
cause," who put the "right emphasis on the right things," when
he wrote vigorously of "the sturdy Roman family, the great
yeomanry of the land, that sturdy citizenry that was the pillar
upon which the great Roman Empire drew its strength." At a
time of great dissension, such as we have today, Stuart pointed
out, Horace was "a steadying influence upon his country." He
urged that youth today be "rebels with a cause—the cause of
helping to keep this country at an even tempo," instead of seeking the sensationalism of marches, riots and flag burnings. The
stirring speech showed his increasing concern for the fight
against Communism.

Most significant in his area of social concern was the honor
paid him by Governor Edward Breathitt of Kentucky, who asked
him to help organize and participate in the Institute for the Education of Teachers in State Government, a special seminar con-
ducted concurrently at all universities and state colleges in Kentucky during the 1956 summer school term at the University of
Louisville. The seminar was named "The Jesse Stuart Seminar On
the Kentucky Constitution" in his honor, "In Implementation of
the Poet Laureate's Conviction that the Future of Kentucky Lies
with the Teachers of Today," as stated on the brochure describing the institute. Governor Breathitt awarded a medallion to Stuart

for the success of the project when he visited Eastern Kentucky University later for the dedication of the new million-dollar library building there, an occasion for which the Poet Laureate was, also, a principal speaker.

Jesse Stuart's past year was a memorable one in literary achievement, also. Late in 1965, McGraw-Hill had published a novel, *Daughter of the Legend*, his only book with a setting outside his native Kentucky hills. Based on a story, or legend, emanating from the strange "Melungeon country" of East Tennessee, this *tour de force* of Stuart's is highly dramatic, written with the intensity and rhythm of a folk ballad. In 1966, Whittlesey House published his book for children, *A Ride With Huey the Engineer*.

The short-story collection, *My Land Has a Voice*, published late in 1966, by McGraw-Hill, brought back the familiar Stuart to his *aficionados*. Here were the characters whom they knew and loved—the wayward Uncle Jeff, Huey, the Engineer, and countless others who recur in Stuart's works. Here was the bardic poet returning to his favorite medium, the short story, portraying with tenderness, alternated wih slashing satire, his land and his people, the rapscallions and heroic figures alike, using the medium of prose, though a poetic prose, as Jesse Stuart is primarily the poet. His portrait of "Corbie"—a small tragic figure from his early school days, a mentally retarded boy who loved to dance, who was loved and protected by his schoolmates, and who won social promotion, to the great pride of his family—is a classic. This story was first published in *The Philippines Free Press*. In "existentialist France," there will be soon, rather amazingly, it would seem, the publication of the Protestant Christian Stuart's autobiographical book, *God's Oddling*, concerning his father, "the earth poet."

A short story, "The Accident," published in *The Saturday Evening Post*, November 19, 1966, has a baroque treatment, an exaggerated humor, reminiscent of Flannery O'Connor, but, with Stuart, one meets the optimistic ending, the basic belief shown here of man's inner goodness, rather than his violence brought on by inner despair.

It is interesting to note the following passage from Donald Davidson, in a letter to the writer, dated March 22, 1967, in relation to Stuart as a short-story writer, "I have been thinking recently that Jesse is the only American short story writer who could be said to be something of an American 'Chekhov'. There's much of the same spirit and range of subjects and characters that leap gustily right out of life, and a similar abundance, almost a profligacy, of creativeness. Jesse is perhaps less under literary influences than the Russian, and less melancholy—though Chekhov started his career with humorous skits and bits."[5]

One might well draw close parallels, too, between Sholokhov's *And Quiet Flows the Don* and some of Jesse Stuart's works, in the opinion of this writer, with the Nobel winner's deep affinity for his region, the land and the people, the strong poetic style, and the sharp, brutal, and tender characterizations. The Big Sandy and the Little Sandy, of the Kentucky hills, invoke a feeling of the timelessness of the Don, though in "the Stuart country" of America, a region most often compared with the Highlands of Scotland. This would seem to be a potent argument for the universality of Stuart, attained through strong regionalism. This writer predicts that Jesse Stuart may well win the Nobel Award for Literature some day.

As for the future, Jesse Stuart will continue his philosophy of action in behalf of his country, as much as his health will permit,, and he will ever pursue his philosophy of optimism so poignantly expressed, in a letter to the writer, written from Cairo, Egypt, on January 1, 1961: "You know, we build our hopes high—We have our dreams—Hopes fade, and dreams never materialize. But such things don't stop us. We build more hopes and have more dreams."[6]

This dynamic spirit of optimism, in the face of the prevailing pessimism and cult of futility advanced in the works of many of today's leading writers, Stuart's daring to be himself, his sin-

---

[5] Quoted by permission.

[6] Jesse Stuart has just this summer realized a great personal dream. He has a grandson. On July 21, 1967, Conrad Stuart Juergensmeyer, was born to Stuart's daughter, Jane, and her husband, Julian.

cerity and his rugged realism, as well as the lyrical beauty of his writing in the tradition of romanticism, his simple, natural diction—these constitute the qualities for which many critics have acknowledged Jesse Stuart to be a vital force in the contemporary literary world. These are the qualities for which he has received his honors. According to a number of America's leading critics, whose statements have been included in this survey, Stuart's works have stood the test of reality, the test of truth, which all literary works must stand if they are to endure.

Jesse Stuart's writing carries the flavor of authenticity because of his innate love for his region. He has believed his destiny to lie there with his own people, and he has spent the greater part of his life there, speaking with bardic fervor for his region. Tragedy, as well as the drama, which permeates the lives of the people who live close to the soil, in addition to the natural beauties of the hills, have been depicted vividly in Stuart's poetry and poetic prose. With piety and a lingering nostalgia for the past, he has, at the same time, exhibited a concern for the future of his region and has led his people in the ways of progress.

He has been the historian for the change in his region from an isolated pocket in the hills off the main road of civilization, where the people clung stubbornly to the eighteenth-century customs and beliefs of their ancestors, to an area now with good roads, scientific farming methods, consolidated schools, television, bookmobiles, and other symbols of modernization. Writing always with deep respect for the best of the past, Stuart has exhibited concern for the problems of the present, particularly in the equalization of educational opportunities in remote areas of America, such as his native region. This humanity expressed in the works of Stuart, which has formed a strong phase of his writing, along with his lyrical portrayals of the life lived close to the soil and the sincerity with which the author invests his words, is, perhaps, the most important reason for the feeling of kinship with the author which his empathic readers enjoy, whatever their nationalities.

As I have shown in this study, Stuart's books and individual short stories have been translated and published in numerous countries of the world, and, as a result of his recent extensive lecture tours overseas, his foreign following may well be expected to increase. As the translations denote, his writing has struck a universal chord.

In the words of Donald Davidson, "The readers of Jesse Stuart must say, 'Here is writing that touches the heart.'"

Since "writing that touches the heart" might be called the basic definition of a classic, of work which attains universality and lives through the ages, one may say of Stuart's best works, "Here is classic writing." One may predict that Stuart's writing of strong, subjective poetry which runs counterstream to today's era of depersonalization, his poetic prose, both rugged and lyrical, his works of deep social concern, *as well as* his writing of broad humor of the frontier type, may well be expected to endure.

Jesse Stuart has carved for himself an individual, an inimitable, place among contemporary American writers. I believe that he is high among those who give promise for achieving permanence in world literature.

Selected Bibliography

....

BOOKS

Adventures in Reading. Chicago and New York: Harcourt Brace and Co., 1952.

BAKER, Ray Stannard. *Woodrow Wilson—Life and Letters*. Vol. I. Garden City, New York: Doubleday, Page and Co., 1927.

BIRMINGHAM, Frederic A. *The Writer's Craft*. New York: Hawthorne Books, Inc., 1948.

BROOKS, Cleanth. *Modern Poetry and the Tradition*. Chapel Hill: The University of North Carolina Press, 1939.

BURNETT, Whit, and Hallie Burnett, eds. *Story—The Fiction of the Forties*. New York: E. P. Dutton & Co., Inc., 1949.

CAMPBELL, Harry Modean, and Ruel Foster. *William Faulkner, A Critical Appraisal*. Norman: University of Oklahoma Press, 1951.

CHAUCER, Geoffrey. *The Canterbury Tales* ed. Rev. Walter W. Skeat. New York: Random House, 1929.

CLARK, Thomas D. *The Kentucky*. New York: Rhinehart & Co., Inc., 1942.

COLLINS, Lewis. *History of Kentucky*. Vol. II. Rev. Richard H. Collins. Louisville: John P. Morton & Co., Inc., 1924.

DAVIDSON, Donald. *American Composition and Rhetoric*. New York: Charles Scribner's Sons, 1953.

DONNE, John. *Holy Sonnets, 1 and 10, Sermon XV and XVII Folio of* 1640.

HOLMAN, C. Hugh. "Thomas Wolfe and the South," *South*, ed. Louis D. Rubin, Jr., and Robert D. Jacobs. Garden City, New York: Doubleday & Co., Inc., 1961.

JILLSON, Willard Rouse. *Kentuckie Country*. Washington: H. L. & J. B. McQueen, Inc., 1931.

Kentucky, A Guide to the Blue Grass State. Compiled by Federal Writers' Project, WPA of the State of Kentucky, sponsored by the University of Kentucky, XXVII, No. 5, 124. New York: Harcourt, Brace and Co., 1939.

KNICKERBOCKER, William S. "Victorian Education and the Idea of Culture," *The Reinterpretation of Victorian Literature*. Princeton: Princeton University Press, 1950.

LEWIS, E. Glyn. "Modern British Writing," *Anglo-Welsh Literature*, ed. Denys Val Baker. New York: Vanguard Press, Inc., 1947.

MAUGHAM, W. Somerset. *Maugham's Choice of Kipling's Best*. New York: Doubleday & Co., Inc., 1953.

MOORE, Arthur K. *The Frontier Mind*. Lexington: University of Kentucky Press, 1957.

O'BRIEN, E. J. *Best Short Stories of* 1938. Boston: Houghton Mifflin, 1938.

O'BRIEN, E. J. *50 Best American Short Stories* 1915–1939. New York: The Literary Guild of America, Inc., 1939.

PLATO. "Ion," *Dialogues,* English trans. W. R. M. Lamb. New York: G. P. Putnam's Sons, 1925.

SHALER, N. S. *Kentucky—A Pioneer Commonwealth.* Boston: Houghton, Mifflin and Co., 1900.

STUART, Jesse. *A Jesse Stuart Reader.* New York: McGraw-Hill Book Co., Inc., 1963.

——. *A Ride with Huey the Engineer.* New York: Whittlesey House, 1966.

——. *A Penny's Worth of Character.* New York: Whittlesey House, 1954.

——. *Album of Destiny.* New York: E. P. Dutton & Co., Inc., 1944.

——. *Andy Finds a Way.* New York: Whittlesey House, 1961.

——. *The Beatinest Boy.* New York: Whittlesey House, 1953.

——. *Beyond Dark Hills.* New York: E. P. Dutton & Co., Inc., 1938.

——. *Clearing in the Sky.* New York: McGraw-Hill Book Co., Inc., 1950.

——. *Daughter of the Legend.* New York: McGraw-Hill Book Co., Inc., 1965.

——. *Forestaste of Glory.* New York: E. P. Dutton & Co., 1946.

——. *God's Oddling.* New York: McGraw-Hill Book Co., Inc., 1960.

——. *The Good Spirit of Laurel Ridge.* New York: McGraw-Hill Book Co., Inc., 1953.

———. *Harvest of Youth.* Howe, Oklahoma: The Scroll Press, 1930.

———. *Head o' W-Hollow.* New York: E. P. Dutton & Co., Inc., 1936.

———. *Hie to the Hunters.* New York: McGraw-Hill Book Co., Inc., 1951.

———. *Hold April.* New York: McGraw-Hill Book Co., Inc., 1962.

———. *Huey, the Engineer.* St. Helena, California: James E. Beard, 1960.

———. *Kentucky Is My Land.* New York: E. P. Dutton & Co., Inc., 1952.

———. *Man With a Bull-Tongue Plow.* New York: E. P. Dutton & Co., 1934.

———. *Men of the Mountains.* New York: E. P. Dutton & Co., 1941.

———. *Mongrel Mettle.* New York: E. P. Dutton & Co., 1952.

———. *My Land Has a Voice.* New York: McGraw-Hill Book Co., Inc., 1966.

———. *Ploughshare in Heaven.* New York: McGraw-Hill Book Co., Inc., 1958.

———. *Red Mule.* New York: Whittlesey House, 1955.

———. *Save Every Lamb.* New York: McGraw-Hill Book Co., Inc., 1964.

———. *The Rightful Owner.* Whittlesey House, 1960.

———. *Tales from the Plum Grove Hills.* New York: E. P. Dutton & Co., 1940.

———. *Taps for Private Tussie.* New York: E. P. Dutton & Co., 1943.

——. *The Thread That Runs So True*. New York: Charles Scribner's Sons, 1949.

——. *Tim*. New York: Robert Lowry, 1958.

——. *Trees of Heaven*. New York: E. P. Dutton & Co., 1940.

——. "Uncle Jeff," *A Vanderbilt Miscellany*, ed. Richmond Croom Beatty. Nashville: Vanderbilt University Press, 1944.

——. "Up the Branch," *This Is the South*, ed. by Robert West Howard. Chicago: Rand McNally, 1959.

——. *The Year of My Rebirth*. New York: McGraw-Hill Book Co., Inc., 1956.

VAN DOREN, Carl. *The American Novel*. New York: The Macmillan Co., 1940.

VAN DOREN, Mark. *Enjoying Poetry*. New York: William Sloane Associates, Inc., 1951.

WALCOTT, Fred G. *Manual*. Minneapolis: Professional Books, Inc., 1949.

WEYGANDT, Cornelius. *A Century of the English Novel*. New York: The Century Company, 1925.

PERIODICALS

AMES, Richard Sheridan. "Thomas Wolfe," *The Saturday Review of Literature*, VIII (June 1938), 21.

ANON. *The New Yorker*, "Book," March 22, 1941, p. 70.

BAKER, Howard. "The Contemporary Short Story," *The Southern Review*, III (Winter 1938), 590.

BENET, William Rose. "Round About Parnassus," *The Saturday Review of Literature*, XI (September 22, 1934), 129.

BIRD, John. "My Friend, Jesse Stuart," *The Saturday Evening Post,* CCXXXII (July 25, 1959), 81.

BRYANT, Cyril Erick. "Kentucky Is His Land," *The Christian Herald,* LXXVII (November, 1954), 74.

BURKE, Thomas. "The Short Story in America," *The American Mercury,* XXXIX (September, 1936), 103–5.

BURNS, Paul C. and Hines, Ruth. "Kentucky Is His Home," *Elementary English,* XXXVIII (March 1951), 138.

CANFIELD, Dorothy. "Jesse Stuart," *News of Books and Authors,* (May–June 1944), 1.

CHENERY, William L. "Picking Popular Fiction," *The Saturday Review of Literature,* XVIII (June 18, 1938), 15.

COWLEY, Malcolm, "Man With a Hoe," *The New Republic,* LXXX (October 31, 1934), 342.

DEAL, Borden. "Mountain Magic," *The Saturday Review,* XLI (September 20, 1958), 10.

ELIOT, T. S. "American Literature and the American Language," *Washington University Studies.* New Series, No. 23, p. 16. An Address delivered at Washington University, June 9, 1953.

FLETCHER, John Gould. "Kentucky Georgics," *Poetry: A Magazine of Verse,* XLV (January 1935), 217.

KOHLER, Dayton. "James Still and Jesse Stuart, Mountain Regionalist," *College English,* III (March 1942), 523–533.

MAUGHAN, A. M. "A Walk Through Scotland's History," *Holiday,* XXVII (May 1960), 74.

MORGAN, Joy Elmer, ed. "Editor's Note," *National Education Association Journal* (January 1950), 7.

Poetry—A Magazine of Verse, XLV (November, 1934), 112.

SALOMAN, I. L. *The Saturday Review,* XXXVI (December 26, 1953), 21.

Stuart, Jesse. "Angel in the Pasture," *Esquire*, LI (June 1959), 49–50.

——. "Are We a Nation of Digits?" *The Saturday Evening Post*, CCXXXV (July 28–August 5, 1962), 8.

——. "Ascend the High Mountain," *Country Beautiful*, I (February 1962), 9.

——. "Backgrounds and Results of Regional Writing," *The Peabody Reflector*, XXVI (January 1953), 4–5.

——. "Challenge in Cairo," *Journal of the National* Education Association of the United States, LI (May 1962), 46.

——. "Colorado," *Best Articles and Stories*, III (October 1959), 50–52.

——. "Comeback from a Heart Attack," *Today's Health*, XXXVI (February 1960), 69.

——. "Do Our Schools Teach Dishonesty?" *Ladies Home Journal*, LXXVII (March 1960), 6.

——. "Freedom Lanes," *Daughters of the American Revolution Magazine*, XCVI (November 1962), 689.

——. "Love That Land," *Readers Digest*, LXII (May 1953), 20.

——. "I Have to Write or Die," *Christian Action*, XIV (December 1959), 20.

——. "Is the Short Story at a Dead End?" *The Peabody Reflector*, XXVI (February 1953), 28.

——. "Kentucky Hill Dance," *The New Republic*, LXXIX (May 16, 1934), 15–16.

——. "My Father Was a Railroad Man," *Tracks* (April 1953).

——. "The Accident," *The Saturday Evening Post*, CCXXXIX (November 19, 1966.

———. "The Man Who Painted Schoolhouses," *Country Gentleman*, CXXIII (July 1953), 30.

———. "Things I Have Loved," *Lyrics from Lincoln Memorial University* (1928), 14.

——— . "What America Means to Me," *American Magazine*, CLI (May 1951), 10.

———. "Why Album is My Best," *Prairie Schooner*, XXX (Spring 1956), 32.

TATE, Allen. "Regionalism and Sectionalism," *The New Republic*, LXIX (December 23, 1931), 158.

WABNITZ, S. "Jesse Stuart and the Old and New in Short Stories," *New Mexico Quarterly Review*, VII (August 1937), 183–8.

NEWSPAPERS

ABEEL, David. *The State* (Columbia, S. C., March 24, 1960, p. 12-C.

ADAMS, George Matthew. "Today's Talk," *The Dallas News*, November 8, 1953, p. 12.

ADAMS, J. Donald. *The New York Times Book Review*, April 14, 1940, p. 3.

ANON. "Jesse Stuart's Kentucky Tales," *The New York Times Book Review*, April 26, 1936.

ANON. *The Chicago Tribune*, June 19, 1944.

ANON. *The Chicago Tribune Book Review*, June 12, 1934, p. 3.

ANON. *The New York Herald-Tribune Books*, June, 1949.

ANON. *The Kansas City Star*, June 5, 1944.

ANON. *The New York Sun*, June 11, 1944.

ANON. *The San Francisco Chronicle*, June 14, 1944.

ANON. *The Winston-Salem Journal* (N. C.), June 12, 1944.

BEMENT, Douglas. *The Philadelphia Inquirer*, July 6, 1938, p. 16.

BURGER, Marjorie. *The New York Times Book Review*, October 29, 1961, p. 6.

CARMER, Carl. *The New York Herald Tribune Books*, November 8, 1953, p. 3.

CANBY, Henry Siedel. *The New York Herald Tribune Books*, April 14, 1940, p. 1.

CREASON, Joe. "The Author Who Writes So True," *The Courier-Journal Magazine* (Louisville, Ky.), January 15, 1950, p. 7.

DIGNAN. *The Courier-Journal* (Louisville, Ky.), November 1, 1953, p. 6.

FADIMAN, Clifton. *The New York World Telegram*, April 16, 1940, p. 12.

FAVRE, George H. *The Christian Science Monitor*, November 1, 1953, p. 15.

GANNETT, Lewis. *The New York Herald Tribune Books*, March 21, 1936, p. 3.

———. *The New York Herald Tribune*, June 23, 1938, p. 2.

GREGORY, Horace. "A Farmer Singing Behind His Plow," *The New York Herald Tribune Books*, October 14 ,1934, p. 128.

GRIFFIN, Gerald. "Jesse Stuart, Prophet Honored in Homeland," *The Courier-Journal* (Louisville, Ky.), October 16, 1955, p. 6.

HANSEN, Harry. *The New York World Telegram Book Review*, April 16, 1936, p. 401.

———. *The New York World Telegram*, June 22, 1938, p. 12.

———. "The First Reader," *The New York World Telegram*, May 14, 1940, p. 5.

H.T.H. "Un Grand Poete Americain," *Le Progres Egyptien,* (Alexandria, Egypt), March 7, 1961, p. 2.

JACKSON, Joseph Henry. *The Los Angeles Times,* "Bookman's Notebook," December 3, 1953, p. 5.

JORDAN, Smith Paul. *The Los Angeles Times,* July 6, 1938, p. 8.

LEVIN, Meyer. "The Candid Critic," *Newark Star Ledger* (N. J.), October 22, 1953, p. 6.

PAULUS, John D. *The New York Times Book Review,* November 1, 1953, p. 3.

RICHEY, Elinor. *The Herald-Advertiser* (Huntington, W. Va.), October 16, 1955.

RUGOFF, Milton. *The New York Herald Tribune Books,* March 16, 1941, p. 2.

SMITH, Henry Nash. *The New York Herald Tribune,* June 5, 1944.

SNYDER, Charles Lee. "Kentucky Portraits," *The New York Times Book Review,* September 21, 1958, p. 3.

STEPHENS, Robert. *The Chicago Tribune,* June 30, 1938, p. 21.

STUART, Jesse. "Italian Diary," *The Huntington Herald-Advertiser* (W. Va.), August 5, 1962, p. 5.

The Campus Caravan, (Cairo, Egypt, American University), February 13, 1961, pp. 1, 4.

THOMPSON, Ralph. *The New York Times Book Review,* March 21, 1936, p. 2.

———. *The New York Times Book Review,* June 23, 1938.

VAN DOREN, Mark. *New York Herald Tribune Books,* June 12, 1934, p. 34.

———. "Good Speech of a Kentucky Hollow," *The New York Herald Tribune Books,* May 3, 1936, p. 7.

VAN GELDER, Robert. *The New York Times*, March 23, 1941, p. 70.

WALSH, Chad. "Magazine of Books," *The Chicago Tribune*, November 15, 1953, p. 19.

UNPUBLISHED THESES

DICKINSON, *Blair*. "Lexicographical Study of the Vocabulary of Greenup County, Kentucky, Set Forth in Jesse Stuart's Beyond Dark Hills." Unpublished Master's Thesis, Department of English, University of Virginia, 1941.

RAMEY, Lee. "An Inquiry Into the Life of Jesse Stuart." Unpublished Master's Thesis, Department of English, University of Ohio, 1941.

WASHINGTON, Mary. "The Folklore of the Cumberlands as Reflected in the Writings of Jesse Stuart." Unpublished Ph. D. Dissertation, Department of English, University of Pennsylvania, 1960.

LETTERS

ADAMS, Donald J. Letter to the writer, October 16, 1960.

DAVIDSON, Donald. Letter to the writer, April 19, 1954.

———. Letter o the writer, March 22, 1967.

———. Letter to the writer, May 11, 1959.

HILLYER, Robert. Letter to the writer from Newark, Delaware, March 3, 1961.

———. Letter to the writer, April 15, 1961.

KHALAF, Nadia. Letter to the writer, June 15, 1961.

MARSH, Lydia Creighton, E. P. Dutton, Publisher, Letter to the writer, April 28, 1953.

Stuart, Jesse. Letter to the writer, April 18, 1953.

——. Letter to the writer, August 13, 1963.

——. Letter to Lydia Creighton Marsh, E. P. Dutton & Company, New York, March 7, 1952.

——. Letter to the writer, February 5, 1961.

——. Letter to the writer, January 30, 1963.

——. Letter to the writer, Ocober 24, 1960.

——. Letter to the writer, June 22, 1953.

——. Letter to the writer, April 20, 1953.
Warren, Robert Penn. Letter to the writer, July 13, 1959.

OTHER SOURCES

Guggenheim Foundation. *John Simon Guggenheim Award Announcement*, released nationally to the press, June 7, 1937.

Hillyer, Robert. "Announcing a Major Work by One of America's Most Gifted Writers." Undated clipping of Stuart puplicity release from E. P. Dutton & Co., Inc., found in Scrapbook 15, p. 2, in the Stuart Room, Murray State College, Murray, Kentucky.

——. "Letters to the Editor," *News and Views About Dutton Books and Authors*," Scrapbook 15, p. 25, in the Stuart Room, Murray State College, Murray, Kentucky.

Levinthal, Sonia. *Information Release*. New York: McGraw-Hill Book Co., Inc., March, 1949.

Masters, Edgar Lee. "To Jesse Stuart," *News and Views About Dutton Books and Authors*. Information pamphlet. New York: E. P. Dutton & Co., Inc., March-April, 1940.

SAROYAN, William. "An Impression of Jesse Stuart," *News and Views About Dutton Books and Authors*. New York: E. P. Dutton & Co., Inc., March-April, 1940.

STUART, Jesse. "Schools to Keep Us Free." An address delivered before the 77th annual convention of The American Association of School Administrators, Atlantic City, New Jersey, 1951.

———. Interview with the writer, Spartanburg, S. C. March, 1953.

———. Interview with the writer, New York City, December, 1956.

———. Interview with the writer, Vanderbilt University, Nashville, Tenn., April, 1959.

———. Interview with the writer, University of South Carolina, Columbia, S. C., March, 1960.

———. Interview with the writer, Greenup, Kentucky, July, 1960.

———. Interview with the writer, New York City, July, 1961.

———. Interview with the writer, New York City, November, 1961.

———. Interview with the writer, Columbia, S. C., November, 1963.

———. Interview with Dr. Havilah Babcock, Mrs. Alice Wyman and the writer, WIS-TV, Columbia, S. C., March, 1960.

———. Interview with President Thomas F. Jones, University of South Carolina, Dr. Havilah Babcock, Don Upton, WIS-TV, Columbia, S. C., November, 1963.

Index

....

Jesse Stuart and Kentucky are inseparable themes throughout the book and there seemed little point in having a main entry on either. References to particular places or regions of Kentucky are indexed by name, e.g., "Greenup and Greenup County, Ky." Stuart's books are listed by title.

THIS BOOK WAS
SET IN JANSON TYPE BY
SCHWARTZ TYPESETTERS
PRINTED AND BOUND BY
THE STATE PRINTING COMPANY
BOTH OF
COLUMBIA, S. C.